D1006841

THE
CONNECTION
GAP

THE CONNECTION GAP

Why Americans Feel So Alone

LAURA PAPPANO

Rutgers University Press
NEW BRUNSWICK, NEW JERSEY,
AND LONDON

Library of Congress Cataloging-in-Publication Data
Pappano, Laura, 1962–
The connection gap : why Americans feel so alone / Laura Pappano.
p.   cm.
Includes bibliographical references and index.
ISBN 0-8135-2979-4 (alk. paper)
1. Loneliness.   2. Alienation (Social psychology)   3. Social isolation.
I. Title.
BF575.L7 P36   2001
155.9'2—dc21
00-068349

British Cataloging-in-Publication data for this book is available from the
British Library

Manufactured in the United States of America

FOR TOM, OLIVIA, MOLLY,
AND DONOVAN

 CONTENTS

ACKNOWLEDGMENTS

A book, even one on loneliness, is not written alone. I am grateful to so many people for their varied contributions. First, this book would not have been possible without my friend and former editor at the *Boston Globe Magazine*, Evelynne Kramer. Her keen sense of a good subject kicked in immediately when I said I wanted to do a piece on loneliness. And her urging, upon seeing the first draft of the story, to "ratchet it up a notch" brought the magazine piece the kind of response that prompted this book.

I am equally indebted to the scholars and staff at the Murray Research Center at the Radcliffe Institutes for Advanced Study at Harvard, who had me as a visiting scholar for four years. Former director Anne Colby offered key guidance early on. Scholar Jackie James was frequently at the ready with a clipping, a reference, or a thought. She also read the manuscript and provided invaluable feedback. I cannot overstate the vital role the individuals and the community of the Murray Center played in the creation of this book. Impromptu conversations with the likes of Evelyn Liberatore, John Laub, Rosalind Barnett, P. J. McGann, Catherine Ellis, Marty Mauzy, Janet Malley, and Erin Phelps—and many others—sent me constantly to new sources. I owe particular thanks to Eileen McDonagh, whose fabulously persistent and encouraging nature helped to bring this book to light.

Harvard students, joining with me through the Radcliffe Research Partnership Program, provided not only dogged research but illuminating ideas and a fresh take on an old world. Their observations, their stories, and their way of looking at the Connection Gap profoundly informed this project. I am grateful to have worked with such dedicated and thoughtful young people as Catherine Malmberg, Bonnie Tsui,

X   ACKNOWLEDGMENTS

Abby Fung, Lisa McTeague, Rebecca Lubens, and Laura Tarter. Thanks also to Cinnamon Stetler. Special thanks to Britte Chang, whose command of data sets and software interfaces is a thing to behold.

I am thankful to my new friends at Rutgers University Press, including editor in chief Leslie Mitchner, whose enthusiasm has won my heart.

The material in this book (that which doesn't come from studies, polls, books, magazines, newspapers, Websites, TV ads, or any number of other cultural sources) comes from my life and my observations. I am indebted to the people I have interviewed for magazine and newspaper stories, to strangers I've seen or overheard, and to people close to me who have borne the scrutiny of my observations. Thanks to my dear friends Eric Schwarz, Maureen Coffey, Chuck Agosta, Lucy McQuilken, and Aime and Jerry Grady. I tried out *The Connection Gap*—or many of its ideas—on them over marathon dinner discussions. Thanks too to Shawna Giggey-Mashal, who is ever in possession of the latest scoop. I am grateful to my siblings, not only for their support and love now but for the fabulous though often hard times we shared in the past. I appreciate the stories from my grandmother Ellie Svehla and the frankness of my grandfather Al Pappano. I feel incredibly grateful for Robert Norton and lucky to have a mom like my mom, JoAnne Pappano, whose strength and generosity are unmatched by anyone I have ever met.

The writing of this book was done with the encouragement, support, and thoughtful critique of my writers' group: Cynthia Dockrell, Linda Freeley, Jane Lawless, and Louise Kennedy. Particular thanks to Louise; her copyediting skills are legend, her knowledge of etiquette and trivia are breathtaking, but she also provides the kind of emotional support we all need.

I owe a great deal to those who urged me to have faith and to persevere. I am thankful to Andrew Martin, Barbara Marks, Nancy Kahan, George Gibson, Peter Karoff, Desmond Morris, and Juliet Schor for their advice and—at times—willingness to commiserate.

To my friend, mentor, and former editor Irene Driscoll I owe tremendous thanks. Her willingness to "fly" has brought me to where I am today. *Boston Globe* editors—former and present—Lincoln Millstein, Paul Hemp, Mark Morrow, Jan Freeman, Marilyn Garateix, John Burke, Nick King, Greg Moore, Peter Canellos, and Matt Storin have provided support, feedback, and a place to practice my trade. Thank you to my colleagues at *CommonWealth*, past and present: Dave Denison, Bob Keough, Tripp Jones, and Matt Malone, who let me air ideas for *The Connection Gap* in their pages.

Finally, I want to thank those closest to me who have lived with my questions, my piles, and my insistent efforts to make sense of the present. My mother-in-law, Nancy Lynch, has been a fan and a believer in the project even during times when my own faith grew thin. My dear friend Peggy Rambach provided ample material as well as the most undying support and faith one could imagine. It is hard to know how to begin to thank my sister Margaret, who applied the considerable firepower of her professorial intellect to the research and reading of the manuscript while never ceasing to be the perfect, loving, supportive sister. I'm lucky to have her in my corner. Thanks to my sister Andrea, who survived being the youngest, and to my brother, Dante, who brought medical research to bear on my arguments. Last, I thank my children, Olivia, Molly, and Donovan, who have given me a joy I could not have imagined—and new eyes through which to see the world and the culture we live in. And for my husband and best friend, Tom Lynch, who has proved himself a worthy researcher—especially now that he is mindful of getting the citations for his findings—a tireless conversationalist, and a true soul mate: my love.

THE
CONNECTION
GAP

 INTRODUCTION

W̲e are losing touch. And we don't even realize it.

On Wednesday evenings, after the children are asleep, I go alone to the third floor of our 105-year-old Victorian and do what no previous inhabitant of this house has ever done. I sit in front of a fourteen-inch color monitor, log on to the Internet, and type in the Web address of my online grocer. When the home page appears, the image of the mother and smiling infant reminds me why this is the best way to shop. This new way of putting food on the table—or at least in the cupboards—should net me more time for playing. Funny, though, I *feel* more rushed than ever.

I enter my password and cruise the virtual aisles, scanning product names under headings like "fresh," "packaged goods," and "household accessories." It takes only about twenty minutes to fill my virtual shopping cart. This approach to tackling the weekly supermarket list has taken some getting used to. (Who knew that Tony Tiger cereal is properly called "Kellogg's Frosted Flakes of Corn"?) Nonetheless, it's remarkably trouble free. There is no heavy lifting, no worries that those two cases of caffeine-free Diet Coke will crush the bread or, as happens to me in the real store by the time I reach the soda aisle, won't even fit in the cart. I even get a running total of how much I'm spending. I don't have to haul anything home; it is all delivered the next day.

But probably the biggest pitch for online grocery shopping is that you don't have to deal with other people. Forget the folks who park in front of the dried pasta or abandon carts in the middle of aisles. There's no wait for the person at the bread counter to select the sourdough baguette with tongs from behind a plastic case. *People* slow things down. And I'm not the only one who feels this way. The appeal of interacting with a computer or a machine instead of a human has caught the fancy of vendors from McDonald's to the local turnpike authority. In my state of Massachusetts, the former turnpike director made no qualms about the draw of skipping the required interaction at the tollbooth by using the Fast Lane transponder. "With as much as people have going on in their lives, sometimes stopping and interacting with other humans is difficult," he said. "You would rather deal with a machine. People would rather not deal with humans if they don't have to."

There is something trying, even exhausting, about human interactions. Why meet when you can e-mail? And digital video makes it *seem* like you're there. Right? Certainly, we are still sorting out all the new technologies we've been endowed with. The novelty is wearing off, and when they become absolutely mundane, we will have incorporated them all into life. It's just the way things are done. Nothing special. It's not special to use a cell phone or to get e-mail. This is how we communicate with each other. But the transition from in-person to online is not just trading slow for fast but is renegotiating the terms of engagement and the ground rules for living. More often than not, the new rules leave less time and less opportunity to connect—with other people, with the physical world, and with ourselves.

A CEO of a firm that helps established companies build and market an online presence works nearly all the time. He spends fourteen-hour days at the office, comes home to eat dinner with his wife and four children, and then goes upstairs to check his e-mail and keep working. He's not so unusual. He loves the speed and the excitement of the work. It *is* fun to be involved with something hot. Problem is, he hardly has time to connect with anything else. He likens his link with his job to a T1 connection—as opposed to a dial-up—and says he won't have any meaningful time of his own until after retirement. (He's only forty-nine.) He savors the forty-five minutes a day he spends commuting because, he says, it is "the only forty-five minutes I can control." The rest of the day, he behaves like a human pinball ricocheting from one thing to the next, reacting instead of contemplating. But that's the way business is today, he says: "We are making half-assed decisions because we are responding to stimuli."

Much has been written about how time-starved Americans are today. Like the CEO, many of us don't have time to think, either. We, too, respond. No wonder e-tailers, hungry for people's attention, must make each Website "stickier" than the last. It is no accident that time is what the e-commerce world peddles: "Spend your money and they'll *give* you time" is the message. Who wouldn't find that appealing?

That's why I bit when the flyer arrived in the mail offering trial online grocery service. But now, months later, I'm not sure what's happened to the time I used to spend grocery shopping. I don't feel as if I have a great surplus of minutes to savor. Other things just seem to fill the space. I don't play with the children any more than I did before. I don't take long, soaking baths. And I seem to have more, not less, trouble finding time to get through two daily newspapers and the scads of magazines that arrive. In the end, I haven't gained that much. And I've lost some.

When I first started grocery shopping online, I thought I would miss handling the food, judging one Granny Smith apple against another or debating the appeal of Cheez-Its over Cheese Nips. But a funny thing has happened: I have found that the ritual of grocery shopping doesn't have much at all to do with the food. As with other aspects of daily life, the value and meaning of this chore are camouflaged by its very ordinariness. I now find it interesting—even fun—to go to a supermarket. There is the *whoosh!* of sensory stimulation that strikes when you enter, those odd bluish lights, the colorful pyramids of fruits, the sheer stunning display of product choices.

More profoundly, what I miss is the *life* of the supermarket. I used to see the same people working the cash registers. I miss hearing the boss, named Joan, coordinate break times or appear momentarily stressed by the absence of an advertised product. Despite my frustration with other shoppers, I realize I do miss peering into other people's carts to see what they're buying. I miss having other shoppers look at me, acknowledging my existence and confirming my inclusion in society. People used to ask me the ages of my children, notice when they helped load food onto the checkout counter, or nod as they managed to absorb their disappointment when I said no to candy. I miss the public experience of the supermarket.

Certainly, it is easy enough to do without grocery shopping in person. But it is less easy to do without what grocery shopping allows us: to be involved in the details of our own lives and to feel part of the human world. I know there are people involved with the process of getting my food to my home, but I do not see them. I order, then go to work. When I get home, the food is there. And what has happened in grocery shopping is happening in other areas of domestic and commercial life: In the name of efficiency and convenience, we are taking the interactions out of our days. The background noise of the supermarket or the chitchat with the cashier may seem meaningless. But it's not. It is exactly what makes us feel connected.

I realized this when I made a supplementary trip to the supermarket where I used to make my weekly bulk purchases. I brought two of my children, my infant son and five-year-old daughter. As we cruised through the aisles, my daughter loved picking items off the shelf and placing them in the cart. People babbled with the baby and asked my daughter how it felt to be a big sister. At the dairy case, I searched with another woman for unsalted butter, which was in short supply because it was near the holidays, when even the least talented bakers feel moved to produce sweets. At the checkout, the cashier watched and chatted as my daughter unloaded the cart onto the conveyor. As we walked out into the cold and dark late autumn afternoon, my son strapped to my chest and my daughter with her small, ungloved hand in mine, she looked up at me and said, "Those people are so, so nice!" Her observation was her own, out of nowhere, a simple thought that tumbled forth. Yet she had captured the experience perfectly. We had both had a wonderful time—yes—grocery shopping, simply because we were there, engaging with other people. Grocery shopping had made me feel happy.

The experience with my daughter came as I found myself increasingly frustrated by online shopping. There were mistakes, especially with produce. The avocados for making guacamole arrived as hard as rocks; more than once I received someone else's chilled food order instead of my own. I resolved to do more grocery shopping in person. This is how I have gotten to know Richard, a supermarket employee who appears to be in his late forties. He is a solid man who often wears khaki pants and strong, sensible shoes. Because he is mentally handicapped, Richard is given jobs like collecting carts, sweeping the parking lot, and raking leaves. His voice has a slight nasal quality. The rhythm of his speech is awkward, perhaps because he grows impassioned about topics many people care too little about to even discuss: the legality of burning leaves and—a favorite—the rules of operating a motor vehicle (I gather he is not allowed to drive). Nonetheless, we have had important conversations, too.

One morning, standing in the parking lot, he told me someone close to him had punched him in the back and called him a "retard."

He didn't know what to do. He leaned over his rake and looked extremely sad, almost excessively so. I felt in that moment a sense of responsibility. He needed to know: What should he do? Was it true? Was he just a retard? Should he strike back? We talked about how he felt and how you can respond when someone hurts you. In the end, Richard decided to explain that they could not remain friends if his friend treated him so hurtfully. It may seem a rather simple problem with an obvious solution. But working through the dilemma made the experience memorable, probably because I could feel him struggle at first and then feel empowered by his solution. I look forward to seeing Richard when I go to the store. I find him refreshing, perhaps because of the very mental handicap that makes him so eager to engage.

I have no illusions. I am not Richard's friend. In truth I do not know him very well. But I do value our interactions, even though they are the kind many people think are best avoided: They take up too much time and energy. But I do believe such interactions give us something for the trouble: the opportunity to connect and to feel part of the world we live in. Granted, connecting with the gas attendant or the library clerk may on first blush not seem worthwhile. Or, as one senior physician put it when asked why he didn't attend his hospital's holiday party, "I don't want to boogie with the elevator man." After all, the bright new world of high technology, the multiplying services, and the strides we have made in elevating the average American lifestyle are ridding our lives of junk so, as my online grocer's home page suggests, we can get to the good stuff. Why muddy it up? Who wouldn't want to cut out the junk and leave just the very best of what each day has to offer?

But such reasoning misses a critical point: The *junk* has value. The junk is what keeps us human—grounded and connected to our lives, to others, and to our world. It is the realm of the impromptu act, the glance, the word, the thrill of being seen as a person, not because of your title, your position, or your money but because you are there and involved. Many people know the feeling. In a moment, verbally or physically, you extend yourself—you empathize, act, or open yourself to listen. The butcher boasts that his girlfriend's mother from Hungary makes the best meatloaf he has ever eaten. He hurriedly rushes through the swinging doors in hopes of finding you the recipe.

We do reach out. But it is growing harder, in part because we have more choices that allow us to eliminate meaningful human interaction from our daily experience. It is easier to slip past Richard, slip past each other. It is easier to shop online, to e-mail the complaints, to not deal with other people. We are busy. We have a lot on our plates and our minds. And, to be honest, we don't want to boogie with the elevator man. What the online, streamlined, customized lifestyle offers is the ability to interact only with people we want to—people, mostly, just like us. Our society may be more diverse, but our experiences are growing narrower, our quarters more ghettoized. We draw the circle of concern closer around ourselves. Reveling in the junk of daily life— grocery shopping in person included—is one way to connect.

This book is about where we have come from and where we are going. It is a book about ideas and the power of the trivial to shape major change. It is a call to consider the junk of daily life, not as a distraction, but as a potential tool for connecting us to things we care about. Like the CEO who has little time to think about the decisions he makes, many people are becoming overbusy executives of their lives. People are willing to be pulled along into the new way of living without considering the trade-offs. There is a great deal of hunger today to find meaning and purpose in life. Some search for meaning in religious commitments; some leap from bridges or scale canyons. I believe these quests are symbolic of the disconnection many of us feel.

In this book, I speak much about "connection." It is a word that means different things to different people. For me, connection is about engagement with ourselves, our physical surroundings, and other people. Connection is about reclaiming our humanness. It is about making better choices and realizing that we—not the new technology or the latest cultural value—have the power to shape a meaningful existence.

This idea is simple, but difficult to hold on to because so much today—from tangible scientific discoveries to basic social constructs— is in flux. Long-held beliefs are called into question and values upended. Once-certain limits of scientific knowledge are shattered. We are living in a special moment, but it is a moment defined not by any parameters but by the speed with which the parameters change. Scholars and experts in various fields intone about the mythic quality of our age. Historians compare the time to the Industrial Revolution. Economists wonder if tried-and-true rules can still apply. The worlds of politics, science, medicine, human rights, communications, advertising, sports, and more are changing as the result of new events and breathtaking discoveries. The world often feels as if it is exploding with new things and new ways of doing old things. The microprocessor that first allowed a lunar module to land on the moon now costs eighteen cents. Today, millions of the chips power children's toys.

Change and stunning new inventions have become so routine that the shock of the new no longer shocks. At the same time, old parameters and standards fall away: Our society has become comfortable with the pornographic, familiar with the violent, and at ease with the crude. The rising cadre of newly minted Internet millionaires (in their twenties and thirties, no less) has shattered old ideas about a proper ascent up the ladder of success. No wonder the notion of calibrating indulgence and self-sacrifice seems hopelessly dated. Rules no longer apply. But amid the chaos and excitement that comes with great new ideas is the more humble—and stable—fact that we each must attend to our own life.

So while many experts, scholars, and writers today have their eyes on the big issues of our time, I intend here to focus on what is less glamorous and less considered: the junk. In the end, I believe small things have a powerful impact. If we can pay attention to the oft-ignored aspects of our lives, we will gain the grassroots ability to construct a future that we're excited about living. In this book I begin with a concern: I believe we are growing apart, unwittingly disconnecting from our world, from others, and from ourselves. We are, in rather base terms, being sucked along. In this book, I will consider the choices we are making and the values we are embracing. I will, for example, examine the way we build and live in our homes, make friends, and socialize. I'll consider how we communicate and how the virtual world alters how we navigate the real world. I'll look at the power of shopping, our hunger for mobility, and how we quietly struggle to find meaning and connection.

As I see it, we have arrived at a moment of opportunity. We have choices about how the future unfolds. Often, though, instead of making choices, many of us react to stimuli. We want the next thing. But the very new, new things and new, new values that promise to make life more comfortable, convenient, efficient, and private also create the reverse: lives that are more isolated, increasingly self-focused, and lonelier.

It may seem ironic, when "connection" has become the buzzword of the moment and anyone at all is immediately reachable from any location, that people are suffering from loneliness. But many of us are.

It is not, of course, loneliness in the traditional sense. I'm not talking here about the widow in the too-quiet house, the lone figure walking unaccompanied on a vacant street. I'm not talking about the listless and the lovelorn, or about the Eleanor Rigby prototype, the lonely one missing out on the party of life, famished for human contact with too much time to wonder what's gone awry.

I am writing about the rest of us: the overstimulated, hyperkinetic, overcommitted, striving, under-cared-for, therapy dependent, plugged in, logged on, sleep deprived. We are the new lonely. This loneliness touches us whether we are married, single, widowed, or divorced; gay, straight, or bisexual; whether we have children or are childless. It touches the urban, the suburban, and the rural; the hip and the hopelessly uncool. It is not a personal character flaw or a reflection of failure. It is simply how we conduct our lives. It is a mindset and a way of being suited to this age. People trust less and keep to themselves more. People seek privacy, fencing in property, installing security systems in homes, and escaping into cars, behind apartment doors, into master bedroom suites and gated communities.

People talk a great deal about "community" but complain of feeling less and less a part of one. People long for rich relationships but find themselves wary of committing to others. Many of us hunger for intimacy but end up paying professionals to listen to, care for, and befriend us. We are a bundle of contradictions, eager to feel rooted but finding ourselves willingly pulled along with the tide. As a society, we face a collective loneliness, an empty feeling that comes not from lack of all human interaction, but from the loss of *meaningful* interaction, the failure to be a part of something real, or to have faith in institutions that might bring us together. This is what I call the Connection Gap.

The Connection Gap is the cumulative cultural consequence of the choices people make and fail to make, the values that are embraced and those that slip away. It is the result of huge forces reshaping our everyday world, from technology and consumerism to the drives for efficiency and self-actualization. I am talking here about the gathered fallout of a thousand frenetic moves: decisions to use a cell phone even when it's unnecessary, to hire professionals to run your life, to "visit" on the Internet when you know you should do it in person, to shop for stuff you don't really need because you have come to think you do need it, to stay later at the office, to buy a bigger home for a smaller household, to not bother to get to know the neighbors or vote in the local election because it has come to feel like it doesn't matter if you do. And yes, to grocery shop online or Ask Jeeves instead of the local librarian. The Connection Gap is that precious moat of space around us. It is both the protection we crave and the barrier we complain about.

Hey, What Happened?

It's easy to strike up a conversation with anyone over thirty about how radically life, the world, society, and the old neighborhood have changed in recent years. There is virtue, in fact, in recalling the alleged simplicity with which even the most privileged among us was raised. Now, of course, it is far different and all a wreck. This is the familiar line that seems endemic to aging. My grandpa didn't tout the virtues of the Clean Plate Club because he was thinking of us. He championed eating watermelon right down to the rind and chicken clear to the bone because he was a product of the Great Depression. It was the way you were supposed to eat; anything less was wasteful. Clearly, our perceptions are colored by our experiences. It would be easy enough to attribute concerns about disconnection to people glorifying the Good Old Days. In fact, you don't have to go far to see marketing aimed at doing just that. The implicit message, of course, is that if you buy you can reclaim that cozy, connected feeling. One has only to step inside Restoration Hardware to see people longing for a romanticized past of Betty Crocker recipes and bright red metal toolboxes.

But there is more to what's going on now than a hunger for Howdy Doody or the Brady Bunch. The current wave of nostalgia is all the more intense because we are at the dawn of the twenty-first century and in the midst of such a rapid change. We are at once exhilarated by new possibilities for living and fearful of leaving the familiarity of what we have known. These dual forces—longing for the past and eagerness for the wondrous future—have created an awkward tension, one that cannot be eased by the purchase of a butterfly chair or a Bobby Sherman lunch box. The truth is that no one wants to look like a Luddite, but people also worry that good stuff, rich stuff, risks being lost forever. The concern is not unfounded. We are experiencing more than the age-old sense of the uncomfortable passing of time. The world really *is* changing—and so are we.

Sven Birkerts argues in *The Gutenberg Elegies* that we are in a time like no other. "The primary relations—to space, time, nature, and to other people—have been subjected to a warping pressure that is something new under the sun," he writes. "Those who argue that the very nature of history is change—that change is constant—are missing the point. Our era has seen an escalation of the rate of change so drastic that all possibilities of evolutionary accommodation have been short-circuited."[1]

We are drowning in our own victorious advances. We are seizing the future and the present but missing what we hold in our hands. Despite the widespread awareness that technology is radically reordering our lives, we have failed to think deeply about how we want to use it—and how we *don't* want to use it. "In hindsight, the situation is clear to everyone," Langdon Winner writes in his book *The Whale and the Reactor: A Search for Limits in an Age of High Technology.* "Individual habits, perceptions, concepts of self, ideas of space and time, social relationships, and moral and political boundaries have all been powerfully restructured in the course of modern technological development." The very things we embrace transform not just the one specific thing they seem to address but a whole constellation of related things. Changes wrought by high technology are profound, and yet, Winner complains, they "have been undertaken with little attention to what those alterations mean."[2]

So are we smarting from the speed of change? Or have we simply failed to pay attention to what was happening? The truth may rest between the two extremes. It's my hope that, while we may be powerless to slow the rate of change, we may at least increase our awareness of its arrival. Right now, we seem stuck in receive mode, accepting all incoming alterations without question. The speed and seamless manner in which the Next New Thing is put into play leads us to focus on learning how to use it, and not on seeing how it shapes our behavior. Initially, I paid more attention to getting the kinks out of my online grocery shopping experience—customizing my electronic shopping list and finding ways of more quickly perusing the virtual aisles—than I did to thinking about how this would change my sense of community and connection. After all, whether in person or electronic, I still call it "grocery shopping." But, in fact, they are two very different activities.

Consider, for example, how the telephone call has evolved—and changed how we converse. Objectively, a phone call is still a phone call: We used the same phrase in 1960 that we do in 2000. But as the once stationary telephone has become first portable, and now completely mobile, the *experience* of speaking on the phone has been irrevocably altered. The phone call that once commanded one's undivided attention has over time become an event to be undertaken chiefly while you are doing something else: driving, ordering coffee, even sitting in the waiting room of the doctor's office. Certainly, people carve out times for focused phone conversations, but such times are growing rare. What was once a fairly intimate exchange is now often overheard in public. I, for example, found myself in the waiting room of my obstetrician's office seated next to a woman making a cell phone call in which she discussed the recent death of a friend—for everyone to hear. And the length of the phone call, once bounded by the conversation itself, is now subject to outside factors: entering a parking garage, traveling into a dead zone, needing to put milk in your coffee, or being called into the doctor's examining room. The "phone call" is not the same phone call one might have made a few decades ago. And the act of conversation—even the rhythm of the conversation itself—has been transformed from a mostly leisurely and attentive talk to an often clipped exchange. People today do not discuss; they get the message and run.

Technology has not altered our lives and our selves completely on its own. Its impact is intersecting with other forces. The relative affluence of our times has spurred new expectations about what kind of car we should drive, how big our home should be, what kind of clothing and other goods we should have. The increasing speed of life, too, along with the portability and mobility of nearly everything, necessarily changes how we interact. One office worker complained that all the advent of the fax machine in the 1980s did was increase the demands placed on him; papers previously mailed then had to be faxed. Now, they must be e-mailed or sent overnight. The office never really closes. Everything has become urgent. The expectation of instantly available everything speeds up the days, truncates interactions, and makes people nervous about squandering minutes or even seconds. There is no waiting anymore without agitation or—in some cases—anger. This shapes the way many of us move in the world, what we notice and what we no longer see.

The day, as we compose it, has become a series of scheduled activities—not of perceptions. When most of us talk about our days, we talk about what we did or crammed in, not what we noticed or thought. My older daughter was given a homework assignment to go outside, look around for five minutes, and then come back in and write down everything she saw; the exercise revealed the difficulty of taking time to do what we might consider "nothing." After two minutes she was ready to stop observing. I pressed her to stick with it. Finally, after five minutes, she came inside and made her list. I was struck by how many items came from memory—the swing set, the fence by the garage—and how few bore the stamp of the moment of her observation. Could it be she looked but didn't really see? I don't think she's alone. We don't need to see—at least not as specifically as we once did. Travel directions once required people to notice the likes of stone walls and chestnut trees to reach a destination. Today, we need only turn left at the McDonald's, get off at the numbered exit, or read the street sign. Are we losing our ability to notice nature? To enjoy an unscheduled moment?

Other changing values are reshaping human relations. Consider the popular drive for self-actualization. Mixed in with the idea that each of us can and should achieve to the best of our ability is the incessant message that each of us "deserves" certain things: the perfect partner, the luxurious vacation, the services of a masseuse, a therapist, and a personal trainer. I list these "necessities" only partly in jest. It may sound excessive, but the notion that each of us has a right to certain inalienable comforts has caught on. Unfortunately, marketing messages aimed at pampering us contradict a quieter call for another human pleasure: the reward of, at times, considering someone else's needs first. Instead, people are encouraged to focus on themselves. In relationships, people worry about being emotionally swindled. No wonder results of a 1999 study at Rutgers University revealed that the United States has hit the lowest rate of marriage in modern history—and that fewer of those who are married consider their unions to be "very happy."[3]

I don't intend to suggest that the forces at work—and our response to them—yield only negative behaviors. They don't. Part of all this change is good, whether it is better technology, faster service, or a belief that it's worth searching out a loving partner instead of settling for a miserable union with a creep. But there is little doubt that, when it all adds up, we are moving toward lives that are more inwardly focused and, ultimately, more alone. This is troubling chiefly because our society relies on human interaction and the natural tendency of people to come together. We need neighbors to talk with, people who care about what's happening next door or down the street. We need people to lend a hand when an elderly woman drops a bag of groceries as she tries to cross the road. We need the other driver to yield in traffic, the guy who is making your coffee to seem human, and partners to be devoted. We need parents to spend time with their children, citizens to debate issues, and friends to take time to sit around and shoot the breeze.

Of course, among many people and in many places, these things are already ticking along nicely. But even in the happiest corners of our nation, we are facing greater challenges to the simple act of connecting. It is harder to carry on the relationships and to support the interactions that make life truly satisfying. Perhaps if we can recognize the pressures we face and the choices we make, we may help each other reconnect. Life *is* making more demands on us. It's time to make some of our own.

Are We More Alone?

Aloneness and disconnection are tough to measure in a single number. There is no national scale of connectivity. Yet scholars, writers, and others are constantly talking about it, describing in various ways the thinning social fabric. Whether in an academic journal paper, an article in the *New York Times,* or a poll on Americans' attitudes, what we hear about again and again is that our society is less cohesive than we want it to be. In fact, we are given lots of numbers—not just one—that point to a dwindling sense of connection. Missing from such news flashes is a way of thinking about what they mean and how these findings relate to other findings. This is what I hope this book offers: not a comprehensive survey of daily life but a way of interpreting and connecting the events and information around us. So while I cannot proclaim a single number that proves that, yes, we are more alone than we were twenty, thirty, fifty, or a hundred years ago, I do believe that we are. And I believe that there is lots of evidence to support this position.

As a journalist, writer, and social observer, I draw my "evidence" from many quarters: academic studies, scholarly books, government publications, interviews, personal observation, poll data, government data, General Social Survey data, data from the Murray Research Center archives at Radcliffe, old periodicals and books, current newspapers and magazines, television, advertising, movies, store catalogues—even what they sell in the supermarket. It was, in fact, several years ago while writing for the *Boston Globe* food section, that I wrote an article on single-serving foods. In the course of browsing store aisles for new products and trends, I noticed a number of new foods designed to serve just one. (By now we've grown accustomed to them, but back then they were news.) When I got to my desk, I started calling the food manufacturers, and again and again I heard the same story. They were reflecting America's changing eating habits. There were more households of singles, and in households of several people, their marketing research showed, people were eating more meals alone; families were eating *in sequence* instead of all at once. The manufacturers were adjusting to suit the market. This shift was obvious to me as I read the copy on the "family size" box of Weaver's Chicken Croquettes, which assumed consumers were heating an individual microwave dinner for each family member. The "family size" offered an added feature: You could microwave all the meals at once.

Although such information seems trivial, it's not. It is, after all, the trivial that reveals the broader picture of what a society cares about. The forces that nudge and press at us, after all, do not confine themselves to a single academic discipline or sector of life; they are manifested in many ways and in many areas of living, in some more dramatically than others. Besides, it's fun and interesting, as well as informative and useful, to subject daily life to scrutiny. The mere act of examining our environment and our actions edges each of us toward looking at life with the eager eyes of a scout.

So *are* we more alone? Much of this book will address the ways in which we are living more solo, more isolated, more inwardly focused lives. Our aloneness is played out in the way we eat, watch TV, work, play, fall in love, marry (or don't), socialize, and shop. Consider, as one example, the automobile. Americans have long loved cars, but our relationship to the vehicles has changed. The car today is not mere transportation but an intimate personal space. It is a mobile home and office—and an escape capsule so we may get away from everyone and everything. Just so, the car experience is increasingly an *interior* event; the action is not outside the vehicle but inside. Car ads focus on interior amenities—the "supple leather-trimmed seats of the new Lincoln Town Car," the stereo systems, leg room, head room, cup holders, global satellite positioning systems, video players, fanny warmers, and the like—because inside is where we spend our time. Some ads never even show the car's exterior profile. And why should they? The outward appearances of so many cars today are nearly indistinguishable. This was not the case a few decades ago, when it was the exterior—the use of chrome, the design of the grille, the length of the fins, the shape of the taillights, the whitewall tires, the curve of the fender, and the slope of the hood—that lured and enraptured.

The story of the car reflects not just technological advances in manufacturing and design but the story of our own changing ways. What does it say when we care more about the cup holders than the fenders? Certainly cars are more personal spaces, in part because we can do more in our cars today than we could fifty years ago. But we have also come to view cars not as belonging to the household but as individual possessions. The car is a private sanctuary and a vehicle of self-discovery. "I never found the companion that was so companionable as solitude— THOREAU" tops a print ad showing a Chevy Tahoe parked deep in the deserted woods with rays of sunlight cutting through a shady canopy of tall pines. What does it say that a "family" car like the Volvo station wagon has been marketed in TV ads as transportation for solo soul searching? Even when we do drive with others, manufacturers create a sense of separation between driver and passengers in the vehicle's interior. Those marketing the Chevy Venture minivan, for example, tout a "Dual Mode Sound System that lets you listen to the radio in the front seat and lets them listen to a CD or whatever they call music in the back. And vice versa. Which means they won't roll their eyes when you sing and you won't have to listen to something that sounds like bees attacking a hippo." No need to fight over the stereo—everyone gets his or her way. Long gone are the images of the family piling into the car for a Sunday drive. Riding with others (when you must) is no longer a communal event but a set of parallel experiences.

Mostly, though, we try not to drive together. Despite aggressive campaigns and specially designated carpool lanes for commuters sharing rides, Census Bureau figures tracking private vehicle occupancy among workers sixteen and older show that the percentage of those driving to work *alone* rose from 76 percent to nearly 85 percent between 1980 and 1990. Carpoolers dropped from 24 to 15 percent of commuters over the same time period. And a Gallup poll released in January 2000 suggests the trend continues: The percentage of respondents using public transportation to get to work fell from 12 percent in 1947 to 1 percent in 1999; the percentage saying they drove a car or truck but did not carpool rose from 32 to 87 percent. There may be a host of reasons for the trend away from sharing rides, including lower gas prices, but the fact remains: More of us are driving alone.[4]

Our cars—the way they are designed and marketed and the way we use them—reflect a growing aloneness, a state mirrored in other parts of our lives. At times, it's true, we may embrace solitude with the eagerness of someone who needs a break from the frenzy of modern living. But as often, we drift toward solo states as a way of being and thinking even when we are not in need of respite. We have a "default mode" for isolation that seems to kick in almost automatically. Perhaps this very instinct may *contribute* to our stresses, instead of providing relief. Often, after all, our isolation is not physical but perceptual.

Because we cannot always control our physical space, we seek to control our mental space by tuning out or shutting out those around us. We routinely ignore other people or do not see them when we look at them. The driver may mechanically stop to allow a pedestrian to cross the street but betray no glimmer of empathy—and may even seem to wait impatiently and rev the engine afterward. It is as if a stoplight has commanded him, not the desire to be decent. People may hold the door for you or allow you to step onto the elevator first, but the kindness is done mechanically—and without kindness. The body acts, but the switch of human engagement is turned to the "off" position. When we exist more in our private mental states than in the world, we can control others, not by physically avoiding them but by choosing not to engage. We pretend not to see the other jogger when we pass, making the Walkman the excuse for not even nodding. We feign concentration. Our attention is pulled elsewhere, into our chosen world—the cell phone, the Watchman, the Discman, papers, private thoughts. And that is the irony: We may be lonelier than ever, more disappointed in the quality of our social interactions but we are tireless in our pursuit of privacy and seclusion.

In a sense, many of us are placing ourselves in self-imposed solitary confinement. We are filtering out the stimuli of everyday encounters, willingly collapsing the possible interactions and explorations around us in our effort to cut through the day in the most efficient manner possible. The effects of sensory deprivation have been well studied, and we know how devastating solitary confinement can be. It is what breaks prisoners of war and sorely tries cancer patients undergoing bone marrow transplants, whose weakened immune systems require them to spend weeks sealed off from the world. High-tech prisons, in which inmates in solitary confinement are locked down by remote-controlled cell doors and monitored by state-of-the-art surveillance equipment with minimal human contact, have been attacked as inhumane.[5]

Most of us will never know what it is to be literally placed in solitary confinement, but we may feel the effects every day of a lesser but not unrelated experience. Consider the rising number of us who suffer from depression, anxiety, or sleeplessness. Is it just the result of better diagnosis? Unfortunate genes? Or does the more solitary way we live our lives bear some blame?

The Connection Gap

People today *are* concerned about their lives and relationships. Many of us feel less connected and more alone. But how did we get here? What can we do? In this book I will argue that we are in the midst of rapid change, not only in how we conduct our lives but also in who we are. I will examine the elements of daily life that are so ordinary they have become invisible. It is their invisibility that makes them threatening. When we see, when we can cast these elements as choices, we gain the power to act. This book is meant not as a fix-your-life guide but as an argument for recognizing the threats to connection and finding ways to reconnect. It does not pretend to provide a comprehensive survey of modern life. Instead, I am focusing on the domestic and the day-to-day. My subjects and sources are vast and varied, but I aim to hit on major themes that resonate with many people. I understand that I cannot write about all people in all situations. My bias is toward examining middle-class life in America. Even "middle-class" is a very general description, and some aspects of daily living I mention may smack of the most upwardly mobile members of this class. Yet at times I find it valid to set forth this economically endowed group as an example relevant to us all. This group sets the tone, the style, the standard of living that so many of us aspire to emulate. Even when we cannot afford all that this upper middle class has, we try. Our age is a study in the marketing of luxuries to the masses. And even people who cannot afford them still buy new cars, expensive clothes, jewelry, and more. A friend who teaches at a vocational-technical high school, who personally knows the economically stressed reality of students' home lives, never fails to marvel at the brand-new cars, including luxury vehicles, parked in the student lot. The presence of new cars, more than an economic statement, is a statement about our times. When I was growing up, in the 1970s, my parents always drove old cars. At times, with my mother at the helm, the four of us children were instructed to offer encouragement (and a little forward rocking didn't hurt) so that "Nellie" might start. And we weren't alone. Everywhere you went there were older cars on the road. Today the story is very different. Take a drive on a major highway, and most of the cars are late models and in good condition. So, even as I might aim often at the upper economic tier, I believe the messages embedded in the analysis speak to a far wider audience.

To begin with, I will look at the culture of *shopping*. Even as many profess distaste for materialism, our society has become addicted to shopping and buying. It has become not merely a means for acquiring goods but a way of negotiating and valuing our relationships. The language and values of commerce pervade daily life. Is it any accident that personal ads read like catalogue copy? No wonder people "shop" for mates and wonder if they could get a "better deal" than they've got. Shopping itself is also a means for seeking the love and attention lacking elsewhere. Why do we so readily submit to the helpful salesclerk? Hunger for the doting chatter and gentle touch of the woman or man at the cosmetic counter? It is no accident that so many products and services are marketed as keys to enhancing relationships. Connection has become a commodity.

The microchip may have invited us into this new world, but it is *screens*—television, PC, laptop, monitor, and others—that we look at and, increasingly, interact with. The screen has become an unquestioned authority people rely on and trust. It has created a new language and new images for describing our world and our human relationships. What does it mean to "meet" someone now that the online world seems as authentic as the real one? How often do we confuse whether we heard something from a friend or on TV? Or has television *become* a friend? We may use screens ostensibly to entertain us or relay information, but they are doing much, much more. Screens are reorienting our sense of time and place. They are shifting our basic understanding of what it means to *relate*—on- and offline. They are becoming our clerks, our information booth attendants, and our personal assistants. It may be just a toy, but the Teletubby with a screen embedded in its fleshy middle is the perfect metaphor for our age.

Technology—particularly the cellular phone, the laptop, and the whole range of minicomputers and organizers—has made us all aware of the increasing portability of our work and our home lives. But our romance with *mobility* has been in the works for more than a century. From the advent of rail travel to the lack of need for travel at all, we have been obsessed with making the world smaller and our reach longer and further. It feels exciting today to negotiate a deal from the beach, call from the street, work in your pajamas. Nearly anything is better if you can do it anywhere. But what effect does a world in which nothing *has* to be anywhere have on relationships? The hunger for speed and portability has opened up a whole raft of expectations for how people live—and constantly move—through the days. As a people, we are no longer oriented to terrain but to motion. What happens, then, when we need to stop?

In the midst of all this change, one would expect *home* to remain a point of stability. But it's not. Just as we are changing, our homes are changing, too. They are becoming places where we seek out privacy and seclusion, not just from those who live next door and down the street but from those who live under the same roof. Why do we need more bathrooms in our homes today? Is it by chance that the living room is no longer for living? And what of the new urban planning efforts to build and design communities with sidewalks and picket fences aimed at bringing back neighborly interactions? Can we, if we try hard enough, build community with wood and nails?

At the heart of the book is the chapter about *relations*. One of the most confusing aspects of life in the present is that the relationships we have long counted on are changing, morphing into hybrids and new forms. What does it mean anymore to be a friend? Neighbor? Parent? Child? Partner? What is a family? It seems to take more work to maintain relationships—and we seem to have less time to build on the in-person experiences that they require. At the same time, the rules are shifting. As a society, we may be more self-aware, but we're also more self-absorbed and less willing—in all our relationships—to compromise. We want to connect, but the dance of relating has grown convoluted. We don't trust. We feel vulnerable. We want to fall in love, but we worry it won't last. We hunger for intimacy but end up confused about what that means. Why do so many—from folks on TV talk shows to people standing in checkout lines or riding on the train—feel the need to spill their innermost secrets to strangers? Why do we ache to confess?

The personal issues facing *us* are not self-contained but color our communal relations and affect our social fabric. We talk a great deal these days about "community" and describe ourselves as living in "a global village," but increasingly these labels seem to be more tricks of language than images that reflect the way things really are. People may, after all, be more closely linked electronically and more carefully tracked by demographers and marketers, but being plugged in, grouped, or identified with a mass of others is not the same as participating in a real community. Certainly we hunger to belong, but where can we find something meaningful to belong to? Why do we trust less and fear more? And what has happened to civility and common decency? It's not by chance that public disruptions have become commonplace: A man douses airline workers with coffee because he can't get an upgrade; the thirtieth anniversary of Woodstock ends with cars and vans set ablaze.

The challenges seem huge. In the final chapter, I offer some thoughts on how we might begin *bridging the gap*. The key is to realize that we *do* have choices. We are making them every day, and they are changing who we are. Already, we see ourselves growing more impatient, more covetous of privacy and seclusion, and less certain of how to reach out to others. In some ways, we are becoming less interesting people, more cloistered in our lifestyle enclaves and more easily satisfied with what we can possess than who we can be. It's time to take back our lives.

Human relationships are vital to our individual and collective happiness. We *need* to engage and connect. We *need* to be inconvenienced, dropped in on, surprised, and called upon. Of course it may be easier for parents to hire a professional baseball coach to polish their child's pitching technique, but it may be more valuable in the end to do it themselves. As a people, we must realize that the craze for perfection, the instinct to pay experts, and the eagerness to delegate the chores of our lives are not making living better—just thinner. As we reap what we feel are the benefits of this age of affluence, we are narrowing our experiences and cutting out interactions and opportunities for connection. It's time to reverse our collective retreat and to reinvolve ourselves in each other's lives. Certainly that's tough, especially when we are constantly presented with the tantalizing opportunity to do more while doing less. But there is good news: The Connection Gap is here not because we invited it but because we have not pushed it away. The challenge seems daunting, and yet the solution is straightforward: Only connect.

 **SHOPPING**

A man whose love affair has ended, in a Lydia Davis short story called "Break It Down," is sitting and staring at a piece of paper and trying to make an accounting of what has happened. His question: Was it, financially speaking, worth it? He's adding up the expenses, of travel, of the hotel, of meals. He figures that ten days of a love affair cost about one thousand dollars, and he's weighing what he got for his money. His first instinct is to balance that expense against lovemaking, once a day on average (or one hundred dollars a shot). But he quickly realizes this is rather shortsighted. There are other things that need to be factored in. There's the feel of her skin, the little questions she whispered in his ear, the pleasure of having breakfast together in a bright white coffeehouse. Maybe it was actually cheap, more like three dollars an hour, he decides. But then, he calculates, there were bad times, some hurt along with the ecstasy. In the end, as he struggles to match money to love, to weigh pleasure against loss, he comes down to an odd equation: He spent one thousand dollars and ended up with one of her old shirts.

The story shows just how complex human relationships, especially love, can be and how emotions resist price tags. Davis plays out the futility of translating the value of a love affair into dollars. But the story also reveals something else: the overwhelming instinct to view relationships through consumer eyes. We may not apply a hard dollar number to each encounter, but we do want to know the value of a relationship. What are we getting? What are we giving? Today, in the marketplace of human relations, we are shoppers all.

The role of shopper is one that suits Americans. And not just when we talk about buying stuff. Shopping today is much more. It is one of

the most familiar and frequent acts we engage in. It is how we negotiate relationships, seek personal fulfillment and make emotional connections. We may "shop around" for friends that please, seek out goods
that enhance our self-image, or buy the professional services of someone to listen, to empathize, and to care. The luxurious venues for shopping, the dazzle of retail displays, the catalogues that evoke daydreams
of perfect Sunday brunches are not merely ways to showcase goods, but
experiences to be consumed, as real in their moment as any life event.
We spend our money and our time according to a consumer ethos.
Partners commune over goods, show their compatibility by agreeing on
what purchase should be next "for the house." Shopping informs our
language, expectations, and notions of life. Singles in search of a partner, in effect, "shop" for a mate. Some comb personal ads, reading the
offerings like so many catalogue entries. Should we someday expect to
see potential mates advertising their moss-colored eyes and hair of saf-
fron or clove? Singles bars have acknowledged the commercial lexicon;
they're "meat markets." In effect, we are constructing personal relationships according to consumer expectations. At the same time, the
intimacy of our commercial relationships—the up-close and personal
advertisers, the attentive salesclerks, the myriad of personal professional
services—is blurring our understanding of what a personal relationship
is. Shopping may offer control over the unpredictability of life, but it
offers no clear distinction between what is a product and what is not.
So people do what feels most comfortable: shopping and buying.

Buying has become as ingrained as the need to eat and sleep—and
not just among the wealthy. Never mind that as a society we own more
stuff than ever—we *want* more. We have discretionary income, and we
spend it. And this is not just a habit of the moneyed class. More than
70 percent of households with incomes over twenty thousand dollars
have money left over after paying for the basics, and all of those earning eighty thousand or more, have discretionary income. Sometimes we
buy more than we can immediately pay for, relying on credit to get
what we want. Between 1989 and 1992, mortgage and home-equity
debt rose an average of more than 15 percent across all income levels,
measured in constant 1992 dollars. Over the same time, the percentage
of American households with credit card debt ticked up to 43 percent,
with the median debt at one thousand dollars.[1]

Spending has not always been so easy for Americans. A hundred years
ago, the Protestant values of self-sacrifice, self-restraint, and a distaste for

waste dominated the belief system. Spending one's earnings was done judiciously, and only when there seemed no other alternative. Such values have been turned on their head. Over the past century, we have moved from being a society utterly suspicious of spending and consumerism to one defined by them. Today we embrace all that our forebears frowned on: the quick fix, immediate gratification, and a lust for the brand-new. Even early industrialists like Henry Ford, who had everything to gain by selling style, beauty, and the installment plan, shunned such values in favor of durability and living within one's income. At one point, Ford boasted of building a car "so strong and so well-made that no one ought ever have to buy a second one." Ford, of course, could not halt the growing tide of consumerist values—values that have brought us a credit card culture and fed the hunger to acquire newer, more luxurious versions of what we already own. What would he think today of the ads for Honda that urge consumers to "simplify," while explaining that "simplifying" doesn't mean you have to live without leather seats or a state-of-the-art sound system? Today, some of us have become like winners of a shopping spree who are given three minutes to fill a cart: We grab for all that instantly appeals. The result is not just overstuffed closets of goods but lives shaped, packed, and penetrated by consumer ideology. In the absence of other unifying values, the consumer ethic describes who we are and how we live. It orders expectations, shapes life goals, and defines behavior. Shopping is not merely a metaphor run amok. It *is* how we live.[2]

What does this have to do with connection? A lot. Just as Davis's story illustrates the impossibility of matching money to love, our consumer-centric way of life, too, fails to grant real value to the little things—the whispers, the feel of a lover's skin, the pleasure of company. It's not that these details of relationships don't exist. They do. But in a system where they can't be given value, they can't be translated. These things—at the heart of human relationships—fade from consciousness. The instinctive quest to apply commercial rules to personal encounters leaves out, devalues, the very human qualities that evoke compassion, love, gratitude, loyalty.

Consider this true incident: My friend has two cats. When she went away for a week, her neighbor looked after them. Afterward, though, my friend grew troubled: She realized she couldn't reciprocate because her neighbor didn't have any pets. So the next time she went away, she hired someone to care for the two cats. When the neighbor found out, he was upset and hurt. He asked her not to ever hire anyone to care for the cats again. He'd be happy to do it for free. My friend, despite being very thoughtful and attuned, had instinctively viewed the neighbor's help as part of an economic equation. He was providing a service of value, and she needed to balance it with payment.

Meanwhile, the possibility that the neighbor gets pleasure out of doing a favor, that it makes him feel needed, trusted, and relied on, is absent from the figuring. Those values are outside of the consumer system and therefore don't register. This is at the heart of our Connection Gap. We short-circuit the very things that deepen a sense of belonging and interdependence. In a culture enamored of control, money frees people from needing others. Many people would rather pay someone to do something for them than to have someone else do it for free. But the cost of this choice is more than the professional's fee. Unaccounted for is the loss of connection.

The consumer ethic—along with the personal cost this ideology extracts—is not confined to the realm of neighborly relations. Its influence is pervasive. It guides people's thinking and actions. It leaves our society with a materialistic language as the basis for our communication: Say you love her with a diamond tennis bracelet! It consumes our time and our thoughts. It redefines our goals in materialistic terms, driving us to reach for the better house, the better car, and the more exotic vacation instead of reaching for the better quality of life, the deeper, more satisfying relationship, or the better society. What's most insidious, though, is that we have so fervently bought into material culture that it seems better and easier to have our lives commodified and sold to us. Instead of fussing to connect with yourself or with others, you can just buy the package that marketers have figured out is right for you. And if you're feeling the itch for community, you can join Sam's Club.

Insidiously, we are being silenced and absorbed by the very consumer ideology we embrace. As Leslie Savan argues in *The Sponsored Life*, the incessant flow of commercial messages mixes "the most intimate processes of individual thought with commercial values, rhythms and expectations." We are living, she says, "the sponsored life," in which commercial culture sells our own experiences back to us. We are not living freely, authentically, but cribbing from the marketers' consumer profile even as they crib from us. This all may appear harmless, or at worst an annoyance. In fact, it represents the translation of life into a shopping model. People silently apply consumer sensibilities to human encounters, monetary values to what should remain outside of such a system. This threatens values that make personal sense but not shopping sense. In the end, many of us are left feeling we have made many transactions but no satisfying connection.[3]

Money Rules

A front-page story in the *New York Times* on October 14, 1998, with the headline "When Money Is Everything, Except Hers," describes the life of a thirteen-year-old girl named Wendy Williams who lives in a trailer park in Dixon, Illinois, called Chateau Estates. This is not the oft-told story of life in abject poverty in a neighborhood rife with drugs and guns. Rather, it is a look at the struggles of a seventh grader who is sneered at, teased, and put down because she cannot afford the designer clothes, the nice home, or the fine vacations her classmates in this town of three-hundred-thousand-dollar homes with three-car garages take for granted. When she remarks to another girl, "That's a really awesome shirt. Where did you get it?" the retort is stinging. Williams recalls: "She looked at me and laughed and said, 'Why would you want to know?'"

She tries to conceal her rummage-sale clothes in a school where the Nike swoosh and Tommy Hilfiger labels are coveted and displayed. She leaves her shirt hanging out to cover the cheap belt; she purses her lips to hide the overbite that has given her the nickname Rabbit. She has asked, but her parents—a welder and a part-time cook for Head Start—cannot afford an orthodontist.

Wendy lives in a time when status or acceptance is determined by what you can afford, not by who you are. It does not matter that she is a voracious reader or talented at math. She is poor in a culture in which wealth—or at least the outward illusion of it—is the price of friendship. As one who twenty-five years ago wore thrift-shop clothes and shoes that crushed my toes, and who ached for a pair of the suede Pumas that were the status symbol of the time, I appreciate the sting of realizing what you cannot have. But my pain was largely private; Wendy lives in an era when material lacking draws public mocking.

One obvious consequence of this is familiar: The expanding gap between the "haves" and the "have nots." In recent decades, the gap in average income between the poorest 20 percent of families and the richest 20 percent has widened. In 1967, for example, the difference in average family income between the poorest fifth and the richest fifth was $66,294, as measured in constant 1994 dollars. The size of that gap increased slightly in the 1970s and more substantially in the 1980s, and it has exploded since. In 1994, the gap was $105,221. Put another way, in 1967, the richest fifth of families earned 7.5 times as much as the poorest fifth. By 1994, the richest fifth were earning more than nineteen times the poorest fifth.[4]

Just as critical as the size of the gap is the meaning that it holds. As Wendy's case shows, the lens through which kids today view each other is largely materialistic. No wonder the 1998 Roper Starch Youth Report, which reported results of interviews with 1,189 American children ages six to seventeen, revealed that for 55 percent "being rich" was their number one daydream, ranking above desires to be famous, smart, or a sports star.

And children are not the only ones who value wealth so dearly. Susan Fornier, an assistant professor at Harvard Business School, says that our culture's preoccupation with consumption prompts most of us to dream of purchases and to maintain active wish lists of things we want to consume. Other researchers before her have established an array of goods that make up "the good life," including desires for career success, exotic experiences, and the acquisition of great wealth or possessions. In her analysis, Fornier links consumer daydreaming to pervasive materialistic beliefs.[5]

So what do people include on their wish lists? A survey Fornier conducted with colleague Michael Guiry of adults of a range of ages, incomes, education, and social classes in the southeastern United States, Massachusetts, Indiana, New York, and Pennsylvania found a hunger for luxuries, consumer goods, and special or exotic experiences. The most popular wish list item was a desire for a new, bigger, or more beautifully situated home, mentioned by 71 percent of respondents. Almost half wanted new cars. More than one in four listed luxury items, including yachts, antiques, jewelry, and designer clothes. A majority also expressed the desire to travel throughout the United States or Europe or to take a vacation in an exotic location. Interestingly, Fornier and Guiry observed the presence of consumption excess (30 percent wanted at least two houses, cars, or vacations), consumption escalation, and trade-up (22 percent stated wishes for newer, bigger, or better possessions and experiences).

What's most startling in the study, though, is that a majority of those surveyed thought they would attain at least 75 percent of their wishes. A third believed they would realize 90 percent of their wishes! The lists, then, are not mere fantasy but real guides and goals that shape and motivate people. The acquisition of goods and the purchase of desired experiences are dominant guideposts along life's journey. We move forward, reaching toward each new consumer goal as a measure of our progress. Although the idea of "moving up" to a better watch, a finer car, a bigger house is an old standard, it has become cemented into the American psyche. If you don't acquire the goods associated with your station in life, the question arises: What's wrong? Why is he driving that old car? Why didn't they go on vacation this year? Why hasn't she replaced that old sofa?

Despite our lust for stuff, Fornier also discovered that the more items people put on their wish lists, the less life satisfaction they reported. Those who wanted the most stuff were the least happy. Fornier suggests that "possession-focused dreaming may reflect a hope that the road to happiness is paved with currently unrealized consumption desires, or a tendency to revert to fantasy for escape." People believe that their unhappiness can be solved by the right purchase, a notion drilled home by marketers who endow products with powers far beyond their physical realities. Perfume can make you mysterious; a car can imbue your life with adventure or romance. The right drink will make you hip; choosing the proper overnight carrier will reveal you to be a genius in your workplace.

The products send signals; our consumption desires telegraph life goals. The message persists: How much money you spend and how you spend it, more than anything else today, describes who you are. We hunger to be unique. We respond to the advertisers who wink at us, who whisper in our ears, who invite us to join the exclusive inner circle and tell us we are part of something big. But we are, in fact, ever more alone, ever less distinct, known to ourselves and others by the cars we drive, the stores we shop in, the catalogues we get, the restaurants we frequent, the vacation spots we know, the brands we buy, and the labels we wear.

The spending of money keeps Wendy Williams apart from her classmates. It keeps her from going to the mall, joining clubs, playing sports, seeing a movie, going out for pizza, or socializing after school. It makes her, in today's culture of abundance, one of the lonely. Her plight is not unique. A seventy-year-old widow who once lived in a five-bedroom home in a tony suburb found herself, after her husband's death, living alone in a small city apartment, watching her few dollars like a hawk. (He had left her with virtually no money.) She told me when I interviewed her how lonely she was for company. "What about the senior center?" I asked, knowing that the woman who ran the local program organized day trips and discount movie days. No, she answered, the three dollars or the six dollars was too much to spend on socializing when she couldn't even afford to buy enough food to eat well. The same point was made in a letter sent to me by a reader who described himself or herself as "one of the lonely." "People don't always have loving families or friends, and it costs a lot of money to be a club member or to socialize or to go on enriching trips," the reader wrote. "It's not fun being lonely."

Money rules.

The power of money to shape the way people relate has long been recognized by other cultures and by scholars of various disciplines. Money, in fact, has often been viewed as a contaminant, poisoning personal relations. That's why, for example, according to sociologists Peter K. Lunt and Sonia M. Livingstone, Malay fishermen avoid commercial transactions with their kin. They will exchange money only with comparative strangers.

Although it's folly to imagine America operating without money as the driving medium, it is interesting to consider what happens when money is introduced into a society. In *Das Kapital*, Karl Marx argued that money had an alienating effect on human relations. Obviously, many have disagreed with Marx, countering that money gives people greater freedom and more choices. One thing is clear, though: Money can organize a society. Money creates a structure for the valuing of goods and services and for the attainment of wealth. In a monetary system, things can have independent and individual values and can be bought or sold on their own. It is unlike a barter or trade system, in which values are relative and connected to the trading relationship. Moving from a barter system to a monetary system alters the way people relate. One classic argument, as described by Lunt and Livingstone, is that money moves "people from a form of social relationships based on emotions and imaginative thinking to a set of relations based on calculation." Because money does not convey human emotion, it rationalizes social relations in the marketplace. And, they and others argue, this new standard becomes the "model for social relations generally."[6]

Do modern Americans treat social encounters like commercial transactions? Some scholars have argued that people can compartmentalize
and keep social relations separate from business relationships. Others say
the two tend to run together. The two ideas seem to oppose each other,
but today they are both at work in daily life. Certainly, there are some
relationships that are kept separate from considerations of money—family, for one. If your child, your sister, or your mother needs you to do
something, chances are you'll do it and not quietly calculate how much
your "gift" of time and effort is worth. Just because individuals may not
tally the value of such efforts doesn't mean others don't. Various surveys
have calculated that the care for elderly or ill relatives is responsible for
eleven to thirty billion dollars a year in absenteeism, tardiness, and lost
production among workers who struggle to hold down a job as they
care for others. Another example of free help came my way when my
stepfather, a handyman, spent a week rebuilding my sagging front
porch. He worked long days, was fussy about doing it right, and never
considered—and would have been offended by—payment. All the
while, of course, I couldn't quell the commercial voice in my head. He
may have been giving me his time and his talent, but I saw a gift worth
several thousand dollars, much as I wished not to see it that way.[7]

We can probably all come up with a group of people in our free-
exchange circle, people whom we have helped for free without keeping a running tab. I would argue, though, that such circles are growing
smaller. Within a family, the idea of "owing" is superseded by duty. You
give because you are asked or you sense that it is necessary. At various
times in history that same sense of duty, at different levels of intensity,
has been applied to neighbors, friends, compatriots, stray children,
travelers, and people in need. Today, it is more challenging to rouse a
sense of obligation to any but a few individuals. Certainly, people do
volunteer, but volunteerism is different from simply doing the thing that
needs doing in an unscripted moment. There are fewer and fewer
people with whom we "trade" favors and help without keeping an
accounting. It feels less comfortable to shovel the neighbors' walk. Do
they want me to do it? Will I be liable if they slip and fall after I'm done?
Would they rather hire someone? A few decades ago, you didn't pause.
My mom would hand me or my brother a shovel and send us over to
our elderly neighbor's house. Imagine trying to orchestrate a barn raising today. Who would volunteer such tremendous amounts of labor?
Who would trust that, in time, they could tap the same pool of labor

for their own benefit? Yet even cooperative efforts on a much smaller scale are powerful experiences. You feel great, exhilarated. You feel like you're a part of things. But there is something that stops many people from joining in, that freezes them in the moment they are contemplating action.

In one of his poems, Robert Bly describes just this idea. He writes of the sudden halting of things, of "Those great sweeps of snow that stop suddenly six feet from the house . . ./ Thoughts that go so far." He writes of the boy who finishes high school and "reads no more books," of the son who stops calling home, of the mother "who puts down her rolling pin and makes no more bread." He sees that "the wife looks at her husband one night at a party and loves him no more." He writes: "It will not come closer—/ the one inside moves back, and the hands touch/ nothing, and are safe."[8]

Disengagement and insularity *do* seem safer than the unpredictability of involvement. And yet, over and over again, we witness what happens when disaster or tragedy strikes. The ordinary rules of behavior are upset, and people act with their hearts. People work together to pile sandbags against the banks of a rising river; people give blood; they send clothes and money to storm victims; some help to clean up damage. When news of the Oklahoma City bombing came across the airwaves, a woman with a headset on in the headquarters of a national telemarketing firm in Cambridge, Massachusetts, stopped pitching a credit card and shared her reaction to the news with the stranger at the other end of the line. It is not that we don't know how to connect. We do. We ache for the chance to suspend the normal social rules that keep us squarely focused on the business at hand.

Most of the time, though, we operate in a market mentality. Even if a friend helps out by picking up a child or lending a set of folding chairs, it is part of a commercial equation. When someone does something for you, the overwhelming concern is to repay and discharge the responsibility of owing as quickly as possible. People *hate* being indebted to someone else, even though the debt has the power to join us.

Daily Transactions

There have been so many cultural and social changes in recent decades that it is no longer safe to make assumptions about what a "family" is, what "friend" really means, even what "marriage" is for or should look like. We confide our most intimate secrets to co-workers who, upon transfer or job change, may disappear from our lives forever. Some spouses hardly converse as they work long hours, live in different cities or countries, or rely on e-mail for whispering sweet nothings. A single friend wondered how long it would be before someone discovered her body if she died. This is not to say we don't have "networks," that clinical-sounding word to describe people who know and care about us. But relationships today aren't so clear. What is required of a friend? A sibling? A parent? A neighbor?

Commercial relationships, on the other hand, are very clear. As the shopper, you are there to be served, to have your needs met, to be thoroughly satisfied and attended to. In fact, being the shopper is generally a very easy and relaxing role. The expectations are clear, and the encounters are mostly quite pleasant. Your needs are the focus, not a trivial point in an era when it can be hard to direct friends and family to drop what they're doing to focus on your issue. It's little surprise, then, that even as polls suggest people today are more reticent about "commitment" in personal relationships, we are charging ahead into long-term committed relationships with corporate America. Commercial relationships are appealing because they're so predictable. You *know* when you dial up to order a sweater from the L. L. Bean catalogue that the person on the other end will be attentive and cheery. Similarly, you can depend on the salesclerk or waitress at your favorite spot to be pleasant and focused on your concern, whether you are trying to find a flattering pair of jeans or are worried about too much cream in the vichyssoise. This also means, of course, that when our expectations of these relationships go awry, we get angry. After a stockboy at one Staples store complained over and over to me about his job, asking if I wanted to work for $6.50 an hour, I avoided the store. He violated the rules: I didn't want to hear about *his* troubles; he was supposed to be concerned about *mine*. The point is, it is supposed to be safe and comfortable to be the consumer. Who, after all, is generally more attentive, more solicitous, more sympathetic than the salesclerk about to receive a commission?

Dealing with someone you are paying is mostly satisfying. As the consumer you're always right, and your issues, however trivial, are treated as very important. Where else can you get such attention? No wonder people hire experts to organize their wardrobes and their lives, to tell them what colors look good, to decorate their homes for the holidays, to drive them to meet personal goals (and browbeat them if they fail), and to listen to their problems. If you hunger for human contact, you can always get a massage. The array of personal services is growing, and it is giving us the ability to have many needs and desires met commercially. As one man in his fifties remarked to me, "Why talk with friends about your problems when you can do it with your therapist?" When we pay, we have the right to good advice and full attention. In a society bent on having "the best," the expectation is that if you hire a professional to listen to you, the quality of advice is better; besides, you don't have to reciprocate. With friends or family, what you get depends on their mood, their issues of the moment, and whether they're still ticked about what you said at Thanksgiving.

The commercial world is efficient and easy. Many of us like the kind of clarity and finality that the consumer role offers. Personal relationships, after all, can be messy, intricate, demanding, and potentially resistant to closure. What's more, it seems natural to tap all the help you need when it's right there, all set up, just for you. Who needs friends to cook meals after a hospital visit when a service will do it—and professionally, too? Why check on an elderly relative at home when someone from a service will change the lightbulbs, drive her to a hair appointment, and sit and chat for an hour every other day? Why ask your partner to give you a back rub when a masseuse will do a more thorough job? Whether out of convenience or indulgence or affluence, it is generally accepted that hiring people to fulfill personal desires is not only all right but even preferable. It's wonderful to have someone give you undivided attention, really look at you, listen to you, think hard about you, touch you gently and thoughtfully—even if you are paying for it.

Mary Lou Andre might be described as a personal shopper or a closet cleaner or an image consultant. Her company, Organization By Design, based in Needham, Massachusetts, has been featured in books and national magazines. She gives conferences and runs fashion shows for major department stores. And yet this petite woman, with auburn hair and the kind of voice that instantly soothes, has discovered that her business is about people wanting to be looked at, considered, and cared for.

There is no denying that Andre has a stunning facility of putting flattering outfits together, a talent that commands $150 an hour. But she readily admits she is not in the fashion business so much as the emotional business. It is the personal and psychological boost she gives clients that has built her such a loyal following. She is the compassionate friend, the fashion-wise big sister—without the baggage, and only up to a point. The relationship is, after all, a business one. This kind of personal service, Andre observes, is challenging. "When you are in the emotional business, you have to have real good boundaries," she says. One woman was calling her several times a day and attempting to give Andre gifts. Andre would not accept the gifts, because she saw it as a move to change the rules of their relationship. What the woman really wanted was a real friend, someone to know and care about her. Andre, thoughtful as she is, has a business to run.

And yet, because businesses like Andre's are all about relationships, the lines get blurred. We think that service providers like Andre are our friends. And they may be, but it is a new form of friendship, one whose commercial bounds make for a one-way flow of compassion. No wonder my friend Lucy, a computer sales representative, was the first to learn that a client's wife was pregnant. It was safe for the client to tell her because he knew she would respond the way he expected: with an abundance of congratulations. No wonder, too, the same client grew very disappointed when Lucy said her accounts were being changed and a different sales representative would be servicing him in the future. He had a relationship with her that he really enjoyed.

The role of shopper is addictive. We know we're paying, but we may feel loved, cared for, and listened to. This is why shopping is such a popular refuge. Some people relieve nearly any excessive emotional state— joy or stress—by soothing themselves with a trip to the mall or some longed-for sales attention. I still remember the release I felt sitting at a makeup counter, feeling the tentative touch of the woman applying concealer below my eyes, dispensing advice about how to make myself look less stressed, less tired. I was in the middle of working on a magazine story in which a woman my age with terminal cancer was deciding to check herself into a hospice. I had been at the hospital that morning to see her. My distressed sister had been visiting, my kids had given me a tough time getting dressed and out the door, and I had a deadline. And yet there I was in Filene's, drinking in the considerate manner of a saleswoman, spilling out my stresses, tentatively at first, then in a torrent. Why is it so satisfying to tell someone you don't know all your troubles? To have her offer advice that is nonthreatening, such as the hint that drinking more water and less caffeine will get rid of the dark rings under your eyes? And, by the way, applying a little tanning powder will erase that wan look. Want to try some?

The problem with the commercial solution to the personal issue is that, of course, it's bogus. It refocuses, redirects, but doesn't address. Yet every day we get the message that our problems can be solved with the right purchase. Our troubles are reduced to one: darkness under the eyes. When we play the role of shopper there are no big problems, just little ones. And there are always soft voices asking, "Can I help?" No wonder we say yes.

The Wonderful World of Shopping

Shopping, of course, is not new. Archeological findings reveal the existence of marketplaces as early as 4000 to 5000 B.C.E. In prehistoric times, some scholars posit, peddlers traveled hundreds of miles from what is now the Baltic Sea to central Europe and the Mediterranean to bring items like salt, flint, amber, and furs to places where they were in short supply. The acquisition of possessions, the desire to have enough stuff, is innately human. We need things. There is security in having things. More recently, we have come to appreciate nice things. We will conquer new lands and sail uncharted seas to get them. But today, of course, we are far from being caught up in the quest for basic survival. Clearly, what is meant by "basics," by "needs" versus "luxuries," has shifted dramatically throughout history, and most strikingly in the past few decades.[9]

When compiling figures on discretionary spending, for example, authors of *The Official Guide to American Incomes* note they did not consider restaurant food discretionary. "Restaurant meals have become a necessary expense for today's busy households," they explain. Although few would disagree with this, just twenty-five or thirty years ago eating out was a big deal, a luxury indulged in on a special occasion. As a child growing up in the 1960s and 1970s, I went out to dinner, for Chinese food, once a year on New Year's Day. I recall the careful preparation for the event: the getting dressed, our best behavior for the ride in the car, and, when we arrived, the large round table draped with a red cloth and set with small ceramic cups and chopsticks. I felt incredibly lucky. Today, my children eat out probably once a week, and that doesn't count the day each week when we have take-out food. Eating out is no longer an extravagance; it's how many today feed a family.[10]

There are so many points in history at which to begin tracing the rise of our modern American consumer culture. Some date it to the colonial era; others, to the birth of the department store in the 1860s, a development that was seen as bringing to the middle class luxuries that had been exclusive to the wealthy. Despite Victorian distrust of spending and abundance, Americans in that era did make purchases, especially to enhance the home, which was considered the family's sanctuary and a moral environment that helped produce good children and citizens. But the consumer culture really took off after 1900, as urban centers grew more established, wages increased, women joined the workforce, and the arrival of mass advertising gave birth to a new consumer ethic. As a result, the amount spent for personal consumption nearly tripled from 1909 to 1929. More and more money was being spent on clothes, personal care, furniture, appliances, cars, and recreation. As historian Elaine Tyler May observes, "Mass consumption offered the promise— or the illusion—that the good life was now within everyone's reach." In particular, May observes, people increasingly spent money on enhancing their private lives. This was the beginning of the emergence of the American middle class.[11]

The Depression and World War II interrupted this trend, but the power of private consumption exploded at the war's end. In fact, some sociologists who study shopping behavior point to the end of WWII as a critical moment in the history of American consumption. It is in these years after the war, for example, that report after report fills the pages of the *New York Times* announcing the construction of new shopping centers. In postwar America, buying was not indulgent but patriotic. Many veterans returning from war went into retailing; others found work making the consumer goods that flowed into American homes. Not only did buying help the economy, but it provided glorious materialistic evidence that America had prevailed and was prospering. In fact, materialism became the very expression of the American Way of Life. When Richard Nixon and Nikita Khrushchev engaged in their famous "kitchen debate" in 1959, Nixon measured America's superiority in the better lifestyle of its citizens, evidenced by the cars, the TV sets, and the radio sets they owned.

And what there was to buy! Two-tone appliances, ever sleeker, ever more modern-looking goods. As Thomas Hine writes in his book on the material culture of the 1950s and 1960s, "the decade from 1954 to 1964 was one of history's great shopping sprees." It was starting in this era that people focused on consuming as never before. "There were so many things to buy—a power lawn mower, a modern dinette set, a washer with a window through which you could see wash water turn disgustingly gray, a family room, a charcoal grill," Hine writes. "Products were available in a lurid rainbow of colors and steadily changing array of styles."[12]

The explosion of spending on consumer goods was observed by a sales executive, William A. Blees, of the Avco Manufacturing Corporation, who noted at the Boston Conference on Distribution in 1953 that the number of potential customers had increased so fast that "most businesses could hardly avoid growing under the sheer pressure of population and its purchasing power." At this same meeting, Earl Puckett, chairman of the board of Allied Stores Corporation, stirred controversy about how to further increase sales. Three years earlier, he had riled the industry by saying that the job of the merchant was to spur obsolescence in order to sell more goods. Now he took to the podium and declared that scientific advances in retail selling were limited. It was not enough to figure inventory, timing of markups and markdowns, and so on.

What a store needed to do, he asserted, was "obtain desired emotional reactions." The remark is years ahead of its time. Today that is how stores appeal and goods are sold: They connect emotionally. Interestingly, another speaker, Robert MacNeal, president of the Curtis Publishing Company, applauded producers for solving many basic production problems. Next, he said, it was time to consider the nation's enormous industrial capacity and find buyers to match their production: "Our need in the future is to 'manufacture' customers for all the goods and services we are equipped to produce and to learn enough about these customers to know what they will buy that hasn't even yet been made."[13]

These men were not the first to plot ways to sell more goods or to cultivate desire among consumers. But their words came as the retail world was exploding. Even as they spoke, the Dayton Development Company was in the midst of constructing the nation's first suburban, enclosed, climate-controlled shopping center in Edina, Minnesota: the Southdale Shopping Center, which opened October 8, 1956.

What's interesting is that even as the messages to buy were multiplying, even as shopping centers were being constructed at the fastest pace in history, the runaway consumer mindset that so completely pervades life today had not yet arrived. Despite the desire for new and better goods, Americans were still thrift-minded. They did not quickly part with money. It still had to be earned, budgeted, earmarked, and then spent. Advertisements in popular magazines of the era suggest a careful American consumer. Ads for clothing boast about low prices and high quality. Ads for food, even in magazines not targeted just to home-makers, feature calculations on the cost per serving. For example, an ad for Ann Page mayonnaise that appeared in *Life* in August 1963, describes how to make "Crispy Crust Chicken" ("No pre-browning, no spat-tering or grease") for only twenty-nine to thirty-one cents a portion. "Once again," the ad reads, "Ann Page proves fine foods needn't be expensive!"

Maybe more to the point is an article in the November 1950 issue of *Good Housekeeping* that challenges the new consumer mindset. "Sorry, We Can't Afford It," by Mary Ellen Chase, is a plea to families to utter these words instead of accelerating spending to, as she puts it, "keep up with the neighbors." The article is notable because now, half a century later, it appears as an unheeded argument for reason in the midst of an increasingly acquisitive society. Chase utters a warning: "Whatever the size of the family purse, there are incalculable and heavy costs that *no* family can afford: The effects on children of the assump-tion that there is plenty of money, the selfishness that lurks in overindul-gence, the carelessness toward possessions easily obtained, the lack of quick understanding for those who have less money than they, the dangerous notion that money alone can purchase values that make the good life. These costs are, or should be, prohibitive for us all."

Chase's concerns capture the struggle of old values—the distaste for waste and overabundance—with the lure of the modern. To be mod-ern was to seek the new or the stylish and discard the old. Although the next two decades—the 1960s and 1970s—brought a stylistic backlash to consumer culture, it seems now to be less of a rebellion than a reckon-ing, the fight before the surrender. We were no longer afraid of being sold, but we wanted to be sold the right things. We wanted—as Puck-ett observed—to have an emotional connection with our purchases. The 1970s brought the credit card and, with it, the rise in shopping as fantasy. It was no longer necessary to compare the contents of your wal-let to the item in front of you and make a judgment: Can I afford it? Is it worth it? Credit urges different questions, questions of desire and the opportunity for immediate gratification: Do I want it? Should I just get it now?

In recent years, we have shed all pretense of shunning consumer cul-ture. The popular bumper sticker suggests that whoever ends up with the most toys wins. No longer do we deny ourselves, plan purchases, hold off. Consuming is not held at arm's length but is wrapped snugly around the body. It is what people do on vacation, during a day off, or while waiting to board a plane. The pursuit of the pseudo bargain, the game of buying for less, spurred the warehouse and outlet store experience. In the 1980s and early 1990s, the mall was declared the new Main Street. This, we were told, is where people meet and congregate. Malls are where people go to hear concerts, to visit a museum, to experience the community they live in. Little is said about the limitations of such civic spaces: They are privately controlled, sometimes have dress codes, and certainly have rules about who can exercise free speech. Today, though, even these spaces are disappearing as public gathering places. In newer malls, there are few seats along the shopping thoroughfares. Instead, they are tucked under stairwells or left to the food courts, where they encourage more spending. Even if seating were not an issue, shopping malls today seem less and less places of leisure. Shoppers, according to one report, spend 20 percent less time in the mall today than several years ago. And, perhaps more critically, the notion of going somewhere to be seen and to see other people, to be present as part of a public scene, is dying. Even in public, we are absorbed by our cell phones, doing the trivial or important business of the day, or focused on our mission and the minutes as they tick off. We don't look at other people, and they don't look at us.[14]

So even as shopping centers and malls continue to be built (according to the International Council of Shopping Centers, there are about forty-three thousand shopping centers in the United States, including about two thousand malls) and sales continue to rise, breaking the trillion-dollar mark in 1997, shopping—at times treated as a very social pursuit—is increasingly a private affair. Even as reports suggest people are spending less time in malls, shopping by catalogue and online has rocketed in popularity. There are hundreds of virtual malls on the Internet, not to mention that most anybody who has something to sell is selling it online. And buying by catalogue is standard practice for millions.

Want Connection? Join the Club!

One reason we shop and spend money is because it's fun. Buying is typically not a chore but an exercise in self-definition, even if it is part fantasy. When you shop—whether by catalogue, in person, or online—you can handle or visually explore the goods, practice, if you will, owning them. Online, you can even fill up your virtual shopping cart—and then delete it all when you reach the checkout. E-tailers send you messages that suggest they know you, recommending a book or some item on sale. In the store, a good clerk sees you and listens. One who knows you by your face or name may even think about you, about which outfits look good on you, which should be avoided. In shopping for an outfit to wear to my brother-in-law's wedding just six weeks after giving birth, it felt heavenly to have someone see me as a potentially pleasant-looking woman and not merely as a fat-padded food source (lovely as that role is). With such attention, it's tough not to feel cared for, even, in a sense, *known and understood.*

If commercial interactions are so pleasant, why bother with real relationships? I'm not entirely serious here, but I want to make the point that increasingly marketers and purveyors of material culture are trying to sell what we crave: social connection. Even if it is not authentic, even if the caring is mere salesmanship and the attention is fleeting, the sales pitch capitalizes on the desire to be more connected. In his book on culture and advertising, *Adcult*, James Twitchell argues that advertising is not, as a whole, on the cutting edge, hypnotizing us into new behaviors. Rather, he says, advertising is "more metronome than trumpet," and the "accumulated force of commercial selling is more like a slow and continuous drumbeat of social norms." Advertising, he argues, is an organizing system: "It externalizes deep, culture-specific, occasionally even biologic, concerns and ties them to specific goods. In so doing, Adcult behaves far more like a religion, gaining power as it colonizes distant aspects of life, making them part of a coherent pattern, than an oppressive dictatorship forcing innocent and helpless consumers to give up their better judgment in order to aggrandize some evil mercantile power."[15]

The desire to connect comes from us. The marketers and the advertisers are rebroadcasting our own wants to us, offering for sale what we hunger for. Nowhere is the message of connection more present than in advertising for new communication technologies, reflecting both the desire for personal connection and a fear that it is growing more remote. Print ads for Nokia digital phones, for example, carry below the logo the tag line "Connecting People." Hewlett Packard's printers are not mere machines but ways, we are told, to "keep in touch with family." HP even offers, in one national ad, a pullout booklet showing all the ways its printers and software can make people closer to loved ones: printing family recipes, creating a family newsletter, sending a polished-looking postcard, making T-shirts, and sending holiday messages online. In other words, you can apply the same office-quality touch and efficiency to your personal relationships as to your professional ones.

Not only is connection a commodity, but it is, we are told, the meat of commercial interaction. There is little more important in the retail and service industries today than building customer relationships. (Dell Computer Corporation, for one, intones in one magazine ad: "At Dell, nothing should stand between you and us.") But what meaning do commercial relationships carry? What role do they have in our lives? And, perhaps most important, how do they affect the way people envision real relationships? Seen on one level, the growing commercial gestures toward personal relationships and attention are nice. You think: Hey, this company really knows me, really cares about me, and really appreciates that I signed up for a store credit card, and they are *so* appreciative that they are inviting *me* to a "members only" sale. The problem is, such faux relationships can come at the expense of real relationships. The marketers are using our personal tools—the phone call, the letter or card (hand-addressed in some cases), the e-mail—to sell us stuff. They are using the tools of friendship—expressed concern, advice, help, loyalty, and personal attention—to build long-term business relationships. In short, they are jamming our personal airwaves. They are selling what we feel we lack. As if they could read people's minds, marketers today are selling not merely goods and services but what so many people really want, like companionship, prestige, hope, youth, and connection.

The number of advertisements selling products as a way of bringing people together and making them feel less isolated and more a part of things is legion. And the products are not only long-distance calling but tangible things such as cotton, nutritional supplements, and superstores, to name but a few. Everywhere the message is that if you buy, you will feel loved, connected, and a part of a functional, joyous community. Marketers know that people want to belong, to feel someone knows them and understands their needs and fantasies. Ads and products today speak directly to you—not people *like* you, but *you*. The mass marketers seem to know everything: not just what car you drive, where you went on vacation last year, or what stores you shop in but how you think of yourself, how you want others to view you, what's in your heart and your mind. The most advanced e-tailing sites, for example, tailor ads to each customer based on what he's shown interest in in the past—or even where he's clicked in the past two minutes. Marketers also know we crave community, so they create imitation communities composed of loyal customers. We fall prey not because we're stupid but because they're singing our song.

Origins, a company that sells makeup and skin care products with a back-to-the-woods slant, wants to be my good friend. In fact, after buying mascara, I learned that in two years Origins would begin sending me a present every year on my birthday. Yahoo! I love getting birthday presents, and even though I'm in my thirties, I still walk around on my birthday like I'm carrying a big, fabulous secret. And, yep, Origins wants to share in that excitement. The great thing for me is that this is truly a no-muss, no-fuss relationship. I don't have to send a gift in exchange. I don't even have to write a thank-you note (don't tell my grandmother)!

But what does it mean when a cosmetics company sends you a birthday present? What is the message? What if I can't help noticing that the present is nicer than what friends or family send? What will *that* mean? Is Origins now part of my close circle? Should I let them know if I win a prize, become an aunt, finish that annual eight-mile road race in record time? The saleswoman was nice enough, but I wouldn't know her if she showed up on my doorstep, gift in hand.

Gift giving, especially for sellers of such intimate goods as cosmetics and perfumes, is a popular marketing practice. But as Mary Lou Andre, the personal organizer, observed, it's one potentially charged with meaning. Gifts, though advertised as such, are never really free but bind the giver and receiver. This is only one way marketers have breached the walls that once made personal communication personal. Now they are flooding our private channels with commercial messages. Tune in to any home shopping channel and you hear the voices of "friends." The hosts, with their insider tips and confessions, hardly seem to be hawking merchandise. Rather, they play the role of guardian angels saving you from social embarrassment. And who hasn't torn into a square ivory laid envelope bearing a handwritten address, with visions of a personal note, only to discover that Bloomingdale's is inviting you to shop and save 10 percent?

We are also having our personal channels jammed by the telemarketers, who in 1997 scored $185 billion in consumer sales, according to the American Telemarketing Association. They have invaded the private domain, walked with their voices right into our kitchens, our family rooms, and our bedrooms. The advent of telemarketing has changed the way I answer the phone. I instinctively prepare for confrontation. I try to temper it, but I know annoyance shows in my voice. The phone is not a means for keeping in touch with friends and family anymore as much as it is a weak link in the armor around the home. Some people have Caller ID and only pick up if a person they are interested in is on the line. (Some people, tired of being identified by Caller ID, block their phone numbers.) Another product promises to screen out telemarketers by requiring callers to identify themselves before someone picks up the receiver. The phone call—once advertised as a way to "reach out and touch someone"—is becoming a way of avoiding communication in part because it has been commandeered by the marketplace. We may love to shop, but we want to do it on our own terms.

The issue is not just the overcleverness of marketers, slipping their way into our lives and affections. It goes the other way, too: We seek relationships with products. Fornier, who has studied the emotional attachments people have to particular brands, speaks of brands having "personalities" with "human characteristics" that are recognized and cherished by the consumers who are loyal to them and even argues that they serve in at least some people's lives as "viable relationship partners."

"Consumers' acceptance of advertisers' attempts to humanize brands and their tendencies to animate products of their own accord suggest a willingness to entertain brands as vital members of the relationship dyad," she writes. At times, she argues, people associate brands with human characteristics, which "animate the brand as a vital entity in the consumer's mind." The relationships between consumers and their brands, she reports from her study findings, mirror various types of human relationships, including marriages of convenience, courtships, flings, secret affairs, best friendships, compartmentalized friendships, and kinships, among others. "The consumers in this study are not just buying brands because they like them or because they work well," she writes. "They are involved in relationships with a collectivity of brands so as to benefit from the meanings they add to their lives."[16]

The idea that we seek emotional connections with products sounds eerie, yet evidence abounds that we are increasingly aligning ourselves with this company or that. It's almost impossible not to. A friend of mine vowed just before her son was born not to dress him in clothes with brand labels (you know, the clothes so boastful of the manufacturer's name that you feel you should be *paid* for wearing the garment). She failed, finding it a losing proposition to keep her son from being a walking ad. Indeed, many of us today *like* showing off where we shop and who we wear. Exclaiming "Oh, he's so J. Crew!" about a guy has been considered a compliment among Harvard undergraduates.

It's not enough today to shop at certain stores or buy a certain brand. We have to join the club. "Are you a member?" is how my conversation begins at the photo shop when I drop off film to be developed. And the scolding I took from the clerk at a chain bookstore when I said I didn't want to become a "preferred reader" exemplifies the aggressive way corporate America is pursuing our allegiance. My wallet, in fact, is bursting with cards showing that I am part of the family at half a dozen stores. When it comes to civic organizations, we may not be a nation of joiners, but we certainly respond when the clerk asks, "Are you a member?" And membership, we are incessantly reminded, has its rewards. You get special privileges, more junk mail and junk e-mail (excuse me, notices), and special prices. Perhaps most important, you generally feel a little cozier at the store, as if you know the score. Some stores and restaurants even circulate newsletters to member customers. And you can be sure these companies know you. You are an insider.

The appeal of this hits you when you shop in a store where you don't have a "preferred customer" card. Consider the time I went to a supermarket where I don't usually shop. I felt like a trespasser, not to mention how disloyal I felt to my old supermarket. As I stood at the checkout, the clerk seemed incredulous that I didn't want to divulge several pages of personal information to join their club. The imitation "community" of preferred customers, club members, or frequent buyers (or whatever term is used) is an affront to the true notion of community. And yet it works. We actually come to feel a sense of affiliation with particular stores. We want to feel connected—even if it's just to the supermarket.

In Search of the Good Life

Consumer culture has trained people to feel entitled to the best. And getting the best means being a good shopper. It is a sign of our society's material obsession that today you can be considered "creative" for having purchased well. Most of us, I'll bet, can call to mind those people in our lives who are the best shoppers. In seeking the best, we accept a definition of life and success that is based on commercial triumphs, not personal relationships.

As a result, shopping is not just about acquiring the goods and services we need. It is, more potently, about acquiring the elements that make up an image, a lifestyle, and an identity. Shopping as an act has become so comfortable that its motions, its values, its rhythm are daily applied to other arenas. "Shopping" describes how we assess human relationships, express our individuality and our identity, order life goals, seek comfort and love, and search for connection. The boundary today between what is real life and what is a purchasable commodity has been whittled to a hair's breadth. Consider that you can now purchase donor eggs from top models, buying for your offspring the promise of physical beauty. In other quarters, some of the most sought-after products are experiences in which the acts of living and consuming become intertwined and indistinguishable.

Shopping is what we do when we walk into a store, log on to a retail Website, or sift through the pages of a catalogue, imagining the items enhancing our own lives. It is also what we do when we interact with others socially or meet someone new. We shop for lovers and friends; we weigh the pros and cons of relationships based on consumer instincts, much as in Davis's short story. We try to decide: How does this person fit with what I already have? Is this relationship *worth* it?

We can blame overclever marketers for this kind of thinking. We can blame ourselves, vulnerable to wanting the good life plotted out in the ads and catalogues that land on the doorstep. But the matter is not so easy as pointing to one or another, a marketer's action or the consumer's response. Shopping has become nothing less than the new definition of modern mass culture. It is who we are. Sociologists Pasi Falk and Colin Campbell argue that in recent decades "the boundary between the world of goods and mass culture has become more and more diffuse." More of daily life has been translated into commodities for sale, and consumerism has become an experience in itself. The authentic and the commercial have been inextricably mixed. "Mass culture transformed experiences into marketable products while advertising turned marketable products into representations, images and then, over time, into experiences once more," Falk and Campbell write. "The consequence of all this has been that the consumption of experience and the experience of consumption have become more and more indistinguishable." So we go to the mall, to the outrageously designed restaurant, to the furniture store with the carnival ride, and we spend not only our money but our time and attention as well. We live and consume our lives in the same breath.[17]

We have become a culture no longer of producers but of consumers. Your station in life is measured not by what you create but by what you can buy. Of course, people have long used goods to display social position, but such displays have intensified, according to Juliet Schor, a Harvard economist and author of *The Overspent American*. She makes a provocative argument that in recent decades we have moved from "keeping up with the Joneses" to trying to keep up with the wealthy. "Today the neighbors are no longer the focus of comparison," she writes. "How could they be? We may not even know them, much less which restaurants they patronize, where they vacation, and how much they spent for a living room couch." Instead we seek to acquire the symbols of wealth: We drive the right cars, go on the right vacations, wear the right clothes, and live in the right neighborhoods. Purchasing power dominates our sense of self-worth. The goal today is not to be interesting but to be rich.

With so much attention trained on nuances of our own and other people's belongings, it is no wonder that shopping commands so much of people's time and attention. Eleanor Uddo, a lawyer with two young children who takes Fridays off to spend with her kids, told me in an interview that the demands of modern life lead her again and again to the same activity: shopping. Uddo, who is very organized, keeps a to-do list on her home computer, which she updates each Thursday night before her day off. Inevitably, she says, "on Friday I am literally dragging my kids from store to store. Eighty percent of the weekend list is buying things, actually purchasing stuff, toys for birthday parties, medicine, lawn care product that has run out." There's so much shopping, in fact, that Uddo has hired Mary Lou Andre to shop for her clothing because she doesn't have time to do it. As she paused on a summer afternoon to consider it all, Uddo was at a loss: "As sick as it is, our society is a buy-buy society, and it's tough to resist it—and I am not so tough."

Most of us aren't. We shop and buy, shop and buy. Amid the excess is a cry for a return to a simpler life. The simplicity movement has gained attention in recent years, and books about cutting back, simplifying, and paring down routinely get prominent display in bookstores. Although the most dedicated in the movement are committed to consuming less, for most of society the message is not so much about consumerism as it is about aesthetics. Simplicity is a fifteen-dollar salad dressed only with oil, lemon, and salt and pepper at an upscale restaurant. It is an architectural style, an interior design aesthetic. It is a rather complicated paring down, if you consider architect John Pawson's book *minimum*, with chapter headings such as "Mass: The uncomplicated beauty of the unadorned wall" or "Expression: Silence as language." In fact, the very desire to simplify that the legitimate movement has tapped into has become, well, just another way to sell more stuff.

Despite the fact that there are some "downshifters" among us, most Americans merely pay lip service to paring down and "getting back to basics." A 1995 study commissioned by the Merck Family Fund, which sought Americans' views on consumption, materialism, and the environment, revealed that 82 percent of respondents agreed that most of us buy and consume far more than we need. Respondents also felt it was a good idea to use possessions longer instead of buying new things and to spend more time working with our neighbors on community service projects and less time shopping. And yet hardly any of them said they felt ready to move ahead with such actions. The message from the survey was that the American consumption habit is so ingrained, so interwoven into our daily lives and family patterns, that we cannot bring ourselves to do anything about it. In fact, mostly people look around and notice who has what they don't and grumble about how people years ago seemed to work less and have more. Labor economist Clair Brown, in her analysis of the American standard of living from 1918 to 1998, observed that we seem to be more and more dissatisfied with what we've got, imagining earlier generations could afford more. It's an incorrect perception, she says, that people today are not living as well as their parents and grandparents. Her data show that families of the same class have done as well as or, in most cases, "considerably better" than families of the same class in 1950 and 1973. So why the unhappiness?[18]

One observation Brown makes is about how people spend money. There is much in everyday life that affects our quality of life, including how many hours we work, how safe we feel, how clean the environment is, and how friendly the neighbors are, to name a few. Brown observes that once people pay for the basics they spend their money not seeking more leisure time or ways to better social conditions that might improve quality of life but pursuing "an ever-higher material standard of living." People buy things for private use that offer more variety and impart greater status but do little to make them more connected to other people or to their community. "What are the forces that propel families to purchase variety and status in recreational goods even though they dread to leave their homes during the day because of smog and at night because of crime?" Brown asks. "Feeling powerless to influence public problems that significantly undermined their own standard of living, people have turned inward to focus on their own private consumption."

The picture is a rather dismal one. Instead of using energy and money to make a difference for everyone, people tend to be isolationist, improving life within their personal territory. People choose to better their own situations because it seems futile to effect greater change. In the end, this means people just burrow deeper. The pervasive thinking becomes: Why share if you can afford your own? Why cooperate if you don't have to? With wealth, people can—and often do—buy isolation. Feelings of discontent and disconnection do not draw people to seek solace in each other but to venture out to find a salve in the marketplace. There, of course, it is sold as a pint of gourmet ice cream or a new shade of lipstick. It is beautifully packaged and ready to take home. But it doesn't last long.

SCREENS

The studio audience at the Ricki Lake show, including me, is getting restless. "I'm sorry, I'm sorry," Ricki says, her basset-hound eyes seeming to communicate real regret for all the goof-ups and filler shots. We have been in the small Manhattan studio with the fake living room onstage for almost two hours, on May 1, 1998, for this, the final taping of the season. Much of the time has been spent applauding on command as the floor director calls out what has, by now, become almost a plea: "Four, three, two, *a-pplause!*" The peppy music jolts us upright, and we appear to come alive, clapping, smiling, and waving for the cameras that pan over our "fine selves," as Ricki has referred to us earlier.

In fact, she started the whole experience off by getting us juiced up, instructing us that our number one goal today was to "get your fine selves on TV!" To be televised is, after all, to be. As Warren Beatty sarcastically observes in *Truth or Dare*, Madonna's film, "Why would you say something off camera? What point is there of existing?" Or as the movie *Wag the Dog* illustrates, if it's on TV, then it must be true.

The problem this day, though, is that few of us are getting our small-screen validation. We came to witness and participate in the final segment of a show whose first part was filmed five weeks earlier. It is called "Lose Weight or the Wedding's Off!" As you might guess, we are here to see if the women have shed pounds (the men's corpulence is not considered here) and are now marriageable. It is a subject that could incite discussion in any gathering. In fact, earlier, as we sat in the greenroom downstairs viewing the first part of the show, my fellow audience members had a hard time keeping it in.

"Better not bring me near him!" one fifty-something woman

warned after seeing one of the men demanding his fiancée lose weight. "I'll kill him!" A soft-spoken young couple from Brooklyn who described their state as "preengaged" delicately probed the subject. And just as we settled in the studio, the size of an elementary school gym with chairs on three sections of risers, a guy on the top row stood up and crowed provocatively, "I don't do fat chicks!"

But when Ricki brings in the slimmed women, she takes only one audience-member comment, from a woman who says the only thing they need to lose is the men. For the audience, the rest of the filming is tedious. We watch Ricki tape scripted comments for a second show, one highlighting her five years on the air. Between commands for *applause!* Ricki banters with staff about the end-of-season party, hardly acknowledging the audience presence. No wonder a woman a few chairs away drifts off to sleep. No wonder others grow hostile, begging for food from platters of take-out sitting beyond camera view. Audience members ache for what we are denied: a chance to engage.

Isn't that, after all, why people came? Even though we're "the audience," we are not here to watch but to step through the imaginary TV barrier and participate. We may not be able to untangle our own relationships, but we sure have something to say about other people's behavior. Shows like this—Jerry Springer's and others that come and go—have become public boudoirs. The intimate is publicized, and secrets are shouted. Relationship issues—parents and children reunited after decades, painful affairs, deceitful friendships—are played out, partly as entertainment and partly as a vicarious experience that offers access to emotion without the vulnerability. Someone else's public pain is much safer than your own. Just as some may attend church for spiritual cleansing, audience members come hungering for catharsis or at least validation of their own emotional life. And when that's done on TV, it becomes suddenly and irrevocably captured and legitimated. It becomes real for guests, audience, and viewers.

But how to create the intimacy—or the illusion of it—so people will speak the private aloud? From the moment we file into the studio, the boundaries between public and private begin to blur. Language within the studio is explicitly sexual. Those charged with warming up the audience speak in an intimate slang, using the word "ass" and the phrase "booty call" over and over until they lose whatever shock value they had and become part of the studio lexicon. The audience eagerly plays along. When three members are brought down for a mock game show as part of the warm-up and asked to invent their own buzzer sound, one woman imitates an orgasmic moan to signal she's got the answer to a question. The implicit understanding between audience and show staff is "We can all talk about anything here—even (and especially) the taboo." But such verbal foreplay arouses expectations.

From where I sit in the studio audience, the boredom and anger are palpable. As the taping creeps along, I see how desperately people want to have their say—on TV. Denied this, their pent-up eagerness grows flaccid. There are now long stretches when the camera eye is not even in the studio but backstage in the control room, shooting Ricki's scripted segments. It does not occur to audience members to speak with those around them. In fact, relations between people sitting in the same place for so long are oddly nonexistent. The TV screen is our only channel of communication. And today, it is failing us.

The single emotion we share is disappointment, which becomes so clear that Ricki apologizes and sends her staff to search for memorabilia to give away. Finally, it ends. Ricki has a 3:30 P.M. appointment uptown, which is our ticket out of the building. As we exit solemnly, silently, section by section, and are herded onto elevators, we are handed a Ricki Lake T-shirt and key ring. Even the elevator operator can feel the discomfort. "Unhappy?" he says as he presses the L button. I am standing beside the guy, a lanky young man in baggy shorts and polo shirt, who doesn't do fat chicks. "This was a terrible, terrible show," he says. "The worst I been to."

I walk a few blocks to a parking garage, there in midtown, and see a group of fellow audience members, women in their forties, including at least one who says she has traveled from Washington State to attend the Ricki Lake show. She shakes her head, clearly upset that this taping did not fulfill expectations. "It was boring," she says. On top of it all, it starts to rain, and rush hour begins in Manhattan.

A Filter and a Frame

As I drive over to the West Side Highway, I keep thinking about the experience. It wasn't what I expected, either. And, most likely, it wasn't a typical show. But somehow, this was more interesting. The lack of opportunity for engagement made it so clear why people had come. The feel of the whole event was far different from the day in the early 1970s when I came from Connecticut with my Girl Scout troop to sit in the studio audience of *Concentration*, the game show. I was awed, as were my fellow audience members, merely to be in the space and to witness real television happening. We relished the chance to clap when the APPLAUSE sign flashed; we didn't feel at all put-upon. What has changed?

To be fair, these were different shows, with different audience expectations. But somehow, too, television has moved closer to us over the decades. It has become more personal. Not only has the content become more intimate—a 1998 *Time*/CNN poll showed that 29 percent of teens get most of their information about sex from TV, up from 11 percent in 1986—but the way it is delivered is more intimate, too. The language is less formal, the presentation styles more streetwise. And the use of super-close-ups makes you feel you are right there, not just in the room but in the moment, a part of the experience. This is not entertainment but life. Imagine such a close-up of Lucille Ball! It seems wrong, indecent. That's because we have altered our relationship to the television, stepping inside the set and taking its "realities" and limitations for our own.[1]

We do not judge TV; we accept it and live by it. Jerry Seinfeld seemed to recognize this when he announced the end of his popular show, *Seinfeld*, after nine seasons. In an interview printed in January 1998, Seinfeld complained about the medium and the way it creates malaise. "It's a habitual medium," he says. "Most people aren't really entertained. What they need is they need to watch TV. Entertainment is almost a luxury item." He goes on to lambaste TV even more pointedly: "Television is like a flyer somebody sticks on your windshield. Who gives a damn what's on it? It's iridescent wallpaper. Sometimes I think people just like the light on their faces."[2]

Indeed, TV is a habitual medium. For decades now John Robinson of the University of Maryland has conducted time-diary studies looking at how Americans spend their time. His results suggest—counter to claims by some—that Americans today have more leisure time, not less, than they did a few decades ago. The time is merely segmented into smaller blocks, he suggests. Questions about how to measure leisure and free time aside, what is notable about Robinson's findings is that, according to the diaries kept by his subjects, Americans spend their added free time chiefly on one thing: watching more TV. In recent decades, his studies show, average weekly hours of TV watching have risen—from 10.4 hours in 1965 to 14.9 hours in 1975 to 15.1 hours in

1985, the latest year for which he has comparable data. At the same time, he reports, people are spending less of their free time socializing, attending sports and cultural events, and participating in formal organizations. What's also interesting about Robinson's findings is that when he questioned subjects about their enjoyment of activities, TV watching rated only a mediocre score—below eating, sleeping, and many more productive activities, like reading and attending cultural events. Robinson and coauthor Geoffrey Godbey suggest that "it may be that the low level of satisfaction with the chief way Americans use free time—television—is a sign of general dissatisfaction with our culture."[3]

Seinfeld was making a similarly harsh critique. While the comedian may be applauded for the content of his episodes, he is focused on the form. The television screen itself, not what it is saying, is the issue. It is a variation on Marshall McLuhan's oft-quoted observation that "the medium is the message." As McLuhan points out in *Understanding the Media*, what he means by this phrase is simply that "any technology gradually creates a totally new human environment." It is the existence of television and the response it demands, to use it, that so powerfully reorders our lives. Even Bill McKibben, who watched two thousand hours of television to write *The Age of Missing Information* and makes fascinating observations about TV content, ultimately blames the thing itself for blunting everyday experience: "I don't fret about TV because it's decadent or shortens your attention span or leads to murder. It worries me because it alters perception. TV, and the culture it anchors, masks and drowns out the subtle and vital information contact with the real world once provided."[4]

By way of contrast he describes the deep learning apprenticeships demand, quoting Buddhist novice Gary Snyder's description of a youngster leaving home to sleep in a potting shed and spend three years learning and perfecting the single task of mixing clay: "In the TV era, we're more comfortable with, say, Robert Warren, who has a cable art show and today is teaching all of America how to paint 'Majestic Mountain Meadow.' No three seasons of watching Robert mix paints!"

Seamlessly, the real experience has been consumed, abbreviated, and repackaged for the screen. To view, today, *is* to do. And while McKibben's example hints at vast differences in knowledge and experience between the real and the televised, those differences are banished from our perception. The screen—along with what happens there—is our cultural truth, the more so because we have less and less firsthand information about other people's lives. Ricki Lake's studio audience also reveals just how much we are in danger of subjugating our lives to the screen, feeling that if an experience is not filmed it does not count, that simple human experience with the old tool of memory is antiquated and faulty. That day at the Ricki Lake show, we could not speak to the camera, so there was no point in speaking with one another. If we could not participate in televised emotions, then we could not have access to our own.

I have focused so far on television, but this chapter is about the many screens in our lives. Despite their differences in construction and function, the TV screen, the computer monitor, the ATM, the Caller ID screen, the video conferencing screen, the laptop, the smart phone, the handheld companion—and any number of other screens we encounter every day—have become our metaphoric windows on the world. It is how children play, how friends talk and colleagues communicate, and how some car owners get directions to where they're going. The cool-hued surfaces have become trusted dispensers of information and the filter through which we transact our lives. It is how, for example, parents at work can log on to a Website and check in on their children at a nearby daycare center. It is the means by which people interact, learn, and judge.

And yet, despite their ubiquitous presence, screens are far from neutral. By its very design, the screen presents information that has been edited and packaged to fit. We become absorbed into the world it shows, forgetting that it is merely a frame, which limits our view. In fact, we seem less and less interested in considering *what isn't shown*, what may lie beyond its edges. It is tempting to believe the screen offers all we need, because it is sleeker and better than anything we have ever had before. It is easy to take what's offered the way it is sold: as "must see TV," as the happening world of dot-com, or, more broadly, as what matters.

Screens give us power and offer shortcuts—but they also take us away from the tedium and the pleasure of the living experience. We see the name on Caller ID and we have new power; don't pick up if you don't want that person. Beam your business card onto my screen and I'll beam mine onto yours; no need to hold a card, feel the raised lettering, run your fingers around the edges as you finish the conversation, making sure you can read it, read the phone number. No need to find a place for it. It's all done. Clean. One student at an Ivy League college doesn't go to the course lectures because you can get them on video (if you want to bother) and the handouts are on the Web. The same student can write an entire research paper without going to the library, without leaving the computer screen, simply by downloading sources and cutting and pasting quotes. And be assured that this student is not alone but is doing what many classmates do. There's less call now for wandering the stacks, peering at call numbers, paging through books that may not have been opened in years, finding something unexpected but interesting. Such a discovery is removed from the experience, as is the sensory experience of smelling books, feeling the presence of so many words, so many ideas, the sensation of time passing and not passing, of things having weight and density.

As McLuhan observes, technology is an extension that allows us to act from a distance. Not only does the screen serve as that extension, but its visual quality gives us the illusion of closeness. Its role as intermediary recedes, and it becomes an original, at times seeming even more authentic than the real scene or information it projects. As a result, the screen has achieved an authority based primarily on the quality of its images. If something is posted on a well-designed Website, we take it to be right. If a screen presents a set of instructions, we follow. A TV ad for B. F. Goodrich tires plays on this role. A car, driving on an open road that stretches off into the distance with an expanse of plains and mountains ahead, halts at a stop sign. At that moment, the asphalt road parts and a screen rises from the earth with instructions: "Select road." Once this task is accomplished, the screen reports that it is "validating tires." When the B. F. Goodrich name is read by the scanner, the final message is rendered: "Approved." The ad couldn't work without the screen. Imagine if, instead of a screen, there was a guy sitting at a roadside stand checking tires! What's more, we have no idea what database or agency the screen is linked to. The screen is not a *tool* for extending the reach of some agency but is *itself* the authority.

As the language in the ad suggests, screen language is a compressed, abbreviated one. But the compact quality of screen interaction is forgotten when intimate issues are communicated through its electrons. It creates the illusion of depth and time. Once people have watched the TV show on alcoholism, teen pregnancy, or welfare reform, they feel themselves experts on the topic; the interview subject's experience becomes our own. Once you have "chatted" online with someone about a life-threatening issue, you "know" him or her. I remember spending time with and writing about Anne Powers, a forty-seven-year-old single mother who was dying of liver cancer. I visited Anne at her sister's home, where she and her sixteen-year-old daughter were living. Because she felt isolated, so far from the South where she had spent most of her life, Anne spent a good deal of time on the Internet, chatting with others with her disease. And while many gush about how real and intimate relationships can be on the Internet, for Anne, a slight woman with auburn hair, riveting blue eyes, and a gentle southern lilt to her voice, the limitations of the screen were painfully, frustratingly clear.

As I watched her online one afternoon, I was struck by the formulaic responses of her "online community." Message after message ordered her to keep fighting, to keep searching for a miracle cure. Hadn't they been listening to Anne? Anyone who spent time with Anne knew that the cancer had spread over more than 75 percent of her liver, that her case was inoperable and beyond the hope of chemotherapy. More important, Anne was comfortable with where she was. She had accepted her dying and was grateful for the time to prepare. In fact, the messages to keep fighting got on her nerves. "I got blasted on the Internet because I said I was dying of cancer," she complained. "Someone said, '*No! You're living* with cancer!' But sometimes you have to face things directly. You can't beat around the mulberry bush with something like this." Although she spent more hours with her online "community" than with her in-person cancer support group, which only met once a week, it was the live contact—the hugs, the body language, the nods and words of understanding—that gave Anne the vital connection she craved as she lived out her last days.[5]

Like a TV special on cancer for which we can summon up sadness without releasing ourselves to the actual gripping fear of such a diagnosis, life is simply less real on the screen—even when someone like Anne is sitting at the monitor on the other end. The screen is, literally, that: a screen that filters and protects. We may choose to change the channel, log off, or ignore the peppy "You've got mail!" Anne craved honesty, and in speaking the truth and not performing for the small screen, she found herself alone and outside the limits of the medium.

I don't mean to suggest that screens and the technologies they represent aren't making us, in some form, more in touch with others. They are. For some, the ability to communicate by typing instead of by speaking is freeing. The problem is that the discussion of such new ways of communicating has focused almost exclusively on these and other benefits while giving little consideration to how this new way of talking is thinning our connections. The Internet can make communication more expedient, but it is limited, a point typically glossed over. Electronic relationships cannot create the kind of social connection that offers people that critical sense of well-being. One has only to consider that any virtual relationship worth its salt is not truly culminated until the correspondents meet face to face. Some virtual relationships aren't worth the effort, a situation that creates a subcategory of shadow relationships—people with whom we have e-mailed but who haven't been elevated to phone or live interactions. Technology broadens and multiplies our reach, but our interactions risk becoming shallow to the point of meaninglessness. Anne may be, literally, electronically connected to others with liver cancer, but what is that worth when they don't know her, don't hear what she's saying? In some ways it's worse than not being connected at all: the illusion of real community. Or, as Jerry Seinfeld might put it, the illusion of being entertained when, in fact, it's merely feeding a habit. It's the failure to acknowledge such limits that makes people less connected despite being more plugged in.

Researchers at Carnegie Mellon University conducted a two-year study of new Internet users—reportedly the first such study of the social and psychological effects of Internet use at home—and published their results in 1998. The study, financed by such companies as Hewlett Packard, Intel, AT&T Research, and Apple Computer, included 169 people in seventy-three households, all of whom had no previous experience with the Internet. The study controlled for loneliness and depression as well as for people who were exceptionally outgoing. The researchers used software to monitor the number of hours of online usage as well as which applications were used. The primary use of the Internet, they discovered, was for social purposes (e-mail, newsgroup participation, chat rooms, etc.). Nonetheless, researchers found that greater use of the Internet was associated with declines in participants' communication with family members, declines in the size of their social circles, and increases in depression and loneliness. Much has been made of the fact that, in general, the Internet represents both a threat and an opportunity for connection—depending on how it's used. But the researchers in this study observed that the most developed features of the Internet do not support or encourage real friendship or social

support. Search engines are most effective in steering us to buy products. Even sites aimed at social interaction either hawk goods or work
to keep conversation controlled and on topic—not always the way
people really want to chat.[6]

The Screen Dream

We take its presence so for granted that it seems impossible
to imagine life without the screen. And yet, in the beginning, the
screen was a dream, a fancy without a purpose. Scientists and inventors
in the 1880s who envisioned transmitting pictures from one place to
another even struggled to find words to describe what they meant.
Some spoke of an "electric telescope," while others imagined "seeing
by radio." Even when the most rudimentary instruments were created
in 1926, allowing the transmission in England of a rough and poorly
articulated image of a human face from one room to the next, it was
viewed as a curiosity. It was not seen as an advancement with a great
future, even among men in commercial telegraphy, members of the
fledgling communications industry.

The story of the race to discover television is a fascinating one, with
a scientist, a roguish inventor, a visionary Russian immigrant, and a
well-read Mormon farmboy all separately pursuing visions despite
naysayers and hopeful but impatient investors. As David E. Fisher and
Marshall Jon Fisher observe in their gripping book *Tube*, there is no
single father of television—and, therefore, of the first screen. From the
start, there was competition to create a means for transmitting moving
pictures that were clear enough to be commercially viable. It is that
hunger for clarity that remains the chief goal today, only the expectations for "clarity" then and now are worlds apart. If people once hoped
for merely being able, for example, to discern the president's features
and being able to tell that it was indeed him, today people want screens
that press at the limits of human perception. The goal is to "be there"
through the screen, perhaps even offering TV and Internet viewers
choices of camera angles on the court, say, at the U.S. Open.

Technologies are fusing—mergers between cable, Internet, and telephone interests are bringing e-mail, TV, Internet access, telephone,
even cell phone via a single supplier. This is blurring distinctions, making the screen itself, more than the distinct technologies, what we perceive as our connection to the world.

Although TV and computer screens are not yet compatible, the two mediums are increasingly overlapping. Soon a single monitor will serve dual purposes, accepting broadcast and online information. Already, movies, home videos, and Webcasts bring TV-like viewing to our computer monitors. Researchers are seeking to build multipurpose screens that are lighter, brighter, and flatter than anything we have ever had. Some promising research is creating screens with active layers only about one-thousandth of the thickness of a human hair and flexible enough to be rolled up. "The weight of a computer monitor could in principle be reduced to a few ounces," writes Alan Sobel in *Scientific American*. The realization of these and other technologies is still unfolding, but the race makes the point: Screens will only proliferate in the years to come. The screen, as Sobel says, is more and more the way the human world communicates: "Whether it washes clothes or controls a satellite launch, a piece of equipment must interact with humans, making a good display"—the screen—"an essential feature."[7]

And "good" may be an understatement. What the new technology is reaching for is to make the screen less an object and more a part of the environment. Resolution will become so breathtakingly fine that it will be ever more difficult to discern where the screen ends and real life begins. And it may not be enough merely to watch. One catchword of our era, after all, is "interactive." Much as Ricki Lake's studio audience wanted to step beyond the role of observer to participant, the next technology more immediately in front of us is digital television. For the first time since Farnsworth and Zworykin developed an electric means of scanning and transmitting signals, the rise of the computer era is pushing a major change to digital scanning. Instead of a scanned image being turned into an electric signal, the image will be broken into a binary signal using the same zeros and ones used by computers or digital devices. There is still controversy about how such technology can be developed and managed, and by whom. But the clear potential is the fusion of screens and the management of the TV signal not as continuous programming but as an offering that can be captured, stored, and used at will, operating as a computer does. It may also send and receive e-mail, run a paging system, operate a videophone, download from the Web, and play movies. As Fisher and Fisher predict: "There will be no reason for people to wait until 11:00 P.M. to see the news, for instance. As soon as a particular news report is prepared, it will be available to be plucked off a worldwide menu for instant viewing. . . . Television will become more like a newspaper, as viewers pick out just the programs and reports that interest them and view them wherever and whenever they want." With expansion of remote technology, they may be in the kitchen, on the patio, or "on a subway, watching a paper-quality laptop screen."[8]

Screens are and will be everywhere. Consider the screens that have proliferated over the landscape just in recent years. Many of us now bank by screen, using an ATM or the click of a mouse to pay the monthly bills. We also view and interact with museum exhibits, check out library books, order deli meats, buy gas, and hold meetings—all via screen technology. We now have laptops, palmtops, pagers, and screen-based information kiosks. You now interact with a screen—not a human—to pick up your new lawnmower at Sears. At some U.S. companies you punch the screen to check in and find out where co-workers are sitting. It has become a common act at retailers: Punch the screen to check the price. Buses now have individual screens for passengers; a screen at every seat is still a selling point for airlines. More and more cars now have screen displays that give directions—no need anymore to stop and ask. We are, with the aid of our multiplying screens, growing ever more self-contained and self-sufficient, eliminating the kind of incidental contact that takes time and seems meaningless but that has the power to connect people.

In the final pages of their book about baseball and television, *Coming Apart at the Seams*, Jack Sands and Peter Gammons gloomily envision a futuristic night at the Milwaukee Brewers ballpark. Milwaukee is playing Boston, and a couple take their eleven-year-old daughter to the game. As the family take their seats along the third base line, "the father prepared the video screens. For no cost, one got the screen and its in-house telecast of the game, complete with statistical information, replays, and, of course, commercials." The father punches his credit card number into the screens to activate these services, along with order-at-your seat meals and shopping. "Box seat shopping includes hats, bats, and all the memorabilia items; push the right button, the MasterCard is billed, and within the half hour your officially licensed Brewers jacket arrives like duty-free goods," they write. The screen also offers access to other televised games, player statistics, news channels, and even an automatically tabulated vote on what the coach should do and what fans want to see on the field. "By the bottom of the seventh, the father became frustrated that he was one of the 87 percent of the paying

customers who'd wanted Red Sox manager Rick Burleson to take out
reliever Craig Bush, who instead had been batted around for six runs in
two and a third innings as Milwaukee upped its lead to 14–4." His
daughter, tired of watching the players, plays baseball Nintendo and then
goes for a walk to the stadium museum, which features a Great Diamond
Moments video room. The father punches up the train schedule on the
screen, rounds up his wife and daughter, and heads home.[9]

Sands and Gammons describe the experience-less experience. In
taking out the trouble—of hearing vendors hawk goods, of passing
strangers' money down the row of seats and then passing hot dogs
back, of talking or debating plays with those nearby—you take out the
sensory contact that makes going to a baseball game such a richly
evocative experience. Screen technology makes it easier. But it's certainly not better. In fact, it is precisely such "advances," I would argue,
that leave us feeling less connected to the experience of being at the
game, to the family members you came with, and to others seated
nearby. The orientation is not to the event and the people but to navigating one's desires via the screen.

Although the Sands-Gammons scenario is invented, it is not far off
the mark. Some of the services they envision are already making their
way into major league ballparks. At the Tampa Bay Devil Rays park, for
example, press agent Carmen Molina says the screens available at the
102 "choice" seats in the stadium allow patrons to choose and change
the camera angle they view, check player statistics, and keep up with the
scores of different games in play. And you can—as at many sports stadiums—order food from your seat, although not yet via screen.

The screen is alluring because it offers the illusion of power. *You
choose; you decide.* But the very engagement is a limiting act. The
"choices" a screen presents are, by its very nature, preselected and limited in scope. You can only choose from among what is offered. Yet the
screen acts with such authority that it makes it seem as if all that is
needed, desired, or worthwhile is right there, packaged and delivered.

The TV Connection

Our first mass experience with the screen, of course, was the
arrival of the television set in the American home. And what a powerful screen it was. As Sonia Livingstone writes, the television "has come
to dominate the hours in our day, the organisation of our living rooms,

the topics of our conversations, our conceptions of pleasure, the things to which we look forward, the way we amuse and occupy our children, and the way we discover the world we live in. Many also argue that television has come to dominate what we think, how we think, and what we think about." It is a stunning medium, one that is a beloved companion to the lonely or temporarily alone. It even provides the very structure to our morning: We measure progress out the door by the timing of particular segments on the morning shows. At night, it keeps us up later, as programming once halted at midnight now just keeps going. When we do drift off, for some, the TV remains a flickering night-light, broadcasting security to its sleeping "viewers."[10]

Television today is so pervasive and so integrated into our culture that it is difficult to discern its influence, because its influence is everywhere. American households now have an average of 2.3 TV sets—about as many sets as household members, according to the U.S. Census Bureau. Although social scientists and critics have spent decades studying television viewing, often declaring its impact "good" or "bad," the matter seems too complex to break cleanly into two camps. Television, after all, has changed and evolved in concert with the rest of modern life. And while some, like author and critic Neil Postman, make a persuasive case for television's deleterious effects, the fact is that TV is also one of the last things we have that unites us. It is the only reliably common language, reference, and activity Americans participate in together—even as they may do it more and more alone.[11]

TV is how we talk to one another, how we exhibit caring, and how we maintain a sense of our place among our fellow citizens. People hardly vote anymore, hardly participate in local politics or the traditional institutions that gave a sense of societal order; fewer and fewer read newspapers. Instead, we spend our time in our homes, watching TV. The pervasiveness of our TV habit struck me on Easter Sunday as I rode home from my mother's house in Connecticut to mine in Massachusetts, taking back roads. As I looked out the car window and into the windows of home after home in the course of three and a half hours of driving, I did not catch vignettes of human activity but instead saw, over and over, darkened windows with the familiar blue glow. Even on a day of prayer, of visiting, of meals, of conversations, it had all come down to the same old thing: what was on TV.

At its best, TV gives us permission to express our membership in the human community. When Princess Diana was killed in a car accident in 1997, people all over the world grieved and mourned via television. The TV took us everywhere we wanted to be and validated our own feelings. The images of flowers and notes, first arriving at and then overwhelming the gates of Kensington Palace and other public sites, prompted the arrival of still more flowers and notes. We saw on our screens that this was what we, as members of the world, should do. We may have failed to send flowers when Aunt Hilda passed on, failed to write the note of condolence to Uncle Eddie, but we do it for Princess Di because our screens tell us that this is how we can interact. I saw the flowers, the notes, the interviews with Everyman as an aching to belong, to be connected to others. Diana's death was the excuse. Obviously, few of us actually knew Princess Di. The mourning, ostensibly for her, was for all of us. We wept for the vulnerability we feel in the face of death, for our own guilt, for the way we crave celebrity, for the ordinary, accumulated pain we have no other legitimate way to express. The television treatment of her death set the stage for a similar response to the tragic death of John F. Kennedy Jr. and his wife and sister-in-law. High-profile, televised tragedy—or victory—allows access to our own latent emotions.

The trouble is that as a society, we have come to need TV so badly in the first place. We may all know intellectually that television is not a reflection of real life—a fact broadcasters work to blur—but emotionally people rely so heavily on television for their experiences that, in some instances, TV offers lives that appear more real, more legitimate, than their own. Livingstone observes that "we often do not remember whether we learnt of a certain fact from a friend or television" and that "we fail to notice that our images of the elderly, for example, derive more from television than from everyday interactions." Livingstone's point here is not the storied confusion of reality versus TV, demonstrated by tales of fans sending soap opera stars wedding and baby gifts when their characters marry or give birth, but is about how we get information about our world. Does it matter that we learn how to lay a stone patio from Bob Vila and not from a skilled neighbor, friend, or relative? Does it matter that we forget that an anecdote we tell is from TV and not from a friend?[12]

I think it does—not because the information is different but because the process of getting it is less rich, less deep, and less open to participation. As a society today we focus more on the ends than the means. But the means, the process, is what provides the opportunity for interaction. The act of telling and retelling—like the acts of teaching and learning—exists not in easily encapsulated broadcast steps but in time and space. It is a shared activity between people. There is value in the slow, human exchange of information and all that goes with it, including the implicit statement that another is worthy of your time and attention. When people repeatedly seek other, quicker mediums to transfer information, they take away a vital vehicle for connection.

The screen is at first blush so appealing—and so is its role as intermediary—precisely because it removes a level of personal negotiation that exists when two people interact. You can do more without investing yourself. This is, perhaps, why people feel it easy enough to flame someone online or criticize a co-worker's performance or deliver bad news via e-mail. The screen lets us hide behind its protective shield. But there is a problem. There are no clear rules beyond common sense and decency about when to e-mail someone and when to deal in person. The screen offers the control and convenience people adore; you may communicate and respond when you choose. But this only heightens our sense of self-importance and threatens one of the most endearing qualities of human relations: the willingness to inconvenience yourself for another. Putting yourself out, subjugating your own immediate desires to serve someone else, is becoming a nearly extinct feature of daily life. It makes friendships harder to forge, diminishes trust, and challenges long-held bonds. Is a friendship still a friendship if two people don't make time to share experiences?

Physical presence matters. There are myriad ways in which screen technology allows people to accomplish more, and accomplish it more speedily. But the screen, with its ease and proliferation, is seductive, and it is an arrow shot to the heart of human relations. Relationships take time to blossom. Conversations need to wander. They are creations that bend this way and then the other, that backtrack and branch off, that have spaces full of thought and no talk, full of eye contact and private visions running parallel to the spoken moment. There is no place in the screen world for this.

But because being wired and technologically fluent means being hip and in demand, we risk reaching the point where we give the screen precedence over the person. We "deal" with people electronically, sorting their needs and desires like so many files, coolly completing one task, then another. It is a fundamentally different way of ordering interactions, and therefore relationships. Sometimes it makes sense. The problem comes when we invoke the screen's efficiencies for too many of our interactions, having one-way conversations simply because it's quicker and it's easier.

The Way We Watch (and Download)

The issue is not just the screen itself but how we have come to use it. Our relationship with the screen is increasingly personal, even intimate. Television is now often watched in solitude, and the tone of programs—especially the chitchat of home shopping—seeks to endow those onscreen with the status of "friend." In the electronic world, screens are not objective tools but personal accessories that amplify and fill in when human capabilities fall short. Screen technology expands our memory, polishes our look, extends our reach, and even gives us the illusion of having more time. (There seems no limit to what one can pack onto a software-generated calendar, while a few pen marks fill the day on the paper version. And a day that is not planned, but merely lived, seems to contain nothing unless it's recorded and checked off.)

When we reformat our lives for the screen, whether by reconstructing a conversation as e-mail or translating the day's activities into an electronic planner, we alter the structure of our experience. Stuff that must be done becomes a set of ordered "tasks." The screen and its requirements become the template for human activities. A day is no longer a stretch of time between waking up and going to bed; it is a series of spaces into which data may be entered and linked to specific times. The screen is the companion that reminds us of appointments and errands, that tells us when we have mail, and that keeps us company. In fact, that phrase is hardly used anymore; it's rare to hear one person say to another: "I'll keep you company." People don't like to do something with someone else—like keep them company—unless it also suits their own desires. But more critically, chances are, if you're electronically plugged in, you've got company enough.

Screen interactions—whether TV or electronic—are mostly solo pursuits. With the exception of home entertainment theaters specifically built for gathering, most screen interactions today are viewed as private moments (despite the fact that the electronic realm is not private at all). It's rude to look at what's on someone else's screen unless you're invited to do so. This one-to-one relationship has made viewing, in general, a less communal experience. Airplanes, even coach buses, now often have a screen at every seat. We surf the Net alone, chat online by ourselves. Mary Ann Liebert, publisher of the journal *CyberPsychology and Behavior*, says the Internet has changed her own life patterns. After dinner, she and her husband go to separate computers and spend the evening online, at times e-mailing each other with information the other would find interesting. What is striking about the arrangement is not just that the couple stops communicating in the old ways—talking, playing games, strolling—but that this new medium seamlessly replaces the old. Their talk, their expressions of caring, are now routed through the screen. This may be perfectly acceptable to many. But I believe such changes fundamentally *change us* as we align the motions of our living with the requirements of the screen. The screen becomes the filter, the parameter; the response is electronic and not human.[13]

And yet the lure of the screen, of the human–electronic interface, is powerful, even intoxicating. Many among us boast about speed and RAM and take pride in navigating the Internet, bookmarking Websites, and finding and downloading something new. The act of "finding" has become an accomplishment in its own right, on a par with actually "creating." Researchers report computer users registering a "high" when finding and downloading information—even when it's relatively useless information. For some, the Internet is actually addictive, prompting diagnosis of Internet Addiction Disorder. Among the symptoms, according to a University of Pittsburgh Web posting, are a need to spend increasing time on the Internet to achieve satisfaction, withdrawal with the cessation of Internet use, fantasies or dreams about the Internet, and continued Internet use despite problems exacerbated or caused by it. These include sleep deprivation, marital difficulties, lateness for early morning meetings, neglect of occupational duties, and feelings of abandonment in significant others. While there is some debate over the legitimacy of such a diagnosis, there is, naturally, a support group to help: the Internet Addiction Support Group, which is, however unhelpfully, online.

Whether the screen is addictive may be irrelevant, though. If forecasts are to be believed, we will all be spending more time interacting with it in the years to come. McDonald's is testing use of screens for ordering food, "betting that many consumers prefer an electronic clerk to a live one," according to a *Wall Street Journal* article. Internet tracking firms like International Data Corporation predict the further saturation of devices like personal digital assistants or handheld companions (even the language is evocative!), along with smart phones, smart pagers, and other portable multiuse gadgets. Already we are carrying screens in our pockets, displaying at our request the disparate elements of our lives. What's to stop the wallet from becoming obsolete, with photos being scanned in instead of slipped into a clear vinyl pocket? Screens are personal keepers of our information. And as we use them not at a distance but inches from our face and for the most personal aspects of living, we invite a profoundly intimate relationship between self and screen. Screens are moving from the status of *tools* to *interfaces*, not held at arm's length but metaphorically integrated into our very being.[14]

While researchers are looking at real computer-human interfaces, the most tangible fusion at present is in the form of a toy and TV show for the preverbal set. Teletubbies, those British-generated characters heralded as the next Barney for the toddler set, have screens embedded in their fleshy bellies, an image that captures the seamless integration of child and screen. It is a powerful metaphor, all the more so because children, more than adults, gravitate to the screen as an unquestioned authority. They seem, at times, oblivious to its limitations. A fourth-grade boy doing a report on Mozart was working at a computer in his school library when a visiting mom mentioned that the composer was married, information he might want to include in his report. The student, though, didn't believe it was true because that fact "didn't show up on the screen" when he did a search. The mom found the fact for the bewildered child—in a book. Anyone with children understands how screen-centered the next generation is already and how proud parents are of their kids' computer skills. Children seem born with the ability to point and click. Just to be sure, parents routinely sign up preschoolers for computer classes and put their infants in front of the screen. According to the *Wall Street Journal*, "lapware"—computer software for those eighteen months to three years old, typically used while sitting on an adult's lap—is "one of the fastest-growing segments of the software market, with sales more than tripling in 1997 to $27 million." We have software marketed for the nine-month-old set, and IBM retails a computer embedded in a plastic desk and designed specifically for youngsters aged four to seven.[15]

The hunger to introduce babies to computers springs from parents' well-intentioned desire to give their children a head start in the race to a top college. But, again, the screen has real limitations that are overlooked. Tufts University professor and child development expert David Elkind has voiced concerns. Very young children, he says, haven't developed the ability to understand that a picture on a computer screen is a symbol for something else in the real world. They can become overstimulated, and he goes so far as to blame early computer use by children as the "most likely culprit" causing the rise in attention deficit disorders. The big question—why do babies and toddlers need to learn how to use a computer before they can even talk?—seems oddly lost in our love-fest with the screen. This is not to say the screen is the enemy, either. But we aren't being objective. We merely embrace.[16]

When television first arrived in the American home, there was a similar tendency to celebrate its wondrous capabilities. In the November 1950 issue of *Good Housekeeping*, Bianca Bradbury wrangles with the arrival of this new medium in her home, posing a question in the headline that might well be posed today: "Is Television Mama's Friend or Foe?" The article is amusing and informative because it so innocently considers what is now the single most influential medium in American culture and because it foreshadows our own grappling with Internet hookups. But Bradbury's piece is particularly interesting for her observations on how people *watch* TV.

In Bradbury's description and in practice, early TV viewing was not what it is today, a personal and private act, but a group activity, like watching a performance or going to the movies. The audience was a unit, present not only to *view* but also to *respond*. The TV, she goes on to explain, has brought a wonderful world into her family's living room. She gushes about the high quality of broadcasts, declaring shows like *Kukla, Fran, and Ollie* "inhabited by gentle people, people of good will. Television has made us a gift of these friends." And TV news, she declares, takes on subjects like housing, rent control, the United Nations, and policy on China—subjects "meaningless to children when heard or read. But when an authority, excited and sincere, sits behind a table, looks into a camera and argues pro or con, vague issues become real." The television she describes is an active medium, one that provokes interaction among family members. TV news drives adults to clarify their views, she reports, describing a scene that would be utterly foreign today: "So, often, when the news clicks off, the living room turns into an arena, and the parents find themselves defending beliefs they didn't even know they held. To the children, the news has become real and personal. Bill, at breakfast, lifts his nose out of his cereal long enough to ask, 'Pop, what's the lowdown on world government?' and Pop searches his mind, trying to remember what he really does think."

This vision of TV—as bringing the world into our living rooms (when, indeed, the TV was in the living room for everyone to watch together)—is not so far from how the Internet is being touted. Computers, we hear, are connecting everyone to everyone else. Literally, in both cases, it's true. TV does bring the world into our home, and computers do electronically link people in faraway places. But, as we have seen with TV, it's a whole lot more complicated. Television has profoundly changed how people relate, how people perceive the world, how people envision themselves fitting in to society. TV has spawned a whole language to describe not the energetic discussions Bradbury envisions but the passivity it encourages. Before TV there were no "couch potatoes."

Although Bradbury envisioned the screen as a spark, we long ago came to view TV as a passive medium, which is not altogether accurate. As scholars in the field of television viewing research observe, the value—or lack of value—of the TV experience has, in part, to do with *how* one watches rather than just what is intrinsic to the medium itself. This goes back to Seinfeld's complaint: that we are too eager to accept what's being fed us. TV has come to be used as an ever-present companion, which can watch over our children and even lull us to sleep. TV represents security in its reliable presence and predictable range of offerings. We, at times, lean on it like a close friend or an older sibling. Home shopping channels invite petty confessions. Other programs, like Ricki Lake's, offer access to intimate issues probed at a safe distance. Sitcoms provide both entertainment and a common language of jokes and references, letting us feel part of a broadcast community. Sitcoms also offer a structure for making sense of all that doesn't make sense in daily life.

The broadcast of mundane moments and trials and tribulations (albeit of TV characters) invites us to envision our own trivial experiences as fodder for the screen, imagining ourselves as the star of our own sitcom. Can't you hear the theme music playing as you become soaked walking in the driving rain from the car to your office? Can you imagine the canned laughter rolling as your child spits out the sticky Starburst candy into her hand, threatening to make everything around her adhesive, as you sit without water in a crowded, sweltering chapel waiting for your sister to be awarded her Ph.D.? TV programming, without our conscious decision, provides a frame and an organizing structure for our real-life experiences. At the Ricki Lake taping, for example, when we were asked to sing the words to "The Brady Bunch," everyone in the studio audience—a group of people diverse in age, sex, socioeconomic level, and race—knew *all* the words. Television culture is unifying. But it is also homogenizing.

Social scientist Tannis M. MacBeth researched television viewing in three similarly situated communities in Canada. One community, by accident of geography, was in a valley out of reach of a transmitter and had no television reception, despite being linked to other communities via rail, bus, and roads. This community was given the name "Notel" in the study, for "No Tel-evision." Another community, "Unitel," received only one broadcast channel, and a third, "Multitel," had multiple television channels. Although the Notel residents did not watch TV regularly, because they were not isolated they knew what TV was and occasionally watched elsewhere. This was important to the study, observes MacBeth, "making it less likely that we would find differences between Notel and other towns, providing a conservative test of the effects of television."[17]

MacBeth and colleagues gave tests to schoolchildren and adults in the three communities to judge their creativity and problem-solving abilities, especially the tendency to find "out of the box" solutions. MacBeth concludes, after much caution about reading too much into the results, that "the availability of television and normal patterns of viewing, had, on average, a negative effect on creative thinking for both children and adults." The tests showed adults and children in Notel outperforming their peers in the two other communities, more often finding answers and showing more persistence in the face of difficult problems. It may be a reach to blame violence on TV for violence in the schools, Pokémon for playground battles, or a flood of Saturday morning TV ads for our kids' insatiable appetite for everything they see. But it is equally faulty to believe that television—the act of viewing itself—doesn't affect the way we view our own world or, as suggested by MacBeth's studies, the way we seek solutions.

The range of possibility in television is limited, in part because the same content, images, and tone are broadcast over and over until the repetition makes it seem true. TV's portrayal of middle-class life in America, for example, is actually a view of life for those at the very top of the economic ladder. Commercials are especially guilty. What is held up as a "normal" or "typical" kitchen, for example, in advertisements for cereal, other food, or appliances is beyond the means of most Americans. And yet, over and over, these luxuriously appointed homes are presented as "what everybody has"—or ought to have. Networks also create programming that lacks racial and ethnic diversity and that increasingly focuses on only the young, white, and beautiful. The reasoning may be economic: Broadcasters realize that advertisers are looking to influence young consumers. (Older consumers with more to spend have already declared brand loyalties.) But the result is that certain groups of people with certain lifestyles are overrepresented on TV. In the end, the small screen shows a very small piece of life. But those who watch don't see the reduction; they see the world that is *supposed* to be—or so the repetition of these images makes us think.

Ask Melvin Sanchez, the resident services coordinator for the Jackson Parkway public housing project in Holyoke, Massachusetts, about the power of TV. He worked with tenants in public housing so dilapidated that when I visited in 1998 the 209 units were about to be bulldozed and completely redeveloped. The brick, barracks-style housing had been built in 1944. Some of the units still had the original kitchens. Because of the redevelopment, there was a lot of anxiety and concern among residents. Naturally, Sanchez spent a great deal of time listening and talking, not just about the relocation but about many aspects of their lives. Part of the redevelopment, after all, was aimed at making this area—and the residents who lived there—part of a viable working middle class. What struck Sanchez, an ambitious and well-spoken man whose family was part of the Puerto Rican migration into the city decades earlier, was how powerful a role television played in residents' conceptions of how their life should look. People, he said, believe what they see on TV: "They look on TV, and on all the shows everybody has a house and all the kids have bikes and they say, 'I'll get that because everybody gets that.'" Residents don't see, he observed, that you've got to work for it.

The ability of TV to gloss over economic hurdles is matched by its ability to gloss over emotional complexities while seeming to deal with real issues—much as the Internet did for cancer patient Anne Powers. The very nature of TV programming calls for segmenting experiences into half-hour or hour chunks, a length of time to which we have become wholly adapted. This demands familiar patterns of revelation: the presentation of the problem, the plan of action, and the resolution.

Things that take time and require hard, soul-searching consideration in real life—being cheated on, the discovery of incest, being stood up at the altar, problems with drug abuse—all fit into one episode of *Beverly Hills 90210.*

It's easy to rail against TV. The American Academy of Pediatrics gave us more ammunition when it said TV should be banned from the lives of children under two. We have long labeled television a "bad" influence, even as we boast when Junior takes to the computer, which has status as the "good" screen. But they are really different forms of the same thing. Early research suggested computer users tended to be highly educated and were not heavy TV watchers, supporting the notion of dual camps of "TV people" and "computer people," but that picture has changed. Research in 1998 by LinkExchange and Hambrecht & Quist showed that TV viewing didn't suffer as a result of the Internet and that heavy TV watchers tend to be heavy Internet users, while light TV watchers tend to be light Internet users. This supports the idea that there are heavy and light "media" users. Use of the TV and use of the PC are complementary, not adversarial. The report's authors cite the common practice of the two mediums advertising for one another. After the 49ers football game ends, TV viewers get the message to check www.49ers. com for postgame stats or even an interview or chat with a player. Before the game, anyone logged on to the 49ers Website gets the message to tune in to Channel 2 to watch them play.

Just as the TV has become a medium of the masses, so has the Internet, accessed from whatever personal venue is most convenient. One screen does not dominate the other, but the two cooperate to build a powerful conduit for information, entertainment, and communication. Together they seek to have more and more of our lives mediated over or through their waves, wires, and cables. Screens are the preferred tool for navigating everyday life and the information superhighway—the two blurring into one screen-guided existence. This is not inherently bad. The screen life is here, and it is, increasingly, the way we live. But, as easily as we tune in or log on, we must be able to set aside the technology. The challenge is to use the technology without being engulfed by its potency. It should not be a replacement for life experiences and face-to-face interactions.

Although it is viewed as a "smarter" medium, we know by now that the computer screen is just as great a threat as TV when it comes to taking us away from our lives—and not just adults. Our children socialize via real-time talk and e-mail and lose hours of sleep and homework time surfing the Web. It's little wonder. The Internet is an astonishing resource. The offerings on the Web are so vast, the promise so great, the high of downloading information so intoxicating, we can lose ourselves even as we imagine we can glimpse the informational zenith. In over-stuffing ourselves with content and undernourishing ourselves with analysis, though, we threaten to cave in under the weight of facts that give us bulk but no meaning. This is important. It takes searching skills, not thinking skills, to amass a mountain of Internet-generated infor-mation. But when do we take the time to judge the quality of what we've downloaded? It is easy in this age to be dazzled by style and miss out on the substance.

Camera, Speakers, Microphone = Eyes, Ears, Mouth

They are thinking out of the box at PictureTel, the Andover, Massachusetts, video-conferencing company. At least, that's what the logo for PictureTel's Living Lab, with its opened box and arrows leap-ing out, seems to suggest. More appropriately, though, they are think-ing *about* the box. Taylor Kew, the lab-coated guide who greets me, heads through heavy doors, down a snaking hallway, and into a series of rooms containing some items I am told I may not write about. In fact, I have to sign a form agreeing not to disclose company secrets.

But for all the fuss, what Kew and his colleagues are trying to do at PictureTel is what everyone is trying to do everywhere: make the screen not just more like real life but *better* than real life. "Our goal is we want it to be better to [meet] over video than in person," says Kew. He uses his well-practiced Super Bowl metaphor to explain. Most people, he says, would rather watch the Super Bowl on TV than be there at the stadium. And he's right. Not growing up with a household of football fans, I was stunned to get to college and discover that Super Bowl Sunday was such a big deal that the dining hall ordered special meals that could be taken off the premises and eaten in front of the TV. Now, as a fan, I see that this is one day of the year when most Ameri-cans are celebrating the same way: watching TV (and actually watching the commercials), drinking beer, and eating nachos.

So will it ever be better to meet via screen than in person? It depends on what you want to accomplish. Kew claims that people who participate in video conferences show up on time and are better prepared than people at old-fashioned face-to-face meetings. That may be so. But Kew concedes that one real problem with video conferencing right now is that, as he says bluntly, "the quality stinks." People don't look like themselves. Indeed, when he and I have a conversation via video—each of us in a different room—the person I am talking to doesn't appear to be the same person I've met before. Kew's features are blurred, which makes him seem less trustworthy to my eye. It is hard to read his expressions. What I have, in essence, is his voice and a poor visual portrait of him, the disappointing quality masked by the fact that I can see him move around as he speaks. Kew says he's felt the same frustration himself. He describes having a video-conferencing relationship with someone at Ford Motors. Because of the way the camera was mounted, Kew was always looking down on him. As a result, he pictured a guy who was five foot eight and portly. When they met in person, Kew says, he was stunned to discover a lanky man six feet two inches tall standing in front of him.

The issue, though, is not just distorted looks. Because it takes so long to transmit video via phone lines—and it's slower than transmitting voice—there is often a delay and a disconnect between the video image and the voice, even when the voice is slowed down to more closely match the screen. "The problem with the delay is you can't have a good argument and you can't tell a good joke," says Kew. "But if you are good at video conferencing, you can keep talking and no one can stop you, because of the delay."

We will, inevitably, reach a time when the speed and quality of transmission will make video conferencing less like watching your high school AV department at work and more like broadcast TV. If it is often preferable to leave a phone message rather than to speak with someone, why wouldn't it also appeal to meet—even visit—via video instead of face to face? Although this technology is now used mostly in business, the most promising market is for home use. Kew says he has already tried some rudimentary video conferencing with a technologically fluent friend of his. Using mounted cameras and control panels, they snooped around each other's homes, zooming in to see, for example, what's sitting on the coffee table. It was also how he and his friend, both new fathers, first introduced members of the next generation to each other. "I'm showing my baby to his baby," says Kew. "We started laughing."

It *is* cool to think about how much we can do and how far we have come. But even as we envision the world growing smaller, the links multiplying, we can also imagine the screen becoming our stand-in, pulling us away—or setting us free, depending on how you see it—from the complicated and meaning-laden experience of being with another person. Kew shows off a new piece of hardware, a souped-up monitor, making the point about how easily we trade real life for screen life. He claps his hands over the components of a set. "Camera, speakers, microphone," he says, pointing out each. "Eyes, ears, mouth."

MOBILITY

An eighty-eight-year-old woman named Mary Kelley was working the switchboard at a local Council on Aging office and flirting with a messenger as I sat nearby, waiting for her to consider my question. I was doing a story on the booming demographic of the "old old"—the eighty-five-plus population—and I wanted to cast her age-mates as not just old folks but a generation rooted in a common youthful experience. I wanted to know in concrete terms how America was different for her than for the Boomers, the GenXers, and those before and since. I was not seeking sweeping political statements or observations about scientific advances. I wanted the junk, the what-you-did-every-day stuff that often seems too trivial to mention. At last, perhaps inspired by the jar of hard candy sitting on her desk, perhaps prompted by the approaching lunch hour, she explained that people didn't use to diet. "Nobody went to Betty [*sic*] Craig or whatever to lose weight or get in shape," she said. "All you had to do was walk. You never heard of a diet. You ate."[1]

If you wanted to go to town, she explained, you walked. If you wanted to visit a friend, you walked. When you went to school, you walked. Her observation stuck with me, not only because of its simplicity but because she had, in an odd way, hit on what we find so wondrous about modern life: our mobility. Today we celebrate the ease with which we can move: be transported, uprooted, rerouted, and, virtually speaking, delivered half a world away without leaving where we are. My neighbor lives in Massachusetts and works in Chicago. My husband in the past two weeks has been in San Diego, L.A., New Jersey, Miami, Cleveland, and Cannes, France—and he doesn't have one of those traveling jobs.

Although it's obvious that we are a more mobile society than twenty-five, fifty, seventy-five, or a hundred years ago, we don't often think about what that mobility means. There is more to it than just getting places more quickly. It reflects a change in how we move through our world and our lives. It reflects changed connections to the land, to the natural world, and to each other. In the broadest terms, we have been transformed from a society bounded by the limits of time, distance, and geography to one so untethered we must labor to make the concrete relevant. Activities of daily living, once rooted in time and place—eating, working, relaxing, shopping, conversing, parenting, among others—are pulled loose from their moorings. It is a point of glee to discover you can do something "anytime or anywhere." We are a culture of willing transients, trading the roots of physical geography for the wings of mobility. But even as such advances offer freedom, they also extract a price, reordering lives without our explicit consent. If you can be anywhere, where are you? Does it—can it—matter?

At its heart, mobility—along with the portability of so many elements of daily living—means that a person no longer *has* to be in a particular place to accomplish a particular task. The technology that makes the office utterly portable has helped make "work" not foremost a place but a verb. One can, for example, work from an office, a home, an airplane, a car, a beach, a mountaintop—anywhere. It is the *what*, the task at hand, that is the focus, and not the *where*. In fact, location is hardly considered any longer as a factor limiting or even defining what you can do. Any entity—whether a retail store, bank, information system, or person—today offers many points of access. The traditional in-person, fixed-location experience is just one means of making contact, and it's one many today find more cumbersome than the electronic option.

Electronic contact, after all, is quicker. You can do more in less time—commuters can do it while in transit. Instead of staring out the window and thinking as the train delivers them uptown, downtown, or out to the suburbs, people pull out cell phones and laptops and get to work, go online, or make plans. In our society, it feels good to be so efficient. But such efficiency, which is noted as a kind of superiority, is not an isolated act. It is a pattern of living that alters the way we relate—or don't relate—to the physical space we inhabit. The cell phone may make you more connected to distant places, but it leaves you less connected to wherever you are at the moment. There is no magic to two people finding themselves together in the same place if one is talking on a cell phone.

In ways concrete and abstract, increasing mobility is changing the experience of time and space and rewriting rules of engagement. It has not happened all at once. We have gained our wings gradually. The invention of the bicycle more than a century ago created a stir because people were suddenly able to travel at four times the speed of walking. So striking was this change that the public was warned about getting "bicycle face" from traveling against the wind at such high speeds. In turn, the advent of the railroad, the automobile, and the airplane brought new opportunities and challenges to people's lives, as did the distance-spanning telephone. Despite debates about the changing pace of American life that accompanied each of these strides, they remained in concept tools for traversing real miles, concrete distance. Today, that connection is vanishing. Mobility is no longer about reaching a destination; it is about motion.[2]

The rise of cyberspace, the ubiquity of air travel, the premium on speed, and the portability of work, entertainment, and communications have emasculated the very notion of fixed space that once organized the everyday world. The environments we inhabit now are more virtual and more fluid. One-to-one interactions are giving way to interfaces with multiples or networks. Travel today is not about distance but about the quality of the mobile event. As a society, we are tuned and addicted to movement, impatient when our progress is stalled. The experience today is not of traveling from one wholly discrete location to the next, pausing once we arrive to get our bearings and scout the surroundings. Rather, we are always in motion, whether close to home or far away. The actual locations are merely the backgrounds that whiz by. Motion—mobility—has become the steady state. Physical places have become like virtual locations that can be accessed from anywhere at any time. We are no longer oriented to terrain and the worlds that may unfold there but to the act of passing through.

This sensation feels new and exhilarating at times. It is heady to realize all the things you can do while in transit or the ease with which you can travel once-great distances. But this new order has unsettling consequences for the time, value, and attention allotted to personal interactions, quiet experiences, and reflection. These, after all, are the things that allow us to make meaning out of the jumble of daily experience. They connect us to our own lives, to other people, and to our world.

Wheels, Rails, and Wings

Mobility is an old dream. For much of human history it was the land, not man, that determined where people settled and with whom they would battle, be friendly, and trade. Waterways, mountain ranges, oceans, and deserts set the agenda and created sometimes insurmountable limits. No wonder epic tales like *The Odyssey* and *The Aeneid* chronicle the challenges of traveling great distances. Triumph—the arrival at one's destination—marked the attainment of heroic stature. Even today, the idea has currency. The record-breaking swim, the mega-distance run, a year-long cross-country journey by a man on his horse—these are reminders of how small we are and how vast and real the earth is.

Most of the time, though, it doesn't feel like that. Most of the time, we gloss over the detail of hard land, skipping from one city, one coast, to the other. We travel easily and quickly. And it promises to get even easier and quicker in the future. High-speed trains boast record travel times between major cities. A supersonic jet in development may one day take travelers from New York to Tokyo in four hours and twenty minutes, compared with the current fourteen hours. Such progress is even more astonishing when you realize that President Dwight D. Eisenhower only approved legislation to create the Interstate Highway System in 1956, and as recently as the 1960s and 1970s, motorists traveling between major cities spent hours winding along narrow roadways, because major thoroughfares were incomplete. Four hours and twenty minutes in those days didn't get you very far in a car—and certainly not to the other side of the globe.[3]

More than a century ago it was the land and the limits of our mobility that defined the size of our world. In his *Memoirs of a Fox-Hunting Man*, the young Siegfried Sassoon observes that because the Dumborough estate was twelve miles from the home he shared with his aunt, she "was fully two miles beyond the radius of Lady Dumborough's round of calls. Those two miles made the difference, and the aristocratic yellow-wheeled barouche never entered our white unassuming gate." One's social circle was literally defined by the distance the carriage and its occupant could travel. In his wonderful book *The Culture of Time and Space, 1880–1918*, Stephen Kern notes that automobile enthusiast Alfred Harmsworth joyfully predicted in 1902 the automobile would change social life in the country because people living more than twenty-five miles apart were able to visit without arranging a change of horses. People once beyond "calling distance" were now in the social loop.[4]

Mobility—or the lack of it—has long organized our social worlds. As train tracks were laid from cities to outlying areas and then across the American West, stations became population centers and gathering places. Streetcars spurred the birth of the inner suburbs, pushing the distribution of urban population out five to fifteen miles, according to one sociologist's estimate in 1895. The car, of course, expanded that distance further and even changed the design and look of neighborhoods and the American landscape. But more on that later. The point here is that even as we became a more mobile society, we remained oriented to the land, creating places that reflected the belief that one's final destination was a concrete location. We were getting better at traversing the miles between here and there, but it was still *miles* that separated two points.[5]

In other words, geography could be made to feel smaller, more passable, but it persisted as the basis for structuring our experiences. Many magazine ads for planes, trains, and cars in the 1940s, 1950s, and 1960s, for example, highlight the marvelous ways in which these new technologies enabled people to travel real miles over real ground. By contrast, ads for air travel today hardly record the fact that the airplane is a means of transportation. Ads boast about comfort (wide seats, leg room), amenities (onboard phones, personal video screens), and convenience (leave every hour on the hour, make connections quicker)— all addressing the *experience* of travel and not the *fact* of travel. There is no longer anything novel about merely being able to go from point A to point B.

That, however, was not the case in 1946. A magazine ad for American Railroads showed a hardware shopkeeper dressed in blazer and tie leaning over the counter to tell a nattily dressed customer that the railroad "connects my store and my business with every other town and city in the whole country. That means I can give my customers the kind of merchandise—the same up-to-the-minute goods—that folks in the big towns enjoy." The railroad spans the miles, connecting small towns with larger population centers. We don't hear how quickly goods arrive—no Federal Express–style promises of delivery the next day before ten A.M.—but merely that the railway can cover the miles that otherwise deny locals access to the same merchandise as city folk. A second ad the same year sounds themes of localism. The railroads are presented as a modern entity at the same time they are "linked in a closely-knit partnership with the communities they serve. For the railroads employ local people, buy supplies locally, own local property and pay local taxes." The message is clear: The railroad may be newfangled and reaching out to distant places, but it is rooted in the community.

Ads for cars offer a more complex picture, in part because the car has long been sold not merely as a means of transportation but as a reflection of one's identity and place in the world. While messages of style, utility, economy, and status surface in old magazine ads, so do messages about what the car actually does: cover distance. A 1946 ad for Nash, for example, states that this "big new Nash 600 takes you an amazing 25 to 30 miles on a gallon of gasoline at moderate highway speeds—500 to 600 miles on a tankful." A 1951 ad for Buick's new "Dynaflow Drive" offers the motorist "freedom from the physical strain of pushing a clutch pedal hundreds of times a day in crowded traffic. . . . You feel a new mastery of time, distance, straight-away, curve, upgrades and the open road—when *your* hands are on the wheel of a Dynaflow Buick." If driving was once a physical act of covering ground (as well as operating a vehicle), it is now (to listen to the ads) about fulfilling fantasies. A 1998 ad for the Isuzu Trooper pictures the SUV in the middle of an iceberg-packed waterway with a ship in the background. The caption: "Explore places. Bring friends." Although Isuzu describes itself as "specialized worldwide builders of adventure machines" and its tag line is "Go farther," the message is not about miles but about pushing one's metaphysical boundaries. The setting for the ad is fantastical, evoking not travel but play.

Ads for air travel around midcentury also echo themes of spanning miles, often celebrating the sheer miracle of traveling great distances at great speeds. A 1952 Pan American Grace Airways ad displays a map of the airline's flight route and boasts that its course from New York to Buenos Aires is "500 miles shorter" than the competition's. A 1956 ad for the Douglas DC-7 plane pictures a man asleep in a hammock with a newspaper opened on his lap. A cactus plant in the background and a thatched roof overhead suggest an exotic location. The DC-7, the ad trumpets, is "your quickest way to the laziest living." This aircraft, we learn, is "the world's fastest airliner" and travels "up to 50 mph faster than any other airliner. Its top speed is 410!" Today typical commercial jets travel 550 miles per hour—but we don't typically care to know the speed; it is simply an unimportant detail. Air travel has become so routine that it is no longer an experience of distance but of time. When you can travel from one city to another and back in a single workday, the miles become abstract. And the use of frequent flier miles as currency to buy goods and pay for hotel rooms further blurs what we mean by a mile. The truth is, we don't really know how far we travel. We know instead how pleasant—or unpleasant—the experience is, what's on the menu, what movie is playing, what technology is on board, and whether the flight is on time.

From Earth to Ethereal

Modern air travel has recast the way we experience distance: as a wait in a comfy (or not so comfy) seat with a personal video screen or laptop and some peanuts and soda. But communications technology is making us truly mobile, plucking our lives from the physical realm altogether. This is about more than the convenience of being able to do many things at once from a variety of locations. It is more critically about living in a new world, a world in which the tangible is being replaced by the virtual. Abstract as this sounds, that is precisely the point: More and more of our experiences *are* abstractions. We are living less in the physical world and depending more on virtual constructs to go about our lives.

Our advances in travel have tamed our nation's—and much of the world's—terrain; communications technology is making distance, and the terrain it spans, utterly irrelevant. Writing more than twenty years ago as a geography professor at Oxford University, Jean Gottman observed that technology has not been aimed—as is often believed— just at "saving human labor and reducing physical exertion. It has also been aimed at making geographical space, the space inhabited by mankind, *fungible*." The idea that any space can be interchanged with any other space, he argues, would be a boon to mankind. "If this state were achieved," he writes, "an infinity of problems that have always plagued individuals and society would be resolved. The fungibility of space would mean that every point in space would for all practical purposes be equivalent to any other point."[6]

Written at a time when many computers were the size of large refrigerators—massive physical objects—the observation was insightful. Today the Internet, the cell phone, the virtual office represent realization of that ideal. It is, after all, the collapse of space—and not the ability to store recipes or do large calculations in a blink, once popular conceptions of how we would use computers—that seems so marvelous. In the past century, we have moved from life organized by land to life organized by signal; from dark to light; from heavy to weightless. Some scholars, notably social historian Carolyn Marvin, mark the start of the modern era with the telegraph. But it is the telephone that more directly affects everyone. The telephone is more than one hundred years old and, more critically, has made the transition from earth to ethereal. The telephone, which began as a heavy, stationary contraption that used wires to transmit the human voice, is today a light, nearly weightless, mobile, portable device. This evolution has been accompanied by an evolution in the way we use and view the telephone. A phone conversation, for example, has evolved from a special occasion, a replacement for a physical visit, to a sometimes annoying and incessant tool in our new roles, no longer as conversationalists but as managers of transmitted information.

For a long time, the telephone was viewed as an instrument for spanning miles and linking distant places. In fact, until recent years, callers might ask each other, "Where are you?" near the beginning of a conversation, as a way of creating a scene in which a dialogue could unfold. Today, the question is more often "What are you doing?"—asked when you can tell by the series of "unh-huhs" that the person on the other end may be present physically but is doing or thinking about something else. Phone calls have also come to represent annoyances. Even when we want to talk, our response to the ring is often negative; hence the rise in screening calls and devices like Caller ID. It is not viewed as a treat to make or receive a phone call, even when the resulting conversation may be wonderful. We have come to perceive the device not as a friend but a necessary intruder.

To be sure, the telephone is indispensable. But when Alexander Graham Bell introduced his invention to the American public in 1876, it was a tough sell. Although he conceived of it as a way to shrink the distance between two points, others at first were confused and put off. It seemed creepy to talk with a disembodied human voice. It looked difficult to use. Besides, who needed a telephone? There was already 214,000 miles of telegraph wire linking 8,500 telegraph offices. Why use a telephone when a telegraph could relay a message *and* leave a written record of what was said?[7]

The telephone, in fact, was first viewed as a plaything, something to amuse and entertain. It was the failure to see its usefulness that left Bell and his associate Thomas A. Watson to make money by lecturing about the telephone and then showing it off to large audiences in a kind of performance. During these shows, the high point would come when Watson played a tune from a separate location and the music was carried over the wire into the auditorium. These displays actually fed public confusion over the use of the telephone. Was it for music? For a kind of broadcasting?

Even as Bell entertained, he kept hold of his vision of the telephone as a way to span distance. In 1878 he wrote of a future in which "it is conceivable that cables of telephone wires could be laid underground, or suspended overhead, communicating by branch wires with private dwellings, country houses, shops, manufactories, etc., etc., uniting them through the main cable with a central office where the wire could be connected as desired, establishing direct connection between any two places in the city. Such a plan as this, though impracticable at the present moment, will, I believe, be the outcome of the introduction of the telephone to the public."

If Bell saw the geographical implications clearly, according to sociologist Sidney H. Aronson, journalists, cartoonists, and the general public were far from understanding how telephones could be useful in their lives. Even when the first lines were laid and the first stations opened, linking businesses to one another, messages were translated (much as telegraph messages had been) and passed on from customer to customer, rather than just giving them a chance to speak with each other directly. When the telephone did at last catch on, obviously it became enormously popular. People discovered that instead of going to the butcher, placing an order, and then returning later, they might call ahead, place an order by phone, and pick it up in one trip. An obvious application, but revolutionary at the time. Farmers—some one-third of Americans lived on farms in the early part of the century—discovered they could gather at the end of the day on a party line (where several homes shared the same phone line) and trade news and information. The operator thus became a kind of newsgatherer and, in some incarnations, the person who knew who was where doing what.

The telephone saved people trips. It was, quite clearly, a way to cover distance—at least with your voice. Advertisements after WWII reminded customers that company phone lines were crossing ground, so they didn't have to. A 1946 ad campaign called "Telephone Tours" took print readers to, for example, Sweden. The ad, laid out like a travel montage of pithy facts and popular destinations, tells the reader that "By phone, Sweden is as near as your nearest neighbor." The use of "nearest neighbor" then evoked both physical and emotional proximity and familiarity; it may not do the same today. Other ads speak relentlessly of "long distance." A 1961 Bell Telephone System ad displays a woman's hand picking up a receiver on a dial phone (which has a four-digit number). "Why not say 'thanks' by Long Distance?" the copy reads. The tag line says, "Keep in touch by Long Distance." This term—long distance—is today nearly meaningless. The proliferation of phone lines and cell phones has multiplied the number of phone numbers and area codes. We now call "long distance" to the next town, even as Internet chats to another continent or cell phone calls between different time zones are made as local calls. Calling is no longer about spanning space. It is instead about numbers, about the right code and the right interface.

The phone call is also no longer a special event. In 1956, Bell Telephone circulated an ad that depicted the phone call as an occasion. An older woman sits at a desk with a photo of her son propped in front of her. She speaks into the receiver, the embodiment of all that phone calls are no longer: She is sitting still, plugged into a nonportable instrument, and she is giving her full attention to the conversation. "It's almost like a real visit, son. Call again soon," the caption reads. The ad copy doesn't refer to the conversation as a "phone call" but as "a telephone visit." Even the rates displayed at the bottom of the ad speak of distance bridged: "Notice how far you can call for a little."

More than forty years later, the phone call is not so much a tool for covering distance as one for making it irrelevant. And the phone set itself has become so portable that we feel free—and even obligated—to do something else as we talk. Call waiting permits us to split our conversations, even as we split our attention. The answering machine and Caller ID allow us to exercise control. Whom do we screen out? Not just telemarketers, but people who want too much. Whom do we let in?

The incessant ring is no longer a summons but a signal like the red flag on a mailbox: information to be exchanged. We speak when we are ready, making appointments for extended conversations. It has become rude to talk for very long without having made a "phone date." The same is true for e-mail. (The medium, over phone lines, makes long missives feel too imposing. They are hard to read on the screen, take up too much physical space, and are most comfortably printed out and put into a form that can handle more than a few short yaps.) Phone calls are no longer conversations but airy transmissions. We take in, manage, respond. The act no longer requires an acknowledgment of the span of space and, in turn, the recognition that a phone call is a visit of the voice. The call is just a call, a voice in your ear.

No Borders, No Boundaries

Like the Coke ads of the 1970s that spurred middle school chorus directors to wave their batons to "I'd Like to Teach the World to Sing," the Internet access companies today are offering a feel-good message of a new world order. This time, though, the ideals of peace and harmony are being achieved not with music or cola but with better and faster electronic communications. A key part of the message is that Internet access overcomes borders, limits, and boundaries so the planet can be one big happy global family. The message plays well as we quest for a new image to define the twenty-first century. It is as if we have been suddenly released from the weight of limits and beliefs that have held us fast for so long; we are now free—indeed expected— to move about the cabin. Despite the fun we are having with retro chic styles and nostalgic reruns of past eras, no one today wants to be caught being rigid or backward-thinking. Movement, fluidity, flexibility are hallmarks of what it means to be modern. We want to "push the envelope" and think "out of the box." We are hungry to tear down walls and reconfigure our environment, whether that means reordering life goals or being able to switch around seats and cargo space in the minivan.

In a sense, we are moving from a world based on one-to-one correspondences to one in which hybrids and networks—repeatable, blendable entities—are the model. In her essay "The Cyborg Manifesto," science historian, cultural theoretician, and feminist writer Donna Haraway declares that we are moving from an "organic, industrial society to a polymorphous information system" in which physical boundaries and old divisions are being breached. "The dichotomies between mind and body, animal and human, organism and machine, public and private, nature and culture, men and women, primitive and civilized are all in question ideologically," she writes. She sees, instead, a new world in which "no objects, spaces or bodies are sacred in themselves; any component can be interfaced with any other if the proper standard, the proper code, can be constructed for processing signals in a common language."[8]

The lure of the interface is powerful, yet the rise of the network as an organizing principle of life demands a different way of conceptualizing relations. It suggests a movement from the single in sequence to the multiple. Such structures, for example, are well suited for business problem solving. A 1998 Microsoft magazine ad describes how "your sales guy," upon hearing the competition has dropped its price by 10 percent, "retreats to the lobby and, with his laptop, sends a spreadsheet to HQ showing where your current pricing structure is being attacked. Your Sales Manager hosts an online discussion. Invitees: Manufacturing, Accounting, Marketing."

To sum up, everyone crunches the numbers, talks, and comes up with a new promotion that "is sent company-wide and your guy in Chicago is out of the lobby and back at the table." Bingo! Presto! Problem solved! But if the network covers distance and collapses time (Microsoft slogan: Where do you want to go today?), it cannot condense human experience. It merely foreshortens it. In a pressured business situation, that may be ideal. But when interactions become interfaces, when humans become hybrids, when location becomes unimportant, the value of the human experience is endangered. The need to make connections with the neighbor simply because she lives on the same floor of your apartment building, or the requirement to acknowledge another person's physical presence as you stand beside him, feels less urgent. The value of the physical encounter is thrown into question when the electronic interface dominates.

Consider a TV ad for the Philips cellular phone with a six-hour battery. In the ad, aired in 1998, a man is located on a remote oil rig while his wife gives birth to their child in a hospital room, presumably miles and miles away. He coos Lamaze breathing instructions over the phone, seeming to *feel* with her. She responds to his voice, seeming to behave no differently than if they were physically together. The scene attempts to demonstrate that geography is a barrier that can be overcome, even rendered invisible—that is, if one has a good cell phone with a long-lasting battery. (What happens if the labor lasts more than six hours?) This is striking because of the occasion. The birth of a child, traditional practice suggests, is one of those profound events when a mobile phone call just won't do. Or will it? The ad suggests that physical presence isn't quite as critical as we believe.

It is a tantalizing idea. If we allow that being there physically isn't so essential, then what happens to the perceived benefit of being anywhere in person? We already use technology to take our place in other instances. Instead of sitting down beside a child and going through the tedious and often frustrating experience of doing homework together, asking her to stop wriggling in the chair, chewing the pencil, and fiddling with a scrunchie, some of us now do it from the road, by phone, fax, or modem. No muss. No fuss. Pure productivity. Junior does the problems, you check them and ask a few questions, and it's over. And you're still a good parent. Or, when you can't be there to say goodnight or tuck a kid in, there's always the cell phone call from the airplane, the cab, the lobby of the hotel. The problem with all this, of course, is that even as we rely on technology to transport us, we have the illusion of doing real things, in part because we accomplish the hoped-for ends. The process, though—the messy stuff in between that sometimes exasperates and sometimes awes but that always engages and forges connections—can be written out of the daily planner.

The tension here is the obvious one: We may be living an increasingly virtual existence, but we inhabit a physical world, and we are physical beings equipped with senses that inform us of texture and nuance. To be sure, we intuitively understand that relating to an e-mail address or someone's electronic agents is not the same as noting how human beings take up space on a chair, bite at the corner of their lips, or raise eyebrows when you say something they are itching to respond to. Yet, without acknowledging the implications, we are redefining the very basis of relating. We are making scarce the tangible and diminishing the availability of relationships built on physical proximity.

One day, I watched two men in shirts and ties walk together at lunchtime down a sidewalk while one spoke into a cell phone. The image, a rather ordinary one, stuck with me. I pitied the phoneless guy. He'd been rejected. Even as he was physically walking beside the other, he looked diminished, a tagalong, alone. I don't mean to make too much of an ordinary occurrence, but the example illustrates how what seems to be a technological convenience, like the cell phone, has consequences in how we relate—or don't relate—to one another and where we are at a given time. The guy with the phone wasn't really walking on the sidewalk. His attention was elsewhere. The loss of conversation, the loss of the feel of the afternoon, may seem inconsequential compared with the convenience of being able to make or take a call away from the office. But it is human nature to mount a protective response to what is an ego blow. If this guy makes a habit of using his cell phone, will the two men stop having lunch? Will they speak differently, of different things? Will the phoneless one speak less for fear of being cut short again and again?

What happens when we mount defenses in response to or in anticipation of coming in second to a cell phone? Or to some other person's more urgent time pressure in a world where we easily grow nervous indulging any one person or activity with too much of our time? There is a profound evolution under way, and it is being played out in a million such forgotten moments, driven, in part, by the technology and the speedy, mobile lifestyle many of us are wowed by. It happens when we e-mail the person sitting next to us instead of speaking. It happens as we bank by ATM or over the Internet. It happens as you order groceries online, no longer bothering to go to the store. You no longer see the cashier named Joan, no longer hear her remark that your infant is now a toddler; that you look like you're having a Fourth of July cookout; that she has never tasted cilantro but it smells so nice. How could she use it? In what dish?

Even the language of technology blurs boundaries and diminishes the authority of real places and experiences. You can "meet" people without ever seeing them; you "know" them without really knowing. Cyberspace has usurped the lexicon of location, taking what it means to *be* somewhere and redefining it in virtual terms. We "surf" the Internet; early users talked of "homesteading." Now we routinely "go" to this "site" or that "room." We even pay our last respects in virtual funeral homes and bury—er, post—our lost loved ones in virtual cemeteries.

The virtual has been rendered physical, in language. If you talk about shopping at the mall, it is no longer clear whether you are speaking about the act of driving, walking, or otherwise physically traveling to a real structure or about pointing and clicking your way to a virtual "mall" with virtual "storefronts." Despite the fact that e-tailing depends on a very physical network of warehouses, workers, and trucking concerns, the shopping itself depends on our accepting the placeless "store" to be every bit as real as the physical store. The art of real merchandise displays has been replaced by the artifice of the screen. I don't mean to suggest that people are confused by the overlap in language—we can handle it—but that the overlap shapes, and ultimately reshapes, the way we transact daily business. What, anymore, is a store? Who or what are we really relating to? This very perceived need for shopping to be a physical experience has some in the e-tail world feeling that it is critical to have a bricks-and-mortar presence—a physical store—in addition to a website. Others, like Amazon.com, have eschewed the physical completely. The giant online retailer, in fact, made its lack of a physical store the point of its 1999 ad campaign, in which company representatives search for a physical site large enough to house all the merchandise. Naturally, for their purpose, the physical world always falls short. The point here is that technology is changing once-reliable reference points. We must adjust. We are quietly, unconsciously, led into thinking and behaving differently.

This is not the first time this has happened. The advent of print and of the telephone altered the experience and skills employed in interacting. The printing press, for example, changed what people meant by memory and how hard they worked—or didn't—to preserve text orally, as some of our most classic works were passed on. The act of remembering in medieval times was a much more formal and detailed pursuit than it is today; the ability to recall long tales now seems incredible. The advent of writing and printing naturally affected how people spoke, why they spoke, and how they relayed information to one another. While such changes happened over years and years, six months now seems like a long time technologically speaking. Change today seems especially rapid, deep, and seamless. The New Thing arrives in our hand at the perfect moment of desire and we seize it, as the trapeze artist clasps the bar before him, not pausing to see how far from the ground he swings. When new technology arrives, it is pressed into service. The questions are practical ones: Is it easy to use? Is it mobile? Most of us focus on what it will do *for* us, not *to* us.

And yet, it alters how we perceive and how we use our world. I find myself annoyed at people who don't have e-mail—or who have it but don't check it frequently. It is easier for me, more efficient, to use e-mail than to have a conversation on the phone or in person. Sometimes that's fine. But there are times I use e-mail to avoid contact that I should make time and energy for. It offers the easy out, and that easy out becomes habitual. Soon, there are some people I only deal with via e-mail, relegating them to a subrelationship in which I can respond when I choose. At some workplaces, e-mail has become a means to break bad news or reprimand an employee, not because it's right or better but because it's easier.

We have achieved an uneasy victory over fixed space. We can interface, rendering distance meaningless. We can travel without observing
miles. We have become so linked, in a sense, that space *is* fungible. We
can all be logged on to the same Website, crammed on the same pin-
head, hundreds of millions of us, all so tightly interfaced we cannot
make out each other's features or even recognize each other's physical
presence. French cultural thinker Jean Baudrillard says we have entered
a new time in which human scale has become archaic and the daily
"scenes" of life extinct.[9]

"This is the time of miniaturization, telecommand and the micro-
procession of time, bodies, pleasures. There is no longer any ideal principle for these things at a higher level, on a human scale. What remains
are only concentrated effects, miniaturized and immediately available,"
he writes. It is a funhouse vision of daily life in which multiple distor-
tions annihilate any sense of how elements relate to one another. In his
usual colorful vision, Baudrillard further argues that we are making our
physical self, our body, "simply superfluous, basically useless in its
extensions, in the multiplicity and complexity of its organs, its tissues
and functions, since today everything is concentrated in the brain and
the genetic codes, which alone sum up the operational definition of
being."

Such reductions, Baudrillard argues, also apply to our experience of
place and time. The landscape, he complains, has in our perception
become "boring to cross even if one leaves the main highways," and
towns are "undergoing a reduction to a few miniaturized highlights."
The speed of communication reorders our sense of time. It has become,
he says, "a dimension henceforth useless in its unfolding, as soon as the
instantaneity of communication has miniaturized our exchanges into a
succession of instants." In all, "the body, landscape, time all progressively
disappear as scenes." He paints our new existence as an empty landscape, uninteresting in its repetitiveness and reductions. Our exchanges,
like our physical selves, are reduced to function, for function is all that
we choose to value and recognize as legitimate. Fading are the
moments that expand almost novelistically, that inspire wonder and
thought, that leave us feeling utterly alive, certain that there is meaning in our existence.

We are collapsing not just space but life itself. In seeking the efficiency that comes of mobility, we are editing out the details that are not,
we believe, essential. Even as we can do more of everything from

everywhere, we are also teaching ourselves not to see anything we're not looking for. We focus on the essentials, the mission at hand, the appropriate speedy response. We are moving from living in the tangible world to existing through the virtual experience. As Haraway writes, we prize machines that are so compact that they seem "made of sunshine; they are all light and clean because they are nothing but signals, electromagnetic waves, a section of a spectrum, and these machines are eminently portable, mobile." She sees the lust for machines that are not only free of fixed space but also nearly free of their own physical existence. It is an aesthetic of speed and portability.[10]

Speed and Portability

We worship the words "to go." They sing. They catch our attention like neon in a clear, dark sky. Even when there is no rush, we want to drive-thru, take the express elevator, flash the E-Z Pass, use the express checkout, get instant credit, and have immediate assistance. We want to gas up our cars while hardly stopping (wave the Speed Pass, fill, and dash). We want lunch in ten minutes or it's free! There is CoffeeGo, chewable little squares of coffee for those times, according to the package, "when you don't have time for coffee!" We want—we have been conditioned to feel that we need—not to stop. All that is fast and portable appeals precisely because it allows us to stay in motion. And motion has become home base, fixed only in our demand for its constant presence.

Objectively, this seems odd. We have all these advances in technology and lifestyle that allow us to do things more quickly and easily—and rather than relish the extra time they might buy us, we want everything to be even faster! In a sense, what technology has done is create a new set of expectations around speediness. The time saved is not an afternoon, open, ripe, and waiting to be filled, but seconds here and there—just enough time to make us aware of the millions of empty spaces between events. With the opportunity, or perhaps the imperative, that we multitask in that quest for an ever more efficient use of every moment, we are left with more to do and not quite enough time to do it in. It is imaginary spare time, the impromptu moments we are now trying to fill: the two minutes at the red light, the ten minutes stuck in traffic at the bridge, the half-hour commute, the forty minutes on the StairMaster. Without considering what we do, we find ourselves stacking our minutes, packing them full to bursting, in hope of . . . what? In hope of feeling like better, more productive people? In hope of justifying our collapse in front of the tube at the end of the day? Or perhaps not in hope of anything. Perhaps we simply can't stop.

We gravitate toward fluidity and all that suggests lightness, portability, flexibility, and speed. This orientation is not limited to one sphere, to a particular form or function, but catches our interest wherever we find it: in design, architecture, food, fashion, color, scheduling, work hours, art, music, personal style, travel, communication, ad copy, television, entertainment, business, finance. Our banks, for example, are no longer densely constructed masonry buildings whose architecture relays a message of stability, the fixed structure planted like an anchor in the center of town. Instead, banks merge and change. Their outlets multiply, and ATMs appear at every corner. The experience of the bank—and of money, for that matter—is hardly physical at all. It is rare to recognize the teller, to have the deposit accompanied by lollipops for the kids. The experience has been reduced to an electronic interface with an unseen corporate identity.

At work, too, people orient their lives to fluid, rather than fixed, relationships. Not only is work more portable, it is more fluid in *when* you do it. The traditional image of a nine-to-five workday measured by the time clock still exists for many, but for many others it has given way to flexible hours or even the utter mingling of work and leisure. The separation between being "at work" and "at home" is becoming as irrelevant as a company "headquarters" in a stately building with a marble lobby. Work is increasingly where you are. Even work itself—the stuff you get paid to do—is for some becoming less visible, known mostly to the supervisor or team they're working with.

Andersen Consulting, for example, no longer refers to its Chicago headquarters as a "headquarters." The company has reinvented its structure as a network, banishing old boundaries and hierarchies, including the trappings of traditional work—like the personal office. Under the new model, there are no permanent desks and offices, even for partners. That is the case at the renovated office in Wellesley, Massachusetts, where high-tech style and 1950s accents create a hybrid design that is both cutting edge and timeless, quirky yet fun and intelligent.

The most interesting thing about the Wellesley office is the way it works. The traditional office with a cherry desk and memorabilia has been banished. (One is preserved on the second floor, cordoned off by velvet rope as a "museum office.") Instead, employees make reservations to use a workspace. Personal belongings are kept in totes, which are delivered nightly by the service staff. They follow employees' standing instructions on where to place the family photo, the college mug, the commemorative pen. What's more, the staff dress and act much like a hotel staff, sporting gold-colored stars on their lapels and stationing themselves at the "concierge desk" or making themselves available from an office phone through the service directory. No more hunting in the supply room or lingering at the copy machine—the service staff will do it for you. For an additional cost, which is subsidized by the company, employees can also have the service staff take care of personal errands. They will wait at your home for the plumber to show, address wedding invitations, or send flowers for a funeral, as one thirty-year-old analyst had them do.

"I know people who literally come in with a to-do list to get their film developed, get their shoes repaired, flowers bought for Mother's Day," says Curt Hilliker, who was overseeing the Wellesley Andersen service staff the day I visited. Work is an organization, an interface that, in Andersen's case, utterly mixes work and life. It is completely fluid. And the office itself—here as elsewhere—is so light and portable that it is just a laptop, a phone, and a link to company software. Andersen even labels the sparest workstations as "Touchdown" spaces, an image that relays a sense of momentary pause in a mobile work world. Mobility means you check in and you check out. Your job is where you are. The office is merely a way station, and it is increasingly an abstraction in the larger definition of what "work" has become: ideas, computer interfaces, communication systems.[11]

Mobility offers adults more flexibility and fluidity in defining and using time. It does just the opposite for children. Life for children, once organized by geography, is now organized by the clock—with some less than freeing results. A thirty-six-year-old mother of three children recalled for me the geographic boundaries her mother set for her after-school play: As long as she didn't go past the top of her street, she could roam the neighborhood, passing the hours with other kids facing similar territorial boundaries. They were, in short, brought together by where they lived and played.

Today, although she lives in a pleasant and safe suburban neighborhood with other children nearby, this mother's children—like many children today—do not play the way she did. Her children's play is not in the neighborhood but in time slots of organized activities. "Play" is scheduled and run by adults: basketball league, ballet class, soccer, skating lessons, jazz, tap, modern dance, Little League, swimming, community theater. Time-slotted activities, not place, provide the structure. This is the norm for many children. In fact, when this mother one summer decided not to schedule any activities for her children, she had a surprise. "I figured summer was a time for swimming pools and hanging out," she says. "But all their friends had plans. There was no one to hang out with." Her children learned the new rules: Sign up or lose out. Organized activities have become the way children socialize and relate to each other. Children no longer merely play, they have "playdates," a new compound word that implies a time element. It is something that the next generation takes in stride. Play is not open-ended but time-marked. "Is it a long playdate or a short playdate?" my daughter asks. She wants to know whether she can play for two hours or four.[12]

Time pressures on children seem particularly troubling because many adults recall childhood as a period when time flowed without worry about schedules. There were open-ended afternoons. You played outdoors in summer until it grew dark, only vaguely aware of the hour. And even when you wanted it to speed up, time stretched out, as you waited and waited for it to be, finally, the day of your birthday party. I now find it oddly sad to hear my children tell me how fast a week, a month, a year went by. My older daughter—still in elementary school—complains about a shortage of time. The norm for many children today is a dizzying schedule of activities. One forty-eight-year-old mother, who is herself a high-powered executive with a communications firm, recalls the day she spotted a Rolodex on her son's desk—there to help keep track of contacts for his "whole raft of activities," as she describes it. "My first reaction was 'Oh, he's so organized,' " she says. "But then I say, 'Why does a fifteen-year-old have to be organized?' "[13]

If the speed of childhood has prompted cries for calm from the likes of David Elkind, author of *The Hurried Child*, and provoked concerns about "overscheduled children," the worries for adults are less well defined. The media acknowledge people's "harried" lifestyles. The regularity of news features detailing the "race" of the modern "go-go lifestyle" have become so commonplace as to barely warrant recognition as news. We hear about "juggling" lives and about "tag-team parenting." But amid the complaints about the speed of life, we keep on speeding, because speed is exhilarating and busyness has cachet.

Questions about the pace of life—and the accelerating impact of new advances and habits—are not new. As Kern writes, the quest for speed was viewed more than a century ago as both tantalizing and sinister. It was the dangerous quest to reach the port of New York ahead of schedule and in record time that many blamed for the sinking of the *Titanic*. At the same time, others celebrated in art, literature, and music the quickening pulse of a quickening world. There was clearly a great deal of ambivalence toward a world that had suddenly begun to run not on human time but on clock time.

"The sinking of the *Titanic* was but the most tragic consequence of speed made possible by a broad technological revolution that also affected how people traveled to work and how fast they worked when they got there, how they met each other and what they did together, the way they danced and walked and even, some said, the way they thought," Kern writes. "There was no question that the pace of life was greatly accelerated, but there was sharp debate about the meaning and value of speed."

In 1881, George M. Beard, who introduced the diagnostic category of neurasthenia (nervous exhaustion) to psychiatry, published his *American Nervousness*, which, Kern notes, "set the tone for literature on the increasing tempo of life and its nefarious consequences." Beard's argument focused on the fact that industrial advances like the telegraph, railroads, and steam power led businessmen to make "a hundred times" more transactions in a span of time than was possible in the eighteenth century. Perhaps most striking, and a bit humorous to us today, Beard argued that all this intensified competition, in turn, was responsible for many problems, including "early tooth decay and even premature baldness."[14]

If such claims appear far-fetched today, his question—how fast is too fast?—is one we still grapple with. Rather than fret, however, we often boast. In the last half century, speed has become the Holy Grail. We want faster service, faster computers, faster fast food, faster athletes. The pace is so frenetic that speed that is merely linear is no longer speedy. Speed must now have bulk. It is not enough for one thing to be done fast; many things must be done fast at the same time or in such tight sequence that one nearly cuts short the next. People pack appointment books, overlapping meetings. Some watch television several channels at a time. On our computers, we click from screen to screen, searching on one, printing on another. Time is not a measure of length, of hours and minutes and seconds, but of bulk. How much can you fit in?

In some cities today, the one-hour business lunch has become a relic of the past, as power lunchers routinely do the job in forty-five, thirty, or even twenty minutes. Another trend is double and even triple lunching. In Manhattan, the deal-making lunch hot spots watch regulars schedule two lunch meetings—say, one at 12:15 P.M. and the second at 1:30 P.M., for the more leisurely. How do people manage this without offending? John Sheedy, day manager of the restaurant 57-57, told a reporter that "the host will inform us: 'Listen, I have two guys; I don't want the one to know the other is here.' We have a very big restaurant—we would arrange to have the second guest at the far end from the first table." Some double lunchers divide their meals—soup and then salad—and even move from one restaurant to another. But that's touchy, because a quick departure sends the message: You're not important enough for a full lunch.[15]

As a society, we have grown so comfortable with mobility that we now *rely* on everything to have inherent motion, which we seamlessly blend with our own. Work moves, meals move, kids move (ferried by fleets of kid transportation vans), phone calls move, groceries move. In our minds, movement equals efficiency. If we are in motion, we are efficient and busy.

Our speed of life today makes a 1956 ad touting an ambitious junior executive's "aura of immediacy" almost humorous. "Right now!" the headline reads, below a photo of a man stepping out of a Checker cab with a briefcase under his arm. We learn that Tom Adams, who is thirty-six and the vice president and general assistant to the president of Campbell-Ewald, is a real go-getter. "He gave up reminder notes long ago," the copy boasts. "Now, whatever comes up—a phone call, a letter to write, a meeting or a trip—Tom does it. Right now! He acts quickly—decisively. He hurries with a purpose and with such organization and skill that there's no taint of haste in it. He doesn't let up."

Imagine juggling a letter, a phone call, a meeting, and a trip? Piece of cake. For many in today's business world, the schedule—and the immediate action it demands—would probably be so lax only during vacation. Technology has not, alas, simply closed the gap of distance—made space fungible, as Professor Gottman had hoped—but it has reoriented us. Where is our new true north? It's not the clock but the microchip. One has only to have experienced the revolution in computer speed and memory to understand that what we understand by "fast" has changed—and dramatically. This change hasn't been confined to our experience with the computer but has spilled into daily life. We want everything to be faster. In turn, each of us is expected to do our own work in a speedier and speedier fashion. Bosses want work done "yesterday." We are the ones—not the machines—who are holding up production.

In *Why Things Bite Back*, Edward Tenner makes the observation that while technology may have provided many advances, it has not made us any happier. Technology has modified our surroundings, he says, but "we are still unhappy about those surroundings, more discontented than when they were inferior." Technology may do some things *for* us, but it also demands more *from* us. Tenner writes that "the social goal of a new Athens, of machine-supported leisure, has proved a noble mirage. Technology demands more, not less, human work to function."[16]

As a society, we have not unburdened ourselves of the struggle described more than a century ago, as speed-loving "futurists" and their adversaries tried to come to terms with an accelerating life experience. What makes it more challenging for today is that time, not place, is the framework into which we arrange our lives and relationships. Friendships exist in time allotments, not on porches during lingering afternoons that remain unmeasured. Now, we always measure. That's how we keep score. A 1997 *New Yorker* cartoon by Robert Mankoff depicts a busy man in his office with his index finger on his datebook. He is speaking into the telephone. "Thursday's no good for me," he says. "How about never? Is never good for you?"

Geographic Mobility

The mobility of daily life has been complemented by the portability of home. Although much has been made of the booming interest in nesting behavior and "cocooning," and of the success of the home furnishings industry, these trends don't change the fact that many of us move—and then move again. Since the close of World War II, Census Bureau figures show that about 20 percent of the U.S. population packs up and moves each year. Although that figure has risen and fallen slightly, it has remained a steady fact of American life, suggesting that the idea of moving, reinventing oneself, and starting over is a fully entrenched habit. While there are some regional differences (people in the South and West tend to move more than people in the Midwest and Northeast), they are not dramatic. It doesn't matter where you live: Opportunity calls from elsewhere.[17]

Relocation has become a routine, if disruptive, part of life. Over time, it has created a kind of family sprawl, where once-concentrated communities of kinfolk have gradually drifted apart. At the beginning of the twentieth century, people typically lived within twenty to forty miles of where they were born. As we reach the next century, even small communities have high turnover. In New Milford, Connecticut, for example, a small town where I spent my adolescent years, more than *half* of the 22,750 residents recorded in the 1990 census had moved into their current homes in the previous five years. One-third of newcomers came from the same county, one-third from elsewhere in the state, and one-third from another state or country. Even in a small, picturesque New England community with a town green, a local summer fair, and the trappings of tradition, mobility is an integral fact of life.

The story is similar in other parts of the country—a situation that cannot fail to have consequences for people's ability to put down roots and feel connected to their community of the moment. In an April 5, 1998, *New York Times* story on a rash of teen suicides in Pierre, South Dakota (eleven young people between the ages of thirteen and twenty-three killed themselves in three years), a mother whose teenage son committed suicide described the capital city of thirteen thousand as "a very transient town." It is an image that counters the seductive myth about small-town America. People glibly speak of tight connections, deep roots, and a well of concern that never runs dry. People want to believe that although the frontier is settled, an emotional frontier awaits. On December 8, 1997, *Time* magazine ran a cover story, "Why More Americans Are Fleeing to Small Towns," which chronicled the lives of several people who wanted to trade in their overbusy and stressful urban/suburban lives for what they saw as the ideal of rural living. They longed for the connections and the simple living that small-town life symbolizes. But as the story suggests, small-town living is just that: an image. The story recounts how small towns, like large urban and suburban communities, struggle with problems of drug use, poor zoning, and environmental threats, among others. What people dream of, it seems, is an idealized relic of a novelized past. As residents of Pierre found, small-town life doesn't always live up to the clichés. Another mother of an eighteen-year-old suicide victim said she felt emotionally isolated because people didn't want to talk about her pain or about problems that were hard to face. Even though others recognized her daughter's troubles, she said, "a lot of people, you know, don't like to ask." They don't, in other words, want to get involved.

In small communities like Pierre and New Milford (which made national news for its own struggle with adolescent suicide threats), as in urban areas, geographic mobility is a way of life. Small towns are not the rocks of stability people like to think they are. Even though it may *look* as though time has stood still, or at least traveled at a more leisurely pace, such images may be a cover for a population as transient as the rest of America. The Census Bureau flatly notes in its report on housing in 1998, "in the second half of this century, we Americans have been prone to change homes frequently." It is how we live. There are simply fewer places that become the permanent, forever home, fewer places where you can walk down Main Street and have people know who you are.

It might seem a trivial matter, but feeling known and knowing others is central to feeling part of a community. In the past thirty years, homeowners have tended to move a little less often, but renters are picking up the pace. Nowadays, 42 percent of renters have moved in the previous fifteen months. This level of mobility—even when we do not ourselves participate in it but merely watch those around us come and go—alters the very meaning of "home" and the connections we make. Why invest in getting to know people when they—or you—will just move again? Home, we are coming to understand, does not stand for a stable location with a root system of relationships. It is a transportable environment. Home can be created and re-created many times over. My sister described how a friend of hers in Manhattan made an instant "home" for herself after a divorce: In the space of days, she rented an apartment, paged through home furnishings catalogues, placed her orders, and soon replaced what she'd lost.[18]

Home can be created in one instant, broken down and packed away in the next. There is something very American about the ability to pick up and go, something romantic about how we Woody Guthrie–style ramblers go where destiny (and a moving train) will deliver us. But while our society celebrates—even holds sacred—the ability to start over, to wander America's vast lands, we have also valued roots. As we play out our contradicting desires—to stay and to go; to cruise the virtual landscape and to be at one with the physical world—there is less romance today in the feats. We are pulled along, acting on what is before us. We worry about being hip. We sigh and accept the transfer. We leave our bags packed and our cell phones on.

Mobility, fluidity, virtuality—things that once offered the bright, shiny possibilities of new chances and new experiences—are now part of the routine, fading into the status of the invisible ordinary. Being in transit is less traumatic: We are not as attuned, as connected, to the places we inhabit, or to the people and the history those places represent. We are on the move: Cleveland, Atlanta, Houston, Seattle, Tampa, Pittsburgh. Houses, apartments, condos change hands—and then change hands again. Moving vans and FOR SALE signs, flip-phones and pagers, palmtops and Touchdown spaces are artifacts of a society on the go, one defined not by roots and relationships but by where we're heading next.

 HOME

In the poem "Fire" (from the collection *Rain*), William Carpenter describes a man who one day notices his neighbor across the river burning down his own house. The man gazes across the water at the flames and discovers that he is not horrified but intrigued, even exhilarated, by the act. Soon he decides that he, too, should set his home ablaze. "Why should I help him," the man rationalizes, "when I have a house myself, which needs burning as much as anyone's?"

Carpenter describes the excitement and energy with which the man feeds his own fire, trying desperately—as so many of us do—to catch up to his neighbor. He tosses his belongings onto the flames, objects both precious and ordinary. He imagines the two columns of smoke rising from each side of the river "like a couple of Algonquins having a dialogue about how much harder it is to destroy than create," how much harder to shed than to acquire. The home, after all, is not mere shelter but life's keeper, containing all the strictures, burdens, pleasures, and self-indulgences of his too familiar existence. The man sees the possibility that "If I burn everything, I can start over, with a future like a white rectangle of paper." Never mind that the fire engines soon arrive and his neighbor, presumably gone scared, bails out of the burning. Our man presses on. In the end, we see a man "laughing and singing in the snow, who has been finally freed from his possessions, who has no clothes, no library, who has gone back to the beginning, when we lived in nature: no refuge from the elements, no fixed address."

This is not the depiction of home that usually comes to mind: the home as albatross. We generally favor a cozy view, something more like Dorothy's conception of an idealized place of comfort and safety. Click your sparkly red shoes and be transported. But, in truth, we have a complicated relationship with the place we call home. We embrace our homes. We flee them. We seek to transform them. We destroy them. And we hope they will inspire, comfort, and protect us. They seem, at times, to be almost living creatures, like a mother, quietly but certainly exerting influence on who one is and who one becomes. We shape our homes and they shape us. They also provide a great deal of information about who we are and what we want; they offer glimpses of our public and private selves. To be sure, they are highly individualized spaces that exhibit our personal quirks. But they are also cultural artifacts.

Like archeological sites, homes offer clues about how our society operates, about what is valued—and what is not. Houses teem with conflicting messages, but they remain windows onto our time, reflecting domestic ideals and social norms. I recall my parents' home in 1968: It didn't matter that it was a two-hundred-year-old Colonial; they filled the interior with red shag carpeting, butterfly chairs, a tabletop sculpture of multicolored plastic balls on springy wire. They painted a huge British flag on their bedroom wall, continuing the design over a closet and two doors. The new homes being built at the time—homes that many of my friends lived in—were split-level ranches with kitchens upstairs, sunken living rooms, and basement rec rooms. Design-wise, the old order had been ousted, the rooms juggled and rearranged. My parents were young and idealistic, ready to question, experiment, and eschew tradition—and so was the nation.

I don't mean to pretend that the home is an easily decipherable domain. It's not. In fact, scholars who study the home environment seem to struggle as much with how to study the venue as with eliciting meaning from the structures. While there is a tradition of considering space by its intended function, adhering to the view that, as one theorist put it, the structure "has an objective meaning that communicates itself to the building user," other researchers argue that inhabitants bring to and create meanings for the spaces. In other words, there's conflict over who imputes meaning to a space—the people who designed it or the people who live in it. For our purposes, I'd argue that both exert a powerful influence. My family's two-hundred-year-old home told its own story of how people lived with its dirt-floor basement and floorboards that never quite managed to keep out the cold air in winter. At the same time, my parents' use of the space reflected a certain rebellion; although they loved old architecture, there was no effort to use the home as was probably intended. The dining room became a sitting room, and the living room accommodated the clean-lined sofa, slat benches, and a dining room table. The onetime pantry became a wet bar.[1]

Often the use—or misuse—of space pushes change in home design. The tendency of guests to congregate in the kitchen has made it, once a private and unadorned space for the hired help (sometimes even built at the basement level), into the showpiece of many homes. The stylish modern kitchen, with its dramatic lighting, polished appliances, and tony countertops, is where people choose to entertain. Adjoining space is often fitted with sofas and easy chairs, bringing the living room into the kitchen. Entertaining may feel less formal with guests no longer excluded from the preparation of the meal. At the same time, the kitchen itself has become a more public space.

The "misuse" of space—using it according to our needs and not just the builder's intent—offers important information, too. When I went to interview an eighty-nine-year-old woman for a magazine story, she met me in her kitchen, which was set up like a beauty salon. This was where she had her hair done every other day and where she applied her makeup in the morning. She rarely cooked. Two freelance architects in Cambridge, Massachusetts, use their bedroom by night for sleeping and by day as an office, with the bed becoming a surface for viewing plans. Many of us today are enamored of fluidity: We want options in how we use rooms. Decorating books like *Spaces for Living: How to Create Multifunctional Rooms for Today's Homes*, by Liz Bauwens and Alexandra Campbell, show readers, for example, how to make the dining room double as an office.

Despite our ability to use a home's space any way we like, it remains useful to look at the way architects and builders design houses. They are, after all, trying to please potential buyers by creating rooms that will fit many people's tastes and living habits. Kitchens—despite the eighty-nine-year-old woman—are generally used for preparing meals. Bedrooms—despite the young architects—are generally for relaxing and sleeping. This all makes it interesting to look at how homes were designed in the past and how they compare with new homes under construction.

So what do our homes and neighborhoods today tell us? What do they reveal about the forces shaping our lives, about the way we're living? A great deal. Consider that many new homes imitate century-old styles with Victorian features. Consider that architects and planners are designing old-style neighborhoods. On the one hand, people today long for classic images of stability and longevity. People seek to re-create the family homestead, packed with heirlooms and neighborly concern that extends beyond a mimed greeting from a distance. One has only to see the very real design efforts aimed at evoking the past to see such yearnings in action. Yet no replication of tradition is exact. People may like the symbols of history right down to the antique kitchen stove, but it must be retrofitted to operate as thoroughly modern. People want the most up-to-date conveniences and appointments: the second-floor laundry, the master suite, larger rooms than our grandmothers could imagine, more bathrooms, and a kitchen/family room on the first floor (with a restaurant-quality kitchen and lots of Internet hookups). Homes are being loaded with technology. There is constant talk of the "smart" home that calls its own repairmen when a system fails or needs cleaning. While that may be in the future for most of us, many have already been persuaded that home security systems and fences are basic needs. And aside from all that is now part of the basic shelter are the services aimed at bringing what you need—whether groceries, dry cleaning, restaurant foods or chefs, or online goods—to you *at* home. In the end, we are left with a rather odd image of the home that evokes a nostalgic history at the same time it ever more resembles a fortress. That is the tension today: As a society we may be grappling with how to become more involved with family, friends, neighbors, the community, but we find ourselves living in homes that, without our wholly intending it, have made it harder—not easier—to connect.

As a society, we live ever more privately, drawing blinds and socializing less with those who live nearby. People may not even know floormates or neighbors. When this happens, there can be little to say when people meet in the hall, on the elevator, or on the sidewalk. We look and nod. How are you, good? Good, good, good. Gotta go. The details of how other people live are becoming a mystery. I often wonder, on nights when we sit at the kitchen table with hastily made bowls of spaghetti with butter and cheese before us, folded paper towels for napkins, and no placemats, if anyone else on my street is having a dinner like this, with no proper calibration of veggies and starch, no pretense at a properly set table, no effort at attractive presentation. Are we the only ones who let this pass for dinner? Our lives are more secret, less revealed. Advances in home construction have replaced corn cobs with fiberglass for insulation. They have eliminated the cold air that used to rush up between the floorboards in our two-hundred-year-old house and others like it. Our homes, like our lives, today are more airtight, more impermeable, more sealed off from the world outside. Lars Eighner, who was homeless for three years and wrote the book *Travels with Lizbeth*, noticed this sort of change when he observed about the new experience of apartment living, "I'm more isolated now." Once exposed at all times, he is now secluded from the daily witness of people's lives and theirs of his. Even when he occasionally sees the neighbors, he says, "you have no idea who they are or what they're doing." It may be an obvious comment coming from someone who has been homeless, but many others of us could echo his words. In a sense, we have all left the street and gone indoors.[2]

Living Large

Home has always been bigger and more influential than the sum of its physical attributes. Important rights like voting were once tied to homeownership. And in Victorian times architects considered the home not a mere structure but the very foundation of a moral society. Architects who produced Victorian pattern books, containing house plans, believed they could convey a moral framework for living along with the physical framework for construction. The physical structure of the home, they asserted, influenced the behavior of its inhabitants. One writer at the time complained about the trouble that could be caused by what he called an "unhandy house." If the home irritated mothers, he asserted, it would "sour the tempers of their children, even *before birth*, thus rendering the whole family bad-dispositioned *by nature*, whereas a convenient one would have rendered them constitutionally amiable and good."[3]

It was not just the design of the home that had the power to shape character. Keeping a tidy and well-maintained property also helped impart proper values. This belief was underscored in advice articles and fictional stories. "What Small Hands May Do," published in an 1851 issue of *The Mother's Assistant, Young Lady's Friend and Family Manual*, made the connection with a tale of a young girl, Lucy Dale, whose heroic handiwork around the house is the spur that turns her drunken and irresponsible father into an attentive provider. It's a rather direct application of the Victorian belief in the transformative power of a well-dispositioned home. In the story, after Lucy notices the sorry state of her family's house and of their family life, she hatches a plan. She persuades her parents to leave town to visit relatives. While they are gone, she has rags woven into a lovely rug. She paints, tears down overgrown vines, gardens, and rearranges furniture. When her parents return and her father, who has offered little support or moral guidance to the family, sees how his daughter has turned their shameful-looking house into a well-ordered home, he is moved to tears. He sets about to transform himself just as his daughter has transformed their home and, in the process, the family. This story may seem like a lot of Victorian moralizing. Today when we speak of the importance of "a good home," we typically mean the intangibles—the quality of the home life—and not the design or look of the property. To some degree, that is true. We may not openly moralize about neatness and well-ordered properties. But it is often the details of filth or poor physical conditions of homes that draw gasps after news reports of authorities entering houses and finding neglected children. As a society, we are certainly less attentive housekeepers who spend less time cleaning than our parents did, but we still acknowledge a relationship between the state of the home and the state of its inhabitants. That link is played out in our judgments of others and in our fantasies for our own lives.

How often are we persuaded that putting on a new addition or buying a piece of new furniture (or even a new tablecloth) will improve our lives—and our disposition, our happiness? We are not dupes, but the message of transformation has some currency. It is obviously an effective way to sell home furnishings. Consider the ad copy for the Jenna Rocking Chair in Pottery Barn's winter 1998 catalogue: "Whether you're reading beside a sunny window or lulling a baby to sleep, time moves at a different pace in our wide, Mission-style rocking chair." If a home can remake a man, why shouldn't a $649 rocking chair give us time to read and snuggle a baby? We may know intellectually that a rocker won't clean out a packed personal organizer. On the other hand, could it make us feel less busy? We may not explicitly connect our moral health with the structural soundness of our house as our forebears did, but we do connect our homes to our sense of well-being. We note the person with the poorly kept home, judge the renovation project, see meaning in lawn ornaments or the installation of iron gates across the driveway.

This is nothing new. Writers from Charles Dickens and George Bernard Shaw to Virginia Woolf and Sam Shepard have exploited the link between one's character or emotional state and one's home. In his time, Henry David Thoreau was particularly attuned to the power of homes and property. He pitied "the young men, my townsmen; whose misfortune it is to have inherited farms, houses, barns." Property, he believed, was a burden, making one a slave to its care and dictating one's course in life. During his stay at Walden Pond, though, he did come to envision a "larger and more populous house." But the home he describes is still rooted in simplicity. It is "without gingerbread work" (a knock at the Victorians), of one room only, a "house which you have got into when you have opened the outside door and the ceremony is over; where the weary traveler may wash, and eat, and converse and sleep, without further journey." In other words, in Thoreau's view a house should be functional shelter, stripped of foyers, little side rooms, and halls—elements he viewed as social decorations and contrivances. You ought to be able to step inside and see the whole house and all the people in it and not, he complained, "be carefully excluded from seven eighths of it, shut up in a particular cell and told to make yourself at home there—in solitary confinement." In such observations, he makes a point that is as relevant today: The way we design our homes, to a great extent, is a means for controlling social interactions.[4]

Despite Thoreau's current popularity and the simplicity he advocated, homes today are anything but simple. They are ever more labyrinthine, more laden with accessories, more equipped with structural and electronic controls, and more charged with symbolic meaning. When it comes to the American home, the most striking trend in new housing reveals not a yearning for a Thoreau-style one-room hut but a lust for palatial accommodations. Stories about the growing size of the new American home are staples of news coverage and zoning board battles across the country. They call them by many names; "monster homes" and "McMansions" are but two. In some areas of the country, debates rage as smaller, more affordable homes are torn down and replaced with mini-manses. In others, new homes reach sizes unfathomable just a few generations ago. Pick up the paper in any part of the country and the story is there. The *Sacramento Bee* reported on five-thousand-square-foot homes (already huge by most standards) being leveled and replaced with fourteen-thousand-square-foot homes. The *Cleveland Plain Dealer, Chicago Tribune, Columbus Dispatch,* and many others have reported on the driving desire for larger and larger homes. The *Boston Globe Magazine* described the construction of an eighteen-room house featuring six full and two half bathrooms, a wine cellar the size of a two-car garage, and electrical demands that called for ten miles of wire to make it operational. No wonder a developer complained that homes have become so massive "you get tired walking around in them." When the *Philadelphia Business Journal* a few years back announced the "Invasion of Monster Houses," it declared that "the single-family home in the suburbs is not what it used to be." Indeed it's not.[5]

The trend is not confined to the top price range, either. Even regular-size homes are growing. According to the National Association of Home Builders, the average size of the new American home increased 41 percent between 1971 and 1997, rising from 1,520 to 2,150 square feet in just over a quarter century. In line with this trend, there are fewer small homes being built today. Those under 1,200 square feet now account for just 8 percent of new homes, down from 25 percent in 1975, and nearly one-third of new homes are more than 2,400 square feet—compared with just 11 percent two decades earlier. There is a similar, if slightly less dramatic, trend in apartment and condo units. In 1977, just 10 percent of new apartments had three bedrooms or more. Some twenty years later, that figure had risen to 16 percent. And the percentage of new apartments with two or more bathrooms rose from 20 percent in 1977 to 49 percent in 1998. This hunger for more space comes even as household size shrinks and the number of large families (those who presumably need a big house) is in decline. There are 25 percent fewer households with six or more people today than there were in 1960, and there are also more single-person households than at any other point in modern history.[6]

We clearly don't *need* more space. But people *want* it. Not only are large homes status symbols (hence the popular description as "trophy homes") for the wealthy, but even those lower down on the economic ladder want more space. The norms are shifting. People increasingly expect that every child should have his or her own room; no more putting two, three, or more to a bedroom, as was common a generation ago.

The change in the American home is not just about wanting more square footage but about wanting more personal space. For much of his childhood in the late 1960s and 1970s, my husband, his brother, and his sister slept three to a single bedroom—despite the fact that the family home was spacious and there were vacant bedrooms. When his childhood home was sold not too many years ago, I walked through the second floor and opened a door to a lovely, white ceramic-tiled full bathroom that was never used in all the years they lived in the house. It simply wasn't necessary when it was possible, even desirable, to share. Homes are now designed, marketed, and bought with the express appeal that they give individual household members more places to be alone and uninterrupted by other family members. We embrace the Aesthetic of Big.

"Are you dreaming of a home on a grand scale?" Tom Seery, senior editor of the 1998 edition of *Better Homes and Gardens Plans*, asks in his letter at the front of the magazine. "Does 5,000 square feet sound like a nice figure to you?" He touts the magazine's main feature, "Large-Scale Living," which features homes from 3,208 square feet to 5,069 square feet, where "huge master suites, kitchen islands, breakfast rooms and separate living rooms and family rooms are the norm."

This is where you find homes with four and five bedrooms, four and five bathrooms, and plenty of private space so "if you want to be alone, you can easily find a quiet spot to call your own." These large homes are striking not for their uniqueness but for how common they have become, integrated into a set of middle-class hopes, dreams, and, in many cases, expectations. To be sure, some of the largest homes are beyond middle-class reach. But *Better Homes and Gardens* is not an elite publication. It speaks to the lives of many Americans today.

The same issue also offers a section on "small retreats"—that is, homes under three thousand square feet. Here in the "small" section, you find a 2,204-square-foot modern "storybook cottage" with three bedrooms and two and a half baths designed by architect Jeremiah Eck, known for his focus on small homes. In another era, "small" would hardly describe his creation. Consider that seventy-eight years earlier, the April 1920 issue of *Good Housekeeping* introduced readers to plans for two "family" homes, the kind, the author touts, that "will last through your children's lives and be theirs indisputably." So how large is the "family" home of 1920? One is a three-bedroom Colonial, and the other is a two-bedroom bungalow. Both have a single bathroom—a notion now considered absurd (50 percent of new homes today have two and a half baths or more). By our standards, this "family" home is a starter house, or perhaps not even that. The *Better Homes and Gardens* plan that most closely compares in size is described as a "vacation cottage." It is not intended as a year-round or permanent home—certainly not considered substantial enough to serve as a homestead worthy of preserving and passing on to children.

There has been a similar space inflation in the size and number of rooms—and, with it, changes in how people use the space. The "large" living room of 1920 was twelve by eighteen feet and a space sold as a place "where the family may gather in the winter evenings." Today a large living room would typically be twice that size, even though living rooms are largely symbolic spaces that are rarely used. The "great room" or the family room is the new gathering place. Unlike the old living room, the new spaces are often attached to the kitchen and arranged so household members may inhabit the same contiguous space but be engaged in their own solo activities. Today, people want space in which they may do many things, even split their attention, multitasking like the most indispensable machines. People want a space that allows them to have many windows on their mental screens open at a given moment, all running independent tasks. In the kitchen/great room, one person may be preparing a meal and speaking on the phone while another watches TV and exercises or checks e-mail while snacking, doing homework, and listening to music on headphones. The old living room, with its essentially single purpose of sitting and talking, has, in effect, been replaced with a room that encourages household members not to gather around the fire on a winter evening but to be privately engaged in separate tasks.

Technology bears some responsibility, for not only making it possible to do many things at once alone but also, by its very presence, expecting that we do so. The home today is wired not only so we may watch TV while talking on the phone or checking e-mail but so that in so doing we may blur the very divisions between work and home, between being busy and being available. Technology, though, is not the only pressure at work. More generally, people simply *want* the flexibility to use social spaces for their own purposes and the mobility to interact on the fly or with only half-hearted effort.

In fact, people rarely engage in what is rapidly becoming an antiquated activity: sitting and giving our full attention to one another. Author Maggie Scarf, speaking about her book *Intimate Worlds: Life Inside the Family*, makes the point that it is critical to family relations to establish intimate understanding and respect. She draws on the relationship set out by Jewish philosopher and theologian Martin Buber in his classic *I and Thou*. Buber described with tenderness the beauty of meeting others on equal footing and recognizing and accepting their wholeness—meeting them as "Thou" as opposed to "He," which is a form of "It." The message is to truly see and accept the other person for the unique being he or she is, not who you wish him or her to be. "With no neighbor, and whole in himself, he is *Thou* and fills the heavens," Buber writes. Scarf's point is that it is critical for loved ones to be able to "truly look into the other person's eyes and say, 'Yes, I know who you are, I know what you are thinking about.'"[7]

There are, of course, other ways of building relationships and that I-Thou connection, but all require, at times, one's undivided attention. Yet such connections are becoming harder to forge, even—and perhaps especially—at home. The growing size and the arrangement of modern homes is cutting out the inconvenience of being brought together to share space, and yet in sharing space we share experiences, mundane and profound. Some of this results from choices made in how we use space. People, for example, increasingly choose to watch TV in private instead of in a more public room, or to have several phone lines. But it also comes about because of the structure of today's homes; the features we consider modern and important to include physically seclude us from one another.

Just consider the very different language the magazine writers use in talking about the homes and which features they emphasize and praise. In 1920, for example, the text describes the home as a place of stability, efficiency, and practicality, where compact design saves "thousands of steps a year." In 1920, the notion of separating bedrooms by placing them on different floors or with a bathroom between them to maximize privacy was not appealing. In fact, putting bedrooms side by side increased efficiency. "Hall space, which is nearly always a waste, has been reduced to a minimum," celebrates the writer describing the 1920s Colonial. "See how cleverly the upstairs hall forms an entrance to each of the three bedrooms and bathroom."

By contrast, in 1998, the writers talk privacy. Space, we read, is "zoned" so various members of the family can have their own, uninterrupted territory. A four-bedroom plan boasts a "secluded master bath" that is "a private paradise for parents." Even the small 1,642-square-foot "Quintessential Country Home" with three bedrooms and two baths boasts that "separating the bedrooms assures privacy for the master suite." It is an obsession. The message is there in the floor plans: We are (perhaps without realizing it) asking to be left alone.

No More Waiting in Line for the Bathroom

We most especially want to be left alone in the bathroom. While a certain amount of privacy has always been desirable, the bathroom is now not so much a utilitarian space for attending to nature's call but a sanctuary for body and soul, a place to escape to. Pottery Barn's summer 1999 catalogue urges: "Transform the bath. This is your personal spa." In real terms, our bathrooms are getting larger, and—most telling—there are more of them in our homes. According to "The House of the Future," a report by the National Association of Home Builders, we are fast approaching a time when two full and two half bathrooms "will be standard in average size homes." That's quite a leap from the single bathroom that was typical in the 1920s family home. In 1975, for example, only one in five new homes had two and a half or more baths; by 1997, half of all new homes did. The report also notes that bathroom finishes—fixtures, tiles, countertops, built-in features—have grown more luxurious. Bathrooms, it says, are "now becoming more opulent with higher quality materials, marble vanities and closets for linens." And consumer surveys show that inside the bathroom people want more compartmentalized space, such as separate showers and baths. No longer a water closet, the bathroom is envisioned as a spacious warren of rooms, a spa within the home. It seems hard to imagine that the now-exalted bathroom was once a lowly outhouse or a mere nook tucked into spare floor space. The loo has come a long way.

The design changes reveal much about us. In essence, the bathroom has evolved from an intimate space we shared sequentially to a space in which, above other spaces, we retreat into privacy—and not just privacy from peeping or intrusion but a deeper privacy that encompasses information about grooming, personal habits, and flaws. It is as if we want to conceal our imperfections even from those we expect to embrace our blemishes. Many master bedroom suites—bed-and-bath combinations ranked among the most popular remodeling projects in the late 1990s—now include two bathrooms, one for each member of a couple. There is no need to enter your partner's territory; doing so may be trespassing.

Not so long ago, of course, there was little choice but to share. It was a hassle. It was frustrating to wait outside the closed door as, in my case, one bathroom served for six people. In my teen years, we battled for bathroom time each morning. There was a schedule posted on the door, but it wasn't always kept. Many mornings I'd be left to shout at my sister Margaret over the roar of the blow dryer that she was *four minutes into my time!* It was frustrating, all right. And yet I can't help believing that I know and love Margaret a little more for the grouchy way she'd stomp into the bathroom—late—and then ignore my pleas. Unpleasant though it sounds, every time I look at a blow dryer I think fondly of our morning battles and of how hard my sisters, my brother, and I struggled every morning to tame our adolescent hair and skin and pull ourselves together to venture out into another awkward day.

Today we prefer not to share if we can afford it. Certainly it is quicker to get ready, to bathe or shower or do your hair and makeup, if you're not fighting for space. But wants today are about more than convenience. Along with the outward drive for efficiency comes a more veiled drive to avoid the messy, or merely unpleasant, parts of being human. We have become uncomfortable with ourselves. We seek sterility (consider the plethora of antibacterial and clear/clean products on the market). The ordinary human stuff that gets left behind—hairs in the drain, beard bits in the sink, toothpaste stuck on the tube, wet handprints left on the towels—is not normal human residue to our new sensibility but evidence of the grotesque human body. We would rather step into a bathroom as clean and well appointed as the one in the Four Seasons, where an attendant stands by to ensure there is nothing at all left behind.

Although the discomfort with human odds and ends is most apparent in the bathroom, it exists throughout the house. We are drawn to the pristine photos in the pages of catalogues and shelter magazines (where the evidence of human living is artfully, cleanly, stylishly created). Even though we know these rooms are set up for the photo shoot, they stir the desire to emulate the perfection they display. They seduce us, promising that such a look *is* achievable. Buy, hire, and you, too, may have this life! This is not to say we like everything to look brand-new. We may shun the unseemliness of living, but we do embrace the aesthetic of the worn. It is fashionable to have home furnishings that seem to bear the imprint of history and life. Perhaps it appeals because we live our own lives so lightly. Whatever the reason, the worn look is, above all, not a reflection of real life but a statement of style. You can buy a dining room table that is "distressed and scored" to *look* used, but the real table that has been scored by sharp objects accidentally dragged across the surface is suspect. Interior designers, furniture makers, and home decorating retailers labor to create the look of the human touch. They offer history lite, safe from the weight and threat posed by real distress.

Consider the *New Yorker* cartoon by Barbara Smaller that shows a couple standing in their living room, greeting an interior designer who is artfully attired in turtleneck and double-breasted blazer. The man of the couple has his hands thrust deep into his pockets, and the woman speaks. "We want it to look lived in," she instructs the designer, "but not necessarily by us." The most obvious reading of the cartoon plays on the penchant of designers to create environments that look as if someone else—not you—inhabits the space. Taken another way, though, it speaks to the distance between our lives and ourselves. The woman in the cartoon is right: We don't want to reveal the intimate way we live but rather to display a fashionably worn-looking life, even if it's not exactly ours. It's safer to embrace the designed version of life than the real one. Or maybe we are confused, unable to decide which parts of ourselves to showcase and which to hide.

I first realized that the "lived-in" look was in vogue a decade ago when my mother-in-law gave my husband and me a pair of threadbare brown chairs. I was bemoaning their sorry state, shaking my head at the stuffing poking through the armrests, and fretting about the high cost of reupholstering when a former colleague, a high-powered publicist from Manhattan, was visiting. She scolded me. Was I joking? Susan immediately seized on the visibility of stuffing and the absence of sheen on the brown velvet seats as fabulous features, strokes of luck. Did I realize what people were paying for a look like that? I've never reupholstered them. Presumably now that they're even more threadbare, they're also even more stylish.

The point here is that for me, as for the cartoon couple, there is comfort in what is codified and standardized. The worn, the lived-in, the weathered, the ravaged is great as long as it's been approved as fashion. In a sense, what we are talking about here is the need for things to be rendered safe. The fashion ads with soiled and wrinkled clothes are not depictions of "the way things are" but highly self-conscious artistic statements. Although many style elements today borrow from the palette of real life, the transformation of them into fashion is not the same as accepting the impromptu part of living. Quite the contrary: They create a code under which even the most mundane life elements require a particular artistic context to be seen and accepted. The dirty brown couch throw I sat on during one two-and-a-half hour interview in a run-down home (as a roach teased, crawling closer to me and then retreating) lacks a legitimizing context. Authenticity is lovely, but only if it has been cleaned and properly marketed.

In a similar way, we find ourselves styling personal interactions at home. We tend to favor the scripted or planned over the impromptu or, certainly, unpleasant; we schedule time for coffee, a TV show, a trip to the museum, or a baseball game. But the conversation that erupts while standing next to the clothes dryer, the need to cry at the kitchen table, or having someone stroke your back unexpectedly while you're sitting on the bathroom floor upends us. Such events are represented in no category; there is no script, no understanding of what kind of time this is supposed to be. Yet these are the moments that build meaning, real history, true connection. Many of us miss good human interaction today because we do not see it or we cannot schedule it in. Other opportunities never germinate because our domestic environments remove the chances for it to happen. They cut down on the need to share space, to cooperate, even to come in contact with one another.

Missed connections are replaced with other things, including design that evokes the *feeling* of what's absent. Designers suggest environments that revel in history, intimacy, love, friendship, caring, time, and will for conversation. Spiritually attuned architect Anthony Lawlor lectures and writes books, including *A Home for the Soul*, which instructs readers on how to arrange "a soulful gathering room." The impulse is nice: Build a space that communicates warmth and connection. But if you build it, will they come? Does declaring a space for "gathering" make it happen more often? Or is it enough to own the appropriate space should the opportunity for gathering arise?

It is in this arena that many of us are vulnerable to the sales pitches. Pottery Barn sells what we miss. We can envision, with the purchase of the Jenna Rocker, the promise in the ad copy: Time will slow long enough to let us enjoy a good book, and the experience will be as beautiful and elemental as the connection of holding a baby. We want the rocking chair, but not because we appreciate the grain of the wood or the way the craftsman has constructed it. We cannot discern that from the catalogue photo. We want it because we ache for the feeling they are selling. We want the companionship we imagine coming along with, for example, the Crate and Barrel Bloomsbury Sofa. "Throw off your scuffs, dear, and just relax," the copy reads. "I'm going to steam these clams for dinner." Never mind that one in four households is home to just one person or that many dual-earner couples are not steaming each other clams but reaching for Lean Cuisine, eating at their desks, or downing a bowl of cereal with the newspaper.

Home furnishing objects, and the way they are sold, address the longing for the past and for connection. We perceive "old" as a code word for "simpler times"—an era that can be called up and relived for the price of a sofa, a rocking chair, a distressed table, a reproduction dial telephone, a replica of a Victorian-era brass closet hook. We are inundated with images that tease us with the come-on of connection, family, and a sense of history and stability. Our actual lives may lack these elements, but if we can buy the props, can't we pretend? Home furnishings stores are jammed with the evocative goods: picture frames, scrapbooks, mirrors. Even moves to stir up less classical interior styles, recalling 1950s "modern" design, evoke the innocent hunger for the future. Remember when newer *was* always better?

In the 1960s the French sociologist Jean Baudrillard studied home furnishings ads and magazine copy. He noted the prevalence of precut furniture components that could be arranged and rearranged to serve many different roles—as bookshelves, bar, radio, cupboards, wardrobe, stereo, and more. He observed that Old World "symbolic values" in furnishing were being replaced by "organizational values." Furnishings were favored for their versatility and function instead of for their traditional role within the home. The new objects—now more than three decades old—"are no longer endowed with a 'soul,' nor do they invade us with their symbolic presence." The furniture, in fact, suggested a lightness in an era when so much else was weighted with meaning. He observed the disappearance of objects like mirrors, family portraits, and clocks (among other items) from home design. These are precisely the objects, shunned in the 1960s, that are filling our homes today. It is as if we are seeking to find some classical reference point (or the illusion of it) from which to move through the new century.[8]

We want our homes to look lived in—but not necessarily by us. We want to imagine a life that could happen within our walls, even if it is not our own. We want more space, more privacy, more control. We arrange our technology and our social conventions to keep ourselves safe from neighbors who would drop by. We have secured the perimeters. And yet we long for what has been banished. We hunger for the history, the worn patinas, the timelessness, and the dangling conversation that many of us find we somehow no longer have time (or patience) for. We long for heirlooms, for connections to past and present. But too often they are most easily gotten in catalogues or designers' stockpiles, created to evoke relationships that may not exist.

I am reminded of a visit to the home of a prominent Boston interior designer. He showed me his classically designed brownstone, the rich fabrics, the playfully painted floors, and his very wonderful bedroom. I remember the deepness of the colors, the soothing browns especially, but what drew my attention was all the framed black-and-white photographs arranged on his bedside tables. They looked old and precious, the kind of belongings that one cherishes above all others. But the photos were not pictures of anyone he knew. They were a decorative accessory. I remember standing there, trying to imagine what it would be like to sleep under the watchful gaze of all those strangers' eyes. In whose lives did they belong? Did they provide him comfort? Or were they just faces that blended into the scheme, as invisible in their familiarity as the wallpaper and the drapes?

Where do we find comfort and connection? We love the symbolism of portraits and of porches, but we are sold on the refuge of fences, blinds, and private baths. It seems like a step up, having so much more space, not having to take turns in the bathroom. We can have our own. We can watch and listen to whichever TV shows and songs we want, when we want, in our own rooms. We can network the computers in the kids' rooms to communicate with our own, use the intercom to ask the kid a question. We can use a surveillance camera to see who is at the front door instead of just looking out the window. It's hard not to celebrate all the neat stuff we have. But we've also lost some. The "betterment" of the American home—most dramatic in larger homes, but present in more modest newer ones as well—is taking away something we didn't even know had value: interruptions, casual and sometimes annoying contact with household members, spontaneous discussions that may or may not have a point. We have grown accustomed to emphasizing the domestic experiences that are planned: the big vacation, watching a movie together, eating a special meal, having a celebration. But over time it is the repeated and the chance encounters, the ungarnished spending of time, that gives us the intimate knowledge of one another that is the foundation of long-term relationships and real love.

In the movie *Good Will Hunting*, Robin Williams's character, whose wife had died of cancer, makes a rather base though profound point about all this. He says what he remembers—and misses—most about her is the way she would fart in her sleep, one time even waking herself up. That, he says, "is the good stuff." It is—as Williams's character suggests—the intangible, the untouchable, and even the unsavory that moves us and reminds us we are human.

My maternal grandfather, an economist for the government and then a high school teacher, had one full bathroom in his house. I remember visiting him and my grandmother in Mentor, Ohio, and waiting in the early morning for him to finish. I would step inside onto the black shag rug, which still held the outlines of his slippers. The air was moist. It smelled of spicy aftershave, of soap, and of time spent on the john. I always noticed the issue of *Prevention* magazine left open on the radiator box by the window. My grandfather did not emerge in the mornings before school fully dressed and perfect but rather in stages, showing me by his leavings the process by which one began a day.

Life today is far more complicated than it once was. We are too important, too busy, to wait in line for the bathroom. New homes acknowledge the new standards we have. Sometimes, though, it seems the new standards—for bathrooms as for so much else—are not merely about convenience or respite or rejuvenation of the soul (whatever that even really means). They seem, rather, to speak of our discomfort with one another. They seem to speak of our fear of recognizing our imperfections. They seem to be about wanting space—and losing touch.

The Threshold

If we can map changing levels of household connection in the home's interior, we can see in the threshold—that borderland—signs of a changed relationship with the world outside. It is here, along the wooden ridge beneath the door, that interior and exterior meet and part. It is also here that a changed vision of the household's role in the apartment building, co-op, or neighborhood is most clearly symbolized. Metaphorically, the door has shifted from a symbol of entry to a symbol of security. Most people today not only lock their doors but also bolt them. The image of the house with the screen door with spring hinges that slaps open and closed, open and closed, while parents insist to children, "In or out—make up your mind!" is fading. We hold on to and even amplify in our minds the image of friendly floormates in an apartment building or neighbors streaming across each other's thresholds, into each other's homes, pausing to snack in each other's kitchens as easily as if they were their own. In this idealized remembrance, the door is the means for entry, the detail that must be got through before one can reach the lemonade and cookies.

The image is nostalgic, to be sure. But we are desperate to re-create that picture, training our attention on signs that, somewhere, such a life may still be alive, though buried under the rubble of current social norms. I remember how excited a neighbor was the day she found her backyard full of playing children, how the image became a symbol of the tremendous efforts she had made in the hope of creating a sense of community on the street. More often, though, our backyards are empty and the screen door is shut tight; sturdy new versions are even equipped with deadbolts.

The door today keeps the action inside the home from spilling out. It also keeps the outside from coming in. The door is the tangible means for allowing each of us to mind our own business. It seems a natural boundary between the troubles of the world and the troubles of our lives. Why not halt one's attention and responsibility at the door, at the perimeter of the home? Certainly there's plenty to attend to inside. The threshold is not a piece of wood to be spanned but a means of marking the end of the territory we feel responsible for patrolling. It has become a physical and psychological boundary that confines the range of concern. It is certainly clearer than the alternative: basing involvement on an ill-defined sense of moral obligation or common sense. We'd have to ask: What *is* the right thing to do? When should one step forward and be involved? Who needs our help? Our attention? When do we listen? In our busy lives it is easier to follow an unspoken command: Keep to yourself. The threshold makes the line clearer.

This is a rather recent conception of neighborly relations. In the 1950s in Cleveland, my grandmother had a neighbor, Mrs. Sanford. Virtually every morning, Mrs. Sanford stepped outside her back door and, still wearing her bathrobe, charged across the vacant lot that separated her home from my grandmother's. She tapped on the side door and, usually without waiting for an answer, stepped inside. She made herself at home at the kitchen table, and then she and my grandmother would sip cup after cup of coffee as they talked.

This most likely wouldn't happen today. Imagine waking up to find a neighbor arriving for morning coffee—even fully dressed. Anyone would be rightfully mortified, not to mention that it would probably take a professional thief to get past deadbolted doors and home security systems. But what has always struck me about this story is that my grandmother always claimed she didn't like having Mrs. Sanford drop over. She wasn't alone with such sentiments. In the March 1940 issue of *Good Housekeeping,* writer Lydia Hewes "confesses" in a column headlined "Dropper-inner?" that "I loathe having people drop in on me." What's more, she says other people feel the same way she does but "stifle their true feelings in the name of friendship." Despite her dislike for the practice, Hewes says it's not so easy to halt what she calls this "unnecessary complication in modern life." She recognizes that, to keep others from dropping in on her, she must first stop dropping in on them. "I suppose I should practice what I preach," she says, indicating that she doesn't. She also must stop thwarting her own efforts by cheerfully inviting people to stop by. "I find myself saying: 'Do drop in and see us sometime! We'd simply love it!'"

Hewes and my grandmother both recognized that social convention is a powerful force. It is not easy to make an isolated stand. In my grandmother's case, although she grew tired of Mrs. Sanford dropping over, she never let on. She understood that it was part of a larger picture of community, one that was not just about identifying or feeling part of a place but also about participating in neighbors' lives. Mrs. Sanford, it turns out, made a point of visiting my grandmother because she knew my grandfather was often out of town. She felt it was her duty as a neighbor to provide company and to be of service. Her sense of obligation did not end at her back door or her property line.

Today, our society has moved far in the opposite direction. It's now considered rude to drop in, and most of us don't even note our neighbor's lack of company. We practice what Hewes and Mrs. Sanford probably couldn't envision: the mind-your-own-business approach to neighborly relations. People today describe themselves as being on good terms with neighbors not as a result of positive interactions but because they note a lack of bad interactions. A "good neighbor" today is one who doesn't bother you. Certainly, this approach has its benefits, including a respect for privacy. But it also has consequences, including an eroded sense of support and community. This point seems to be brought home every time a major crime makes national news. Reporters inevitably contact neighbors, who express real surprise that the serial killer lived right next door. "He seemed so nice!" we hear. "He kept to himself and didn't bother anyone. How could this be?" The fact

is that we don't really know our neighbors. We might—and I emphasize *might*—know them by sight or name. But we don't know who they
are, and certainly not well enough to insert ourselves into the fray. The
neighbor who heard teenage killers Dylan Klebold and Eric Harris
smashing glass in the garage—glass used as shrapnel in bombs that
would kill a dozen students and a teacher the next day at Columbine
High School in Littleton, Colorado—didn't feel compelled to cross the
threshold and get involved, even if only to ask, "Hey, kids, whatcha
doing?" This is not to blame the neighbor, who publicly acknowledged
his struggle with not acting, but to demonstrate the extent to which we
today are willing—and even expected—to turn inward and mind our
own business.

That's not to say people don't express concern or empathy for a
neighbor. But we do not feel the *obligation* to act. It is today the neighbor's job to acquire support, not ours to perceive the need and provide
it. A hospice worker spoke to me about this changed dynamic. She told
me of leaving the home of a woman who was dying. As she stepped out
into the daylight in an urban neighborhood with homes packed tight
against one another, she realized that no one on the street knew what
was happening behind the woman's front door. Old conventions of
bringing food and offering support still persist, but they are fading.
There are still caretakers and well-wishers, but just as we are less comfortable with hairs left in the bathroom sink, we are less comfortable
with the act of dying. It is more palatable to stay away and order flowers by phone. Increasingly, the hospice worker observed, support for the
dying is given over to professionals.

What, then, are neighbors for? We no longer expect them to be
involved in our day-to-day lives, watching out for our children, visiting when we are lonely, or lending a cup of sugar. Such active neighboring requires a sense of interdependence and trust that has grown
rare. In places where it does exist, where neighbors are conscious of
themselves as part of a whole, participants find they have not only
neighbors but also a sense of community and belonging. I think of a
section of Boston where friends live. On Ashmont Hill in Dorchester,
neighbors have removed back fences so children can run through all
their backyards. No doubt there are other examples of such efforts, but
they are not the norm. More often, we read about people erecting
fences to mark off property and provide more visual and social separation. Even this practice is taking on a problematic edge as homeown-

ers install fences with the "bad side" facing out. As a result, some suburban boards are debating the civil installation of fencing, in some cases
drafting ordinances to enforce neighborly behavior.

Yet people like to talk about where they live as a "neighborhood."
People yearn to be part of a "community." So what does that actually
mean? One study suggests that we have indeed adapted to the "virtuality" of modern life and are willing to say we feel part of a community
without actually having to participate in communal relations at all.
Researchers Mark Baldassare and Georjeanna Wilson at the University
of California at Irvine asked a compelling question: What gives people
a "sense of community"? The researchers assert that the suburbs have
long attracted settlers because they allow people to experience privacy
(the ability to regulate social interaction) and, at the same time, a "small-
town feel" (the ability to know others and be known). This balance of
benefits—the ability to retreat into privacy and yet feel a part of things—
has drawn millions to the suburbs since the close of World War II.[9]

More recently, the researchers posit, the urbanization of suburbia has
upset a piece of that equation. "Although suburban residents continue
to prefer small communities that offer a sense of community, many find
their ideals are in conflict with the reality of living in a suburban
region," they write. The suburban home offers refuge against increased
life stress, but one would expect the sense of community to be diminished in this new, more urbanized suburban environment. When
researchers questioned residents about what was required to view their
community as "unified" and active, however, they discovered residents
did not need to be active themselves but merely aware of "the opportunity to be active" to feel these positive attributes of their town. This
view of community—and, really, of neighborhood—is virtual. It is
viewed not from the street or even from one's yard but from within the
perimeter of the home. Involvement is theoretical, not actual, and the
home is the individual command center rather than a stop along a
connected circuit.

There is, of course, plenty of evidence that the "neighborhood" is
not the cohesive unit it once was. The notion that living next door to
or within earshot or sight of people obligated you to look out for
them, to know them, even to socialize with them, is dead. Somehow,
in our quest to do better in our own lives, to work harder and be successful, our relationships with people who live next door have become
expendable. Whether our schedules are jammed or not, there is little

time today for talking over the back fence or lingering over coffee. But probably more powerful than the time crunch we blame for so much in our lives is an inescapable truth: We aren't in the *habit* of taking time with people, either.

We don't socialize with neighbors as much as we once did. Data from the General Social Survey shows that over the past twenty years we have gathered and interacted less and less with those who live nearby. In 1974, nearly one-third of respondents in this national sampling reported spending a social evening with a neighbor every day or once or twice a week. In 1994, only one-fifth made a similar report. Over the same time, the percentage of those who said they never socialized with neighbors or did so just once a year rose from 28 percent to more than 40 percent. The scales have tipped. There is a growing disconnection between us and the people who live around us.

Even the most basic things neighbors once did for each other—such as paying attention and noticing when something seemed wrong—we can no longer count on. Who is home anymore? Or feels obligated to note that the older man next door who uses a cane is struggling with the bag of groceries? That the three-year-old boy crying on the sidewalk in front of his house isn't safe so close to the busy street? That the woman who lives alone hasn't been seen in days? That the sound of shattering glass in the garage next door might mean trouble?

The problem is not just that we mind our own business but that as a society we are losing any sense that we have a responsibility to act, or even to pay attention. It is easier, safer, to believe it's better not to intrude. Intrusion, after all, is a horrible faux pas in a society that has put privacy on a pedestal. A certain amount of privacy, of course, is essential. But our obsession with privacy has gone overboard, breeding a general mistrust and—perhaps most critical here—making our lives more mysterious to one another. We can look at polls that show how many people agree or disagree with our views on a particular topic, but we lack the kind of everyday information about our neighbors' lives that brings people together: the struggles, the observations, the beliefs that at one time might have been shared over a cup of morning coffee.

The New Neighborhoods

Our willingness to retreat into our homes and have our needs "ordered in" has not been lost on the people who design neighborhoods. In fact, the question of how—and how much—people want to or should relate to neighbors is at the heart of debate among architects and planners. Everywhere the talk is of "community," a word alternately used as catchphrase, advertising slogan, and guiding philosophy behind a design movement. But what should a community, a neighborhood, look like? The debate is active at many levels among many people, from designers to politicians. Two trends are striking for their frank focus on the question: the rise of gated communities and the growing popularity of New Urbanism or neo-traditional planning, which aims to create communal behavior through design.

The two would appear to espouse nearly opposite philosophies—one to keep the broader community out of a private enclave and the other to build communities that draw different people together. But in many ways, they are not so disparate. Proponents of gated communities argue that they are not just excluding outsiders but also building a sense of community within their walls. The New Urbanists, the neighbor builders, may try but cannot force people to interact. What's more, despite the rhetoric about community, New Urbanist communities can themselves be isolated from the outside world, physically, stylistically, or practically. Most interesting, though, is the fact that planners, architects, designers, and residents are looking for design solutions to what they see as a crisis of community. What *should* a modern neighborhood be like?

Edward J. Blakely, dean of the School of Urban and Regional Planning at the University of Southern California, and Mary Gail Snyder, member of the department of City and Regional Planning at Berkeley, study gated communities and are the authors of *Fortress America: Gated Communities in the United States.* They estimated in 1997 that eight million Americans lived in gated communities (there are no official statistics for this neighborhood designation). In the mid-1980s, such communities existed in only a handful of places; now, observe the authors, they can be found in every major metropolitan area. For Blakely and Snyder, the creation of walled or gated communities is far more than a design scheme. It raises serious questions about the state of social and civic relations.[10]

"The real issue," they write, "is not about the actual gates and walls, but why so many feel they need them. What is the measure of nationhood when the divisions between neighborhoods require guards and fences to keep out other citizens? When public services and even local government are privatized, when the community of responsibility stops at the subdivision gates, what happens to the function and the very idea of social and political democracy? Can this nation fulfill its social contract in the absence of social contact?"

These are provocative questions, yet they are not necessarily the questions that propel residents into buying homes in gated communities. More often the impetus is personal: a belief that gates will increase security, protect property values, or increase status. Gated communities—that is, developments with gates, guardhouses, and perimeter barriers, or ones carved out of existing neighborhoods to control traffic and bar outsiders—may speak to personal wants. But they also reflect a broader social state. Why do so many people want to live this way?

I'd argue it's more of what we see in so many aspects of modern life: the desire to make life more comfortable, controllable, and private. Certainly, zoning laws have for years accomplished the job of creating barriers and excluding outsiders, but a gate is a far more powerful statement about where people's concerns and allegiances begin and end. The barriers are not just physical but psychological, social, and political. Gated communities, to varying degrees, are self-governing enclaves that may privatize typically public services. The deeper meaning of gating has not been lost on Fort Collins, Colorado, which banned gated developments as "disruptive to a sense of community." In Dallas, four suburbs outlawed gated communities on the grounds that they would give their residents security denied to others. And in one Las Vegas neighborhood, a plan to erect gates set off fierce debate among residents.[11]

Despite the exclusionary nature of gated communities, they are often marketed—and residents declare their appeal—as creating a sense of community. Within the gates, that is. Blakely and Snyder write that creating a sense of territoriality, of a distinction between what's "ours" and what's outside the gates, does increase the sense of community for some residents. Their survey of gated residents' attitudes, for example, reveals that most think their development "friendly" and one-third feel it is more neighborly than most other developments around them. Still, Blakely and Snyder observe that only 8 percent find their gated community "neighborly and tight-knit," and 28 percent actually say it is "distant or private" in feeling. Residents of gated communities are somewhat more likely than people who live in nongated private developments to say their developments are friendly—68 percent compared with 58 percent.

But as Blakely and Snyder point out, it is one thing to *feel* a sense of community and another to be involved with neighbors. In findings that are in keeping with the research of Baldassare and Wilson, Blakely and Snyder saw that residents of gated communities might have a sense of comfort with other residents—but that it often does not extend to being active. When they surveyed board members of gated communities, they found only 6 percent reporting residents were "very active" in governance; 55 percent said residents were not active. They were slightly more involved in social and nongovernance activities, but the vast majority—87 percent—were only "somewhat" or "not" active. Gated communities, the researchers suggest, offer a way for people to segregate and isolate themselves, to surround themselves with similar people and to embrace a very narrow experience of community. "Gated communities have created a new housing option for some of us," they write, "but they have also created a new social dilemma for all of us." They are, Blakely and Snyder argue, a way of limiting social contact and weakening critical ties.[12]

The value of social contact and the importance of the ties that result are at the center of the New Urbanist approach to development. New Urbanism embraces the idea that bad design has made for social isolation and that better design can bring people together and rebuild community. It is a concept that is catching fire across the country, in inner cities and suburbs; for the purpose of revitalizing housing projects, improving suburban life, and even creating whole new towns. In some ways, New Urbanism is not really new at all. The tenets that define the movement call for building communities that adopt the look and design of older city neighborhoods, places where homes are close together, where people can walk to shop, and where automobiles are tucked in back alleys. New Urbanist design creates a streetscape of sidewalks and front porches, instead of the driveways and garages that often face the street in conventional developments. It is rooted in a nostalgic view of the past, when people were more visible—not cloistered behind locked doors—and therefore more involved in each others' lives.

Although New Urbanists are selling design, they are peddling community. Consider the sales brochure for Kentlands, a New Urbanist community in Maryland, built by husband-and-wife team Andres Duany and Elizabeth Plater-Zyberk, among the movement's most visible architects. The brochure copy reads like a monograph on the All-American Hometown as it describes local residents "visiting on their front porches, talking over white picket fences, fishing from the pier at Inspiration Lake, and celebrating at festivals on the village green." The portrait is so perfect, one wonders, *Is this for real?*

But New Urbanism is not just about the *look* of neighborhoods. It is, perhaps more critically—and more controversially—also about the power of design to influence human behavior. New Urbanists believe that designing pedestrian-centered communities will lead residents to experience the everyday interactions, impromptu chats, and human contact that help forge neighborliness and civic bonds. The same sales brochure makes clear the connection: Homes in Kentlands, it reads, "are built close to the street—and close to each other—to encourage friendships." At its heart, New Urbanism is an attempt to repair neighborhoods by repairing the way communities are designed, built, and lived in. By designing streets with a variety of housing types—"Condominiums share the same street with colonials. Townhomes face estate homes. Cottages and mansions stand side by side"—designers maintain, "a closer community results."

The Kentlands brochure, like the sales pitches for other New Urbanist developments, unabashedly draws on the clichés of the past. New Urbanists are selling not just real estate but a lifestyle. Nowhere is this ideal more evident than in Celebration, Florida, a New Urbanist community created by the Walt Disney company. One brochure proclaims that "Celebration is designed to help people make connections—with their school, their jobs and their neighbors"; another boasts about the town's "front-porch friendliness." Indeed, if you take a walk or ride through the town, the place does look like the perfect *Leave It to Beaver* community. Everywhere you look there are white picket fences, fresh-looking sidewalks, and homes with front porches. It seems almost *too* perfect, like another Disney kingdom.

The relevant question is not about authenticity, however, but about connection. Can design change behavior? Will banishing cars create more pedestrians and, in turn, more social interaction? It may be too early to draw conclusions. One study by researchers at the University of California at Irvine and George Mason University in Virginia asked, "Does neighborhood design influence travel?" In their comments, the researchers noted that urban designers too often make the assumption that creating more pedestrian-friendly environments cuts down on automobile use, when "remarkably there is little empirical and theoretical support for these claims." The researchers, who used travel diaries and other data for San Diego, concluded that there was "little role for land use in explaining travel behavior and no evidence that the street network pattern affects either short or long non-work travel decisions." It may be harder to drive around a town designed for pedestrians, but it doesn't keep people out of their cars. Although the study does not speak to social interaction—an interesting area for research—it does raise questions about the assumption that designing a neighborhood for neighborliness will yield the desired results.[13]

Such an experiment in living is under way on Cape Cod. Just over the Bourne Bridge, on land that was once dominated by the Wampanoag tribe, a 1960s strip shopping center is being redesigned into Cape Cod's first New Urbanist community. It is the first New Urbanist project in the nation to start with a commercial center and build residential housing around it. (Other New Urbanist projects build housing first and import shops and businesses later.) As residents moved into the first thirteen housing units in the spring of 1998, there was a great deal of anticipation about how it would all work. Unlike typical New Urbanist communities, often built on large tracts of uninhabited land, this place—Mashpee Commons—is being built on old Cape Cod, where there are many communities with long histories. What's more, because New Urbanism draws on some of the same principles and tries to create the same feel as many traditional small towns, it raises questions about what it means to replicate an old New England town right beside the real ones that dot the Cape.

For the first residents, the benefits of urban living on rural Cape Cod are evident. A forty-three-year-old pharmacy technician who lives above a Banana Republic store likes the ease of walking to work, the post office, church, the library, restaurants, supermarkets, the movie theater, and Starbucks. "It's really nice to wake up at six A.M. and go have coffee," she says. A twenty-eight-year-old documentary film producer likes the urban street sounds that come through his open apartment windows—the sounds of people laughing, talking, dining, which are foreign to most residents of Cape Cod. But is this a community? Does it feel like one? Certainly, it looks like one, with buildings constructed to mimic an old downtown with different architectural styles for various shop facades and apartments on the second floor. But it may be too early to judge. Several months after moving in, the film producer said he still hadn't had much contact with neighbors in the other rental units. "Everyone goes their different ways," he said. "It's not like I've gone out of my way to meet anyone or anyone's gone out of their way to meet me."[14]

New Urbanist communities look appealing, and some who live in them are quick to offer testimonials about the friendly environment. But the job of forging real connections between neighbors may be too great for design alone. White picket fences, front porches, even a community-wide intranet like Celebration's, are limited: They evoke the longing for neighborliness but do not demand it. Some may take the images to heart. But even in Celebration, backyards are enclosed with high privacy fences. As Blakely and Snyder observe, "It is no accident developers refer to their products as 'communities.'" The word is a trigger that sets off a flood of good feeling and longing. People want what they feel is missing, but people are ambivalent about participating.[15]

We mustn't too quickly accept the declarations of developers, the "community" newsletter, or quaint allusions to bygone days. We mustn't allow mere words to stand in for the hard work of exposing ourselves and committing ourselves to be involved in other people's lives. It has become easier and more comfortable—inside the home and out—to retreat to private quarters and witness less of other people's lives. Builders create private suites, little apartments within our homes. We buy them. Outside, we erect fences for no other reason than to keep us from seeing our neighbors' lives and them from seeing ours. We may debate the design of a neighborhood and whether front porches and sidewalks will bring people together. But ultimately, making a real neighborhood requires people to venture outside and meet the folks next door.

# RELATIONS

Surveys asking what's most important in life routinely find relationships at the top of the list. Connections with other people sustain us, enrich us, and allow us to know who we are. They make life worth living. Studies show they can make us healthier, happier, and more successful at our jobs. Despite such certainty about the benefits of relationships, though, we are not always so clear about what a relationship is or ought to be. The neat words—spouse, friend, acquaintance, neighbor, sister, brother, partner, caretaker—do not evoke universal understanding. A sister may be your closest friend, the one who knows you better than anyone else in the world. Or she may simply share your genes.

Some confusion has always existed, but the labels we lean on are less and less reliable. Telling a friend that your brother is coming to visit for a week might prompt a question: "Is that *good?*" Our relationships are in flux, morphing into hybrids and new forms. We might ask: What, anymore, is a family? What is marriage for? Who is a neighbor, and what does that connection mean? What do friends owe each other? When are you a couple?

A certain amount of morphing has been going on for years. Just consider the family. Back in 1943, a time that evokes a stable image of family for many, people were observing all kinds of dramatic change. Sociologist Marvin K. Opler declared the "transformation of the American family" in the *American Journal of Sociology,* and he was not talking about new family formations like stepfamilies, or multiracial, ethnically mixed, or interfaith families. Rather, he was struck by the changing domestic landscape. He saw the rising numbers of working mothers and of families who bought bread and baked goods instead of making them. He noted those who even purchased ready-made clothes and joined recreation clubs. No longer was the family producing the things that families had always produced. Instead, "the more complete dependence on factory-made goods and on extra-familial agencies providing services and recreation" was shaking up the old order. He would certainly be surprised today. Not only do we rarely make anything from scratch—even meals—but we increasingly rely on services to shop for, prepare, and deliver our food, run our households, host our parties, raise and entertain our children. And, obviously, the American "family" is more diverse in its composition than at any time in history.[1]

Clearly, much about family life has changed in recent decades. It's fun to marvel wide-eyed at the transformation, but it's also worth looking critically at what these changes tell us about where we are headed. What road have we taken? Why do we seem more alone in the world—more surrounded by people, but less connected? There is no doubt that as a society we have in recent decades experienced a profound shift in the way we interact with others and perceive our roles as neighbor, family member, citizen, spouse, friend, lover, parent. One has only to look at the Whitney Darrow *New Yorker* cartoon from July 1951 in which two youngsters stop by an older neighbor's home to ask if he'd like to come to the funeral of their turtle to realize how much has changed in half a century. Not only would we never let young children—these look barely older than tots—visit neighbors on their own, chances are our children don't know their older neighbors well enough to extend such an invitation. Then there is the observation about childhood. Is there time anymore to plan funerals for dead turtles? More and more of our children's play is organized, scheduled, and supervised by professionals.

We did not arrive at this moment in history completely by chance. Rather, our relationships have been cast and recast again, moved in small steps by the choices we make and fail to make (even unconsciously), the messages we take in, and the bump and grind of daily living. At the heart of this chapter—and the Connection Gap—is the idea that we have the power to guide our lives. But we must assert that power. Now, more than ever, the tide pulls us along. We must recognize that the landscape is altered. We must be responsible for digging our heels into the sand and making choices that will lead us closer to the kinds of meaningful connections that give life lasting value. In the end, we have the power to pick up the phone, to get in the car, to step on the plane. We each decide whether to be involved or merely to stand by and silently sympathize. What is new today is the context. If we were once *expected* to put our needs aside for another, we are today assured that putting ourselves first is all right, even proper. If we were once *expected* to socialize with neighbors and watch out for their children, we are today conditioned to keeping our distance. In the decades since Opler's paper, we have been given greater license to focus our concern inward and to look the other way.

The America we live in is more tolerant, diverse, and respectful of the individual than the America of a half century ago. But it is also more socially separate, sometimes excessively individualistic. Many have chronicled these changes. Some argue that we are growing too isolated, others that greater focus on the individual promotes freedom, creativity, and new opportunities for bonding. Both may be true. There *is* real opportunity for connection. But the choices we make and the changes we embrace—the things that make our lives more comfortable, private, efficient, convenient, and enjoyable—demand more, not less, effort from us to make that connection happen.

The Rising "I"

In his essay "Two Hundred Million Egos," Andrew Hacker describes the "New American" as part of a middle class whose unprecedented size has given the majority access to material comforts that were once enjoyed by only a few. This New American is better educated, more informed, and more sophisticated than ordinary citizens have ever been. "He has heard everything even if, at times, he does not like what he hears," writes Hacker. But along with these broadened horizons has come a whole new set of heightened expectations— expectations not only of goods and services but also of how one ought to be treated.[2]

The New Americans, Hacker observes, "are upset when taxis are unavailable, when planes fall behind schedule, and when roads and recreational facilities are overcrowded. They object to the quality of service they receive from others and the lack of people prepared to wait on them in return for a reasonable payment." Success and comfort have brought not just merely elevated lifestyles but an elevated view of the self. As Hacker writes, "the egos of two hundred million Americans have expanded to dimensions never before considered appropriate for ordinary citizens."

It is not enough to want things. We also want elbow room, privacy, respect, and the freedom from worrying about other people's problems. We may be a great mass, recognizable to one another by the late-model cars we drive, the brand of clothes we wear, the food we eat, the stores we patronize. But we are ever focused inward. Seeing others like us does not spur community, merely a sense of validation. Our neighborhoods are not any longer about relationships but about real estate values and zip codes. Families are increasingly isolated units; our personal relationships are more and more all about *us*. And it's little wonder. We are trained from early on to be independent and to look out for ourselves. We worry more about what we're getting than about what we're giving. From the pages of magazines and academic journals, the voice-overs of television commercials, the surveys of pollsters, and the words of regular people, the message resounds: You—the individual—come first. We are constantly fed reminders of our own elevated importance. Make your own road. Call the shots. Get what *you* want—and *faster*. No wonder we have swelled heads.

While Americans have long been viewed as individualistic, in recent years, as Hacker suggests, we have moved far beyond that. We have become the champions of our worlds, the stars of our own fantasies and real-life dramas. We can blame the values of our age: the hunger for acquiring wealth, power, and material goods far beyond personal need. Or blame globalization and its accompanying fear of insignificance. Or blame marketing and the incessant mantra of self-focus. Or even blame the rise of a therapeutic culture. Whatever the sources, we are drawn into an ethos in which the individual is encouraged to reign supreme, regardless of the cost. We all ache to be celebrities, to be Number One—not merely the good or competent, but the superstar with the huge multiyear contract and the sneaker endorsement. The society we inhabit today allows—or perhaps insists—that we be rulers, that we not back down or inconvenience ourselves for another. Power and status now reside in the ability to demand and instantly get material things, attention, and service.

A *New York Times Magazine* special issue on status gives an example: getting what you want in a snap. Writer Steven Gaines describes a young investor who is frustrated at having trouble turning around his new Ferrari in the drive of his three-million-dollar Bridgehampton vacation home. He calls a contractor to see how much it would cost to have the driveway widened by ten feet—by day's end. As Gaines relates it, the contractor, accustomed to such requests, names an exorbitant price. By late afternoon, for that price, the job is complete. The newly rich, Gaines observes, "are enthralled with the velocity of money, obsessed not only with owning new and shiny things but also with the speed they can obtain and dispose of them." The anecdote focuses on the young investor, but the contractor has bought into the same set of values. He has status, too. He can demand—and get—his price.[3]

In a world where hierarchy matters, where status is divined by a hundred subtle and not so subtle signals, we are expected to behave as masters all. We are told incessantly that we "deserve" leather seats and hideously expensive cosmetics. We "deserve" doting partners who send flowers or buy diamonds when they have something really important to say. We "deserve" a break from our hectic lives, to retreat to the five-star getaway or at least have a car that can do zero to sixty miles per hour in 2.4 microseconds to make escape seem more possible. You would think we were all toiling under the hot sun, cooking for families of twelve, and darning socks at night by candlelight. Or that we had all become landed gentry. The declaration of self-entitlement is part of the new American norm, but it is a vision of life in which relationships with others are garnishes, not the meat of existence. The watchword of our age is self-fulfillment. It almost feels like a duty to expand personal experiences and horizons. We strive harder to get in touch with our inner child. We hire the personal trainer to optimize our physique. Some of us even hire people to develop our own personal style.

The "I" focus that dominates is, in some ways, refreshing. To study consumer magazines from the 1940s, 1950s, and early 1960s is to be subjected to the mantra of self-sacrifice and strict gender roles. The teenage girl who double-dated in 1945 is instructed in the pages of *Seventeen* magazine that "it's part of your dating duty to see that the other girl has as much fun as you do." A 1951 article in *Woman's Day* called "Another Time, I Wouldn't" is a first-person saga of regret over ending what sounds like a horrible marriage. The writer, a woman, concludes that even though staying together "might well have been heartbreaking many times" she now realizes "that emotional security, made together, outstrips individual satisfactions." While we might today view this as a dismal admission, the thrust of the article suggests that marriage—even one in which the husband takes little interest in his own children or family celebrations—is worth preserving at all costs.

Few would return to a time when we essentially played out scripted roles, when *Playboy* told its readers that women were time-consuming burdens who could be easily duped. The observation is only half in jest in a 1956 piece: "With most females it is possible to put on a dazzling display of intellectual virtuosity with a minimum of research." It is a relief to believe we are past such oppressive sets of beliefs and expectations. On the other hand, our emancipation has become a no-holds-barred quest for self-expression, self-definition, and self-gratification. A 1977 piece in *Woman's Day* called "Me First" gives a taste of the then fresh struggle between obligation and personal freedom:

"In the last few years we've been learning—through psychotherapy, human potential workshops, the woman's movement and assertiveness training—to get in touch with our own needs and to stop feeling guilty about satisfying them," the article reads. "We don't have to serve as doormats to our spouses, our children or our friends, we're told. We don't have to say yes when we mean no."[4]

For the generation of women so well described by Betty Friedan in *The Feminine Mystique* such talk was not merely about liberation but about survival. And while the *Woman's Day* article addressed women, the idea that individual freedom and choice should be paramount has ignited both sexes. The men's tale has not been as well articulated, but I suspect that even as women felt trapped in the homemaker role of the 1950s, men felt equally trapped in the role of stoic provider. We might argue that one role has more power than the other, but neither can be construed as terribly satisfying. The point here is not to argue gender role construction but to derive from the complexity of the debate an observation about a changing sensibility: In the 1970s, it was becoming acceptable to put individual needs first. But what began as a healthy cry for personal freedom has become an obsessive whine for personal satisfaction. What we need today is balance. The writer of the 1977 article seemed to anticipate the challenge we now face. "It's not as simple as it sounds," the writer warns. "We all accumulate obligations and commitments to other people as we go through life. We need one another as much as we need the freedom to be ourselves. If we don't want to end up isolated and alienated from each other, we have to find a balance between what we want and what we owe others."

The concerns of the time now seem amusing. It is as if this new perspective was so powerful that it was hard to imagine how best to employ it. In the era of sexual freedom, one woman cited in the article wonders if she should have an affair because she is frustrated about a lack-luster sex life with husband Maynard. She puzzles: What is more impor-tant, her sexual needs or her commitment to Maynard? Another couple wonders if they should give up their cabin cruiser to pay for their daughter to attend an expensive private college—or keep it and send her to the local college. These debates seem to miss more pressing issues about equality in relationships, personal identity, life goals, shar-ing household responsibilities. But to help readers handle this intoxi-cating new freedom and the tough decisions that inevitably lay ahead, a Denver psychologist offered a list of guidelines to help one distinguish self-assertion from selfishness. At the heart of the guidelines is some-thing we consider less and less today: How will our behavior affect oth-ers? What will be the consequences of the decision? Will we cause a little annoyance or real emotional trauma?

Our questions today are not about others but about ourselves. Are we getting what we want and need? Are we living up to our potential? Are our relationships hurting or helping us? This makes it a confusing time for forging strong bonds. How much should we give up—and for whom? If we bend too easily, we're being used or are losing face. Our "self-esteem" is in trouble. High self-regard, after all, has become syn-onymous with success, power, and assertiveness. Instead of fitting our wants into context, we expect to consider our needs above all. So how much room and weight to give our relationships? Friends are evaluated: Is this worthwhile, or am I giving more than I'm getting? Potential partners are scrutinized: Will that person give me what I want? Does he/she have the right looks? The right lifestyle? A comfortable standard of living? What if you want to live in California and your partner is wedded to the East Coast: Who gives in? Do you have a commuter rela-tionship? Converse via e-mail? Break up and find what you're looking for nearby? And then there's family. What if your mom, who's getting older and lives halfway across the country, suddenly needs more care: What do you do? Give up your job? Hire someone? Have her move closer to you? Put her in a nursing home?

These are not easy questions, but they are everyday questions. The need—as well as the pleasure—of giving to another is made harder in our times because it is often colored as weakness, not strength. As a cul-ture, we don't advertise the pleasure that comes from some self-sacri-fice. A few years ago I interviewed a Massachusetts woman whose mother lived in Columbus, Ohio, and suffered from Parkinson's disease, a stroke, and a bleeding ulcer. Her mother wanted to stay in her home; the daughter had a job and family in Massachusetts. In the end, she respected her mother's desires, but at a cost. She flew out to care for her mother on many weekends and was daily consumed with the responsibilities of long-distance caregiving. Despite the strain, the daughter came to find real worth in her effort, in part by thinking about how much and how well her mother had cared for her as a child. "When you can turn the tables and care for someone who has cared so much for you, you feel good about that," she observed. This woman's story stayed with me, not only for the matter of caring for aging parents—something more and more of us experience—but for the message it has to my generation of parents. It made me wonder: Are we caring for our children today in a way that will make them want to care for us in the future?

People may give lip service to the cozy ideas of giving, caring, and sharing, but daily life is rife with images and attitudes that run counter to them. We yearn to avoid demands, psychic engagement, obligation; we try to "get away from it all," sealing ourselves off from the needs of others. We drink in the messages of self-indulgence, lavish success, and the intoxicating joy of self-sufficiency. In a TV ad for an American car, a father finds himself set upon by his family all talking at once. He escapes to his car, slips into the driver's seat, and shuts the door, rendering them mute. He breathes a great sigh of bliss. Isolation, we understand, is the new image of freedom. He doesn't have to drive anywhere; being alone offers pleasure enough. It is an image that cuts to our dilemma between needing to be connected and wanting to be left alone.

Autonomy

The executive who occupies the corner office of a Fortune 500 company's regional office in Boston is a woman, this day in a buttery yellow linen suit. I'll call her Caroline. She is attractive, athletic, a former college basketball player, and now, at thirty-seven, a mother of three. In many ways, she has achieved what women twenty and thirty years ago talked and theorized about. She has it all. Family, career, power.

From her seat, she sees a host of demands that sometimes seem insatiable. Yet it is easy to tell by the way she talks that Caroline is thrilled with her own success and filled with the pleasure of hard work and competition. She revels in the speed and certainty with which she moves. "I always live a hectic life and in an environment where busy is the only thing I know," she says. "My husband says, 'When are you going to sit down and relax?' I am not happy being still."

At the same time that she—like so many men and women—thrives on the adrenaline rush of jammed schedules, she acknowledges making trade-offs. And those trade-offs typically involve relationships. She relies on paid help—as many of us do—to care for her children, drive them to piano lessons, and make their lunches. She has less time for visiting friends and spending with extended family, feeling more as if she is "managing relationships" rather than really connecting. "It comes down to the way we run our lives these days, the unrelaxed, rushed format. It is hard to have very intimate relationships when you are looking at your watch," she says. And she does live by the clock. "There are very few times in my life where I say, 'Oh, the time got away from me!' I am, unfortunately, very painfully aware of the time. Time to talk, time to lis-ten, time to really communicate with family and with your whole family unit—extended family or whatever—is very, very, I don't want to say expendable, but it is being challenged a great deal. If I look at the time my husband and I spend talking, it is very, very limited."

Yet, in all this, Caroline sees the emergence of strength. She sees new rules of living that demand more flexibility and new definitions. One of the most important positive things Caroline considers in recasting her image of family is their autonomy. "I find I enjoy being able to say to my daughters, 'We're self-sufficient people. We don't need to depend on anyone,' " she says. Caroline also points out to her children that she doesn't *need* to be married but *chooses* to be married. In fact, she believes that marriage itself will become less important in the future and that, increasingly, people have "a lack of need for each other." Many would agree with her assessment, and demographics are bearing out such forecasts.

On the one hand, her frankness is refreshing. Caroline is unencum-bered by feelings of guilt for focusing so much of her life on her work—guilt that stereotypically plagues successful women. On the other hand, regardless of her gender, Caroline's vision of life, in which autonomy is valued above interdependence, sounds lonely. But in our culture today, we don't see the loneliness. We are focused on the success, the job title, and the fine home stuffed with all the things a high salary can buy.

Certainly, it's nice to be able to take care of yourself comfortably and not to be dependent on other people. The fear many have in times of crisis, illness, or old age is that we won't be able to do for ourselves and will be a burden to others. At some point, all of us must reckon with the fact that we will need to rely on others. It is, we forget, a natural thing. When we talk about autonomy, however, the greater issue is with the young and able-bodied. Those who are able seek not just independence but insularity. It is not enough to provide for the family. People want to limit the need for public goods, services—and even contact.

People build home theaters so they don't have to watch movies with strangers. Others install putting greens and—for those with the space— a few holes so they don't have to wait for a tee time. Some construct weight rooms and hire personal trainers so they can work out without interruption, when they want, and without interactions with strangers. Much of this may be superficial and for the rich, but the increasing availability and proliferation of private versions of public and commercial goods and services speaks to a desire for autonomy—even as we might find real benefits to sharing. None of us wants to wait or share if we can afford not to. This has always been true in some measure— the wealthy were the first to get telephones, private cars, and private jets—but the desire is escalating. We don't want to wait at the copy shop or make our kids compete for attention if we can afford our own machine or one-on-one tutoring. We shop online to avoid the crowds at the store. Private schools are seeing a boom, not merely because of slipping faith in public schools (which are fighting back with tougher standards and more testing in many states) but because we want the control and autonomy a tailor-made education offers. The idea of getting our own even extends to things like fundraising auctions, where some of the most popular items are "private" experiences—lunches, coffee, meetings—with local celebrities. Just about anything is better if it doesn't have to be shared.

The urge to privatize goods and experiences that were once communal may be a mark of modern life. But it is precisely such new values that threaten important connections, on a broad social level and a personal level. We may not recognize the incessant messages to "have your own" as a threat, but they are. They degrade the quality of our community and personal lives. They build walls where there were no walls. Mostly, though, we don't consider such decisions in these terms. Typically, we want our own because it's easier or faster or because it imparts special status to us. That is one of the chief challenges: Things that lead to connection and community-making are often inefficient and typically low-status because they are available to many. We choose autonomy not because we are nasty and cranky but because it is more expedient or makes us feel special.

Philosopher Richard Schmitt observes that we live in a society today that is "committed to separateness." Over and over, people choose separateness over what he terms being "in-relation." Even though people may work with others, identify themselves with a group, be married, be in love, or otherwise be engaged with others, people typically operate as separate, autonomous beings, never truly allowing themselves to mesh and become interdependent. In his book *Beyond Separateness*, Schmitt says separateness is not inherent but a choice people make. He gets at a perceptual issue about how we engage with others, not just by our physical presence but by our emotional involvement—a point that rarely hits the radar screen in polls and studies. If we know the names of some neighbors and facts about them, he seems to be asking, does that make us neighborly? We may stand with our bodies in the group circle, may have the conversation with the friend, but if we remain buried in ourselves, how can we connect?[5]

To explain the power of being in-relation, Schmitt describes acts that are not *yours* and *mine* but *ours*. He describes the power of two people in-relation as they frame a roof. One needs the other's help because the rafters are too heavy to lift alone. If one merely provides strength for the other, remaining separate, then it doesn't matter who helps. It could be Jane one day and Bob the next. If the two work together in-relation, however, they become a team far more effective than two separate individuals. In this scenario, neither is replaceable. Many of us can call to mind examples that support this distinction. Most know the feeling of appearing to be engaged with someone while remaining separate—providing strength but not the intangibles that define real teamwork.

This state, Schmitt reports, also exists in intimate relationships. People keep themselves at an emotional distance, separate, even as they profess to be united. "Separate love is very common" in marriage and partnering, says Schmitt. In such cases, he explains, "the other often is as much a creature of fantasy as a real flesh-and-blood person." Relationships today demand a challenging balance. On the one hand, you want to assert a unique and independent self, and on the other, you want to engage. Traditional gender roles made these two appear mutually exclusive; the way to engage was through one's role. I suspect, in our eagerness to flee such strict expectations, we have overreacted. We now celebrate autonomy and boldly seek to be our "own person." Much as our therapists may applaud, Schmitt argues the flaws in elevating such values. We are, he mourns, becoming *too autonomous*. We're disconnecting from others, growing excessively self-consumed. "The autonomous person is self-centered in so far as her or his decisions are always the most decisive sources of choice and action," he says. "Nothing else—moral obligations, prior promises, love or desire—can overrule the careful, deliberate and rational choices of the autonomous person. But the autonomous person is self-centered in another way: The decisions that shape his or her life are never joint decisions made with another."

The autonomous person, unswayed by emotions and demands of others, ultimately lives alone, struggles alone, makes choices alone. When this happens, others remain on the periphery of our lives. The notion of ourselves—alone—at the center of our decisions affects how we operate socially. The self, he seems to suggest, is all that the autonomous person trusts. All other things, whether love, marriage, or hope, are unreliable. In the end, if we are separate—and not in-relation—we can never truly become part of a community, a marriage, a family, a network of friends. Clearly, this is not how we all operate at all times. Schmitt's separateness, though, warns of a new norm, a state in which we look like we're connecting while our hearts and minds are held back.

The state Schmitt describes may seem stark and extreme, but some of the situations that play out in people's personal lives suggest that our society does value autonomy over connection. Many people today fear commitment and seek no-strings-attached relationships. Some choose commuter and e-mail marriages. Some families gather just once a year—or less. People leave home early and work late. It is a matter of practice that career-climbers take the new job and move—again, and again, and again. Friends promise to get together but don't make the time. People put off calling and fail to visit. Every day, often without consciously considering it, we make choices about how we will relate—or not relate—to the people in our lives.

Sadly, dropping a relationship or, more typically, merely letting it wither away is hardly a noteworthy event. Even important relationships can be lost without more than a little regret. The loss probably deserves more acknowledgment. A very close friend of mine has an admirable habit of never allowing relationships to wither. If a friendship ends, it ends. She writes a letter to clarify and close the relationship. It may be a rather unusual practice, but there is something both bold and tender about it. Friendships, her practice suggests, are too valuable to give over to neglect. If there is a parting of ways, let's acknowledge the parting. For the rest of us—myself included—relationships fade and disappear with little acknowledged mourning. They die of starvation, lacking fresh encounters and experiences to keep them alive. The schedule's too jammed to make time. Besides, relationships distract from the stuff you have to get done. A Robert Mankoff cartoon in the *New Yorker* shows a man at an office desk talking into the phone. He could be speaking to his wife, friend, ex-lover, business associate, brother, sister, mother, father, or his own child. "No need to remind me," he says into the receiver. "I'm well aware that I've forgotten completely about you."

Family

Mere mention of the word "family" evokes cozy images so reliably that political rhetoric calling for the restoration of "family values" seems universally understood. Family, we have come to accept, is everything that is good, stable, and loving. Perhaps this modern belief has its roots in the Victorian era, when the family was viewed as the moral classroom of society, the place where admirable values were modeled and instilled. Despite the milk-and-honey public image, we know family has a dark and complicated side, a side written about in literature, woven into movies, blurted out in sensational news stories, but hardly acknowledged in everyday life. At its most basic, the family gives individuals a sense of identity, lineage, and belonging. At its best, family is an anchor in tragedy, a cheering section in victory, and a place where support and love are unconditional. But what we mean by "family" has changed through the ages, from generations collected under a roof to the 1950s nuclear hyper-ideal to what amounts today to a chosen composition of loved ones.

Now when we speak of "family" we often do so with quotation marks around the label, suggesting that blood relation is not an exclusive nor implicit ticket to admission. We like to believe, whether it is true or not, that we can create our own families, a network of people we care for and care about. What's notable here is the belief that *we may choose*. If Uncle Ed drives you crazy—forget him. He's out. But if your friend Helen is your intimate, your buddy, she's in. The malleability of family has its benefits and drawbacks. On the upside, we are now free— in practical terms—from folks who get on our nerves. There is no requirement to extend yourself to unpleasant relations. More than ever before, we regulate the terms and conditions of familial relationships. The downside is that we are all more alone, granted no guarantee of kinship by right of birth. We cannot presume familial support, aid, comfort, or even company.

This has not happened overnight but over years. There is today more space between kin. We are less intimately involved in each other's lives. We don't live on top of one another. We don't sit around each other's kitchen tables, don't often know the composition of one another's days or thoughts. Some of this represents a real freedom from an era of family lives so intensely intertwined that one felt constantly watched, judged, and talked about, even stifled. But there is more to the story than yearning for the beautiful fresh breath of freedom. We have done more than carve out our own personal space. We have altered our familial relations, placing our individual wants and needs not merely a notch above familial duty but far out front. In *The Grapes of Wrath*, Ma Joad mourns not just the hunger and deprivation that haunt the Joads' futile hunt for a living wage but the loss of the one thing they do have: each other. "We're crackin' up, Tom," she says. "There ain't no fambly now." Ma Joad speaks the words, can see the dissolution and mourn it. We see only the sparkle of progress and upward mobility. Why is it that family has become so hard to be around? Why is it that, far from chewing the fat and telling stories, we feel anxious when too many gather in our living room and stay too long?

The SkyMall advertisement in the in-flight magazine peddles what someone has imagined is family closeness: signing up for a family Website with its own e-mail, chat rooms, news, and—of course—the chance to purchase all kinds of customized products. The ad copy lures with the simple observation: "Your brother lives in Winnemucca. You don't want to visit Winnemucca." The message is that you want to be connected, but the effort of face-to-face visits is just too much (aside from the implication that your bro's chosen home isn't a draw). The solution, the ad suggests, is to fulfill visitation duties online. And, naturally, online "family" is a matter not of blood but of your selection. Even if Uncle Ed is plugged in, if you don't select him, he may be out of luck.

The idea of defining family not by blood but by choice seems second nature. When families are far-flung, it takes effort to visit or phone. There is no need to "have it out"; you can just pretend the out-of-favor relative doesn't exist. We choose by our actions who is in our family and who is left out. As with pleas for nonprofit donations, we may select our level of membership. Figures from the General Social Survey, an annual sampling of Americans, show more than 40 percent of adult children live *within a half hour's travel time* of their fathers. Nonetheless, the majority of respondents visit with their fathers only sporadically—choosing as answers "at least once a month," "several times a year," or "less often." Those answering "less often" than several times a year constituted the largest single group of respondents—one in five—while those reporting daily visits with fathers were the smallest group: 8 percent of all respondents. While mothers fared better with more frequent visits, similar patterns surfaced in figures on siblings. Brothers and sisters most often reported visiting "several times a year" or "less often," even though many reported living within an hour's travel time of the sibling.

Other figures from the General Social Survey show that between 1978 and 1994 the number of people spending the least time socializing with family rose dramatically. Over that time, the percentage of people who said they spent a social evening with their parents only "about once a year" or "never" rose from 15 to 25 percent. Those who spent a social evening with a brother or sister "about once a year" or "never" rose from about one-quarter to about one-third of respondents.

What's important here is that it's not so shocking. Of course we are too busy to be popping in every day or week to see Dad, Mom, Brother, or Sis. We have our own lives. But that is just the point: Our lives are our own. They are not part of a family web that includes our sphere. Many of us today consider this a wonderful feature of our times—living without family eyeing your every move—but the flip side to such freedom is that family is a less integral part of our lives. Those who live near family know the benefits of babysitting, of having someone to call in case of emergency, when the basement is flooding or the washing machine breaks. While this is a benefit of physical proximity, more important than the human equivalent of AAA roadside assistance is the less tangible lift that familial contact offers: a sense of belonging.

When I first began working on ideas that would lead to this book, I spoke with a man named Ed DeMarrais. He understood what I was talking about and explained to me what I sensed better than I could have done myself. He described the changes he saw in his own life, family, and home. He recalled life in the three-decker in Jersey City where he grew up surrounded by family. On Sundays, his Aunt Grace, who lived downstairs, put out rolls and cold cuts. Uncle Arthur arrived with crates of fruit. Aunt Helen came with her husband and six children. The house would be ringing with the laughter of children and the voices of adults talking politics in the kitchen.

"It was just so intensely exciting," DeMarrais, a retired insurance manager, said of those Sundays more than a half century ago. He still dreams about that house and those gatherings. But the adults who bantered by the warmth of the coal stove have passed on. The cousins have all gone their own ways. And when he looks around the neighborhood where he has lived since 1964, he sees a far quieter place than the Jersey block where neighbors moved from stoop to stoop, talking their way down the row houses on a summer evening. Quieter than when his kids made the DeMarrais house the neighborhood social center. Now it is hard to get to know other people, even though he tries. He helps one elderly woman pick up debris in her yard; he shovels snow for another. Mostly, though, he no longer hears the sounds of families and neighbors visiting one another. "I just see little groups of people living alone," he says.

His point—that we don't visit anymore on Sundays, or anytime, for that matter—has since been echoed by others, who have recalled for me this now defunct weekly ritual of visiting. Not only did such contact draw families together, but it provided a stage for passing on stories and knowledge. Today, we do not know each other as well. We don't take time for long conversations. We don't tell stories; we don't value the knack for turning the stuff of everyday life into news, insight, and entertainment.

We are also harder on family members today, more quick to judge and exclude. Like special prosecutors, we feel the need to review our lives and the roles of various relations, then render an indictment. It is not enough to make our own choices in life; we reserve the right to hold family members responsible for our failures. While both the news and real life are peppered with stories of derelict and selfish parents, and politicians everywhere along the spectrum find fault with abandonment and abuse, it is troubling to see the eagerness with which we seek to assign blame. The rise of the therapeutic culture, essential in helping some deal with wretched home lives, abuse, and neglect, or even mere uncertainty, has also invited an exhausting scrutiny of parents, siblings, and kin. Adult unhappiness, defects, and struggles can now be traced to the behavior of others. We may sit in judgment completely on our own terms, with our memories serving as the evidence. We alone render the final judgment, a verdict that allows us to hold others accountable—at least in our own conception—for dire wrongs. In the end, the court of family fault is so highly charged, the dockets so full, that relations are being sorely strained. The expectation of being judged by children is so great that one friend jokes about selling insurance to parents of infants and toddlers to cover the cost of future therapy sessions.

This is not a condemnation of therapy, which serves an important and even critical role for many people in need. This is merely an observation about what many take from it. Perhaps I'm biased. It was his therapist my father cited one evening in his small Brooklyn apartment when he looked up and said by way of severing our relationship: "Sorry, kiddo, but I'm just not into being your father." This was not so much a shock to my twenty-one-year-old sensibilities as confirmation of a stunning belief on his part: that he could *choose* whether or not to be a father. My experience is not so unusual. And my father is not at the starting point nor the endpoint of an unraveled family. In my own extended family there are siblings who have not spoken in years, cousins who are lost to each other, other children estranged from other fathers. "We're not a very close family," my paternal grandfather said one Sunday on the telephone. "But there's nothing we can do about that now." Indeed, I have no feeling, no time, no use for my father anymore in my life. Cousins, once close, are dispersed and no longer known. There is no connection, only the faintest curiosity.

In life there seems a chasm between the "family" of public dialogue and the family we experience in private. Because this is America, a land of stories of triumph and new beginnings, we yearn to have such histories of our own—even as we demand our distance and our freedom. We do, despite the trouble relations can cause, want to be connected, not just in the present, but down through generations. We do want roots. Today, for many of us, those roots seem tenuous, thinned to a hair's width. The thirst to build family connections to the past—and future—has become an important pursuit. Just a few decades ago, we looked obsessively ahead, hungry for all that was new. From the styling of cars to the razing of old buildings, sleeker and fresher was better. Today, we hold the opposite sensibility. We consider the old precious. We restore historic homes; some spend thousands of dollars researching original paint colors. We orchestrate genealogical searches and chart family trees.

The desire to have a family, to feel that sense of history and connection, is driving us to create what we long for. In my case, the lack of a cohesive extended family has self-consciously drawn my three siblings and me to labor to create a big old family anew. We preserve things. My brother transferred 1970s Super 8 movies to video. We take more pictures, and instead of stuffing them in shoeboxes—as my mom did when we were kids—my brother and I in particular are meticulous about keeping up our photo albums. It is if we are proving our existence as a family, not just to ourselves but to generations we imagine coming after.

The danger in our quest—one shared by many today—is that the urge to package and smooth out the rough edges is strong. I want a history more coherent than the one I inherited. I imagine family gatherings that Martha Stewart and the editors of *Bon Appetit* would look on with envy. And, this being the consumer age, we can purchase the means for making our lives appear that way. No wonder scrapbooks, elaborately decorated and self-consciously created as future heirlooms, are all the rage. Edit out the troubles, the struggles, the cutting remarks. Create the history you want to have. One student at Harvard, so dedicated to her scrapbook, admitted to planning events just so she could record them. I am guilty, too. Even though I enjoy apple picking, I have trouble seeing it as anything other than one big photo op. And what of the birthday party entertainers who pause from their work and point out to parents that *this* is the moment to snap, *this* is the well-practiced image they will want to look back on?

More than our desire for connection, we seem to crave perfection. But we risk recording junk, creating the illusion of family connection without the substance. We risk gathering in the online chat room and leaving the living room vacant. Family relationships are built on stories and experiences, on knowing not just what someone tells you but what you see and understand from being together. We may paste up scrapbooks, fall prey to desires to collect china and silver worthy of being heirlooms, but only deep knowing is really worth being passed on. What is to be saved?

On a long car ride, my younger daughter demanded, "Mommy, tell me a story about when you were little." I tell and tell and tell. And then I ask her, at four, to tell me a story about *her* childhood. For some reason, she always tells the same one: about making muffins on Mother's Day, bringing them upstairs to me, and then cuddling up in bed to eat them and drink juice. My children, in their minds and hearts, imagine themselves part of a huge family, the most recent chapter of an ongoing history. They tick off the members, they weave them into everyday descriptions, they decide college plans years away because they imagine Aunt Margaret will be their professor and grandmother "Hush" will visit every Sunday for brunch. For them, there is little more comforting than the security of being part of something so grand as their family. What is family? It is, I think, what we decide to make of it.

Family II

The nuclear family—whatever that really means anymore— is today grappling with questions of connection, self-definition, and history-making. What is a family? How do we stay connected? And how can we create a future? The family may feel itself these days in a rather inchoate stage of formation, breaking new ground and making sense of the old. But from the outside, the family unit itself appears clad in a hard outer shell. More than ever before, the family appears as a closed unit set down in a neighborhood or community. The family is an entity unto itself, a self-contained refuge from the outside world, the keeper of "family values."

The family and the home, whose once-permeable borders made for the back-and-forth flow of cooperation with the school, church, and community, is now a closed shop. Homes are less open to inspection. We know less and less about what it is like behind other people's doors, what beliefs our neighbors hold, what sits on their kitchen table at dinnertime. We learn about families from the media, the feature story on the news or in the magazine, and not from firsthand knowing.

It was not always so. The Puritan family, historians and communication theorists tell us, did not operate as a private unit but as an outpost, a department of civic and religious government. Single adults were ordered by the courts to live in family households. Living alone was thought to undermine a consensus of beliefs, whereas the family enforced and upheld community thought and practice.[6]

The family and home continued in a similar role through the nineteenth century and well into the twentieth, albeit with some alterations. The notion of family as societal adjunct was especially apparent in the raising of children. Parents were reminded that they were not merely rearing their own progeny but bringing up future citizens. Articles like "The Power of Home Influence" in the January 1851 issue of *Mother's Assistant, Young Lady's Friend and Family Manual*, a women's magazine of the day, were typical. They browbeat parents about the importance of teaching good lessons at home to complement lessons at school. Failure at home, parents were warned, meant failure in the school—not just for their child but for the whole school. "A home characterized by ignorance, ill-manners, insubordination, slovenliness and uncleanliness, will make such traits upon the youthful inmates and send their children to the common school with those traits upon them," the author warns. The preachy tone would be unacceptable today, in part because parents are not agents of the school or the community. Yet for parents in 1851 the reminders were constant: The family is one link in the chain, and the whole community depends on the quality of the home life. "Other things being equal," the article states, "the common school will be what those homes are."

We can follow this home-school-community connection into the twentieth century with the birth of the home economics movement. Although concerns about health, cleanliness, and food safety dominated, course curriculums reflect a desire to teach children—girls and boys—about their roles as adults, parents, and members of a community. Courses included lessons on practical skills as well as behavior, including public etiquette, childcare, and running a home.

A required course in Tulsa's high school in 1930, for example, taught units on how to live in a family, the "social significance of the home," and the workings of the community, including the "board of health, milk supply, water supply and sewerage system." It seems silly today to think of teaching children about the sewerage system, but this reflects a belief of the time that young adults needed to understand not only how to live within the home but how home life meshed with community life. A 1925 home economics curriculum for the Denver schools taught boys "the foundation for right living." The aim, according to a government report, was to "give the boy a realization of the meaning and value of homemaking, the important part it plays in citizenship of the community and the Nation, and to develop him into an appreciative member of his household." It is an ambitious agenda, one that explicitly draws the connection between the home and the rest of the world.[7]

Such courses did not imply parents and others were relinquishing their duties. On the contrary. Surveys sought comments from parents to be certain school lessons meshed with home teaching. Other organizations, too, made youth part of their agenda. In Boston, on May 1 and 2, 1934, parents, school officials, health professionals, clergy, and other leaders gathered for a symposium, "The Problems of Youth as Challenge to the Home, Church, School, and Community." According to conference notes, the themes sounded stressed joint responsibility for helping youths adjust in a changing world, one that had plunged into the Great Depression and was headed for war. "The Home, isolated, is not equipped to meet the present situation," one speaker observed.

Even as the end of World War II brought what now seems to be a frightening sense of order to family life (at least on the surface), efforts continued to emphasize the family-community link. A 1958 study of junior high home economics programs showed that a major goal was "to give boys and girls experiences to help them become more satisfactory family members." The report goes on to describe courses that rely on the family unit as the foundation upon which society was built. Given such links, schools had a real interest in making sure youths understood their future responsibilities.[8]

These are not the lessons we hear about today. The emphasis is no longer on the family as part of the community. The goal is to equip individuals for survival in the wilderness of society. One teacher described her challenge: making students understand that a nice car, home, and designer clothes don't just happen. You have to work—and hard—to buy them, and not just any job will yield that kind of lifestyle. "Many aren't aware of what's happening in the real world," observed a high school counselor and teacher who organized a life skills course at a vocational-technical school in western Massachusetts. "You throw out ten thousand dollars, and that seems like a lot of money." But, she says, it takes practical discussions to get at what that amount of money will pay for. "They say, 'I want a Jeep.' We will say, 'Those cars cost X amount.'" While home economics courses still do teach about dating, childcare, relationships, and nutrition—staples for decades—there are more urgent lessons about sexual harassment and acquiring job skills. There is much youths must learn to make it on their own.

Such a focus on survival needs reflects what we have seen elsewhere: a rising emphasis on the individual and a diminished focus on forging and maintaining connections. More critical to youths today than the operation of the sewer system is what jobs pay and how much it costs to live. How can they chart a course that will lead them to personal success and happiness? Thinking about how our lives meld with others isn't as important as it once was. And lessons on getting along are not about etiquette and personal duty but more likely lessons given by the local police department on conflict resolution: Talk before you punch—or shoot.

Our society has moved from the "we" to the "I," from the family as a subunit to the family as its own closed circle. This is not wholly a negative development, but it is a change that has implications for community and connection. Families today are free and independent agents. People pay taxes so they can have municipal services. There is little sense of obligation to serve on town boards, to volunteer in the schools, even to vote in local elections. We are not communing but consuming. We pay, therefore we get schools, fire, police, trash pickup, snow removal, street sweeping, parks. As Robert Bellah and his colleagues observe in *Habits of the Heart*, "the family is no longer an integral part of the larger moral ecology tying the individual to the community, church and nation. The family is the core of the private sphere, whose aim is not to link individuals to the public world, but to avoid it as far as possible."[9]

Then there is the fact that more people today are finding themselves alone—and not part of a family unit at all. Again, this is not a negative or a positive, but it is a development that reflects our changed focus. Many people who in a different era might have endured horrible unions are free to end them—or to avoid them in the first place. Score one for personal well-being. At the same time, though, the very fact of a rising single population means that more people are spending more of their lives alone.

The Single Life

When Cindy Nigro, a hospital neurology and neurosurgery nurse case manager, who is forty-four, bought a dining room table several years ago, her mom was puzzled. "She said, 'But your husband will buy you one,'" recalls Nigro, who pointed out that even though she wasn't married, she still needed a place to eat her meals. When she then bought a three-bedroom house, her mother wondered aloud whether this wasn't something she would want to choose with her husband. But what really baffled Mom was when Nigro purchased a strand of pearls. "She said, 'Oh, but that's what your husband gives you for a wedding present!'" says Nigro. "She just didn't understand."

Nigro's mom didn't understand that the rules had changed. That unmarried women can buy dining room tables, homes, pearls, and much more for themselves. That single men can handle quite nicely the household tasks once viewed as the domain of wives. And that these superficial shifts in lifestyle are signs of a broader change: It has become socially acceptable—and increasingly popular—to live alone. It is all right to be single at an age when many people traditionally have been married.

More people today are single, either by choice or chance, than at any other time in history. In a dramatic departure from the past, there are today as many single-person households as there are households of married couples with children. Between 1960 and 1995, single-person households rose from 13 to 25 percent of the total, while households of married couples with children dropped from 44 to 25 percent, according to the U.S. Census Bureau. And census projections suggest the number of people living alone will increase 12.8 percent between 2000 and 2010, even as the population at large increases only 8.4 percent.

The numbers, in part, reflect an aging population and the rising number of single older women. Higher divorce rates contribute to the rise. So does the increased acceptance of gays and lesbians, which means many people no longer marry as a way of camouflaging or repressing their sexual orientation. But one big factor is the decision of many people to postpone marriage—sometimes indefinitely. For example, according to the Census Bureau, nearly half of single women and three-quarters of single men are twenty-five to sixty-four years old, the years during which people have traditionally been married. In 1995, there were forty-four million never-married adults in the United States, or 23 percent of the over-eighteen population, up from 16 percent in 1970. And the projections for the numbers of people living alone show a greater percentage increase in the population twenty-five to sixty-four years old than in the sixty-five-plus population.[10]

The numbers represent not just a demographic shift but a cultural shift. If Abraham Lincoln's father needed a new wife in order to survive in the wilderness after his first wife died, there are no such mandates today. As Caroline, the Fortune 500 executive, observed, we are experiencing "a lack of need for each other." The forces that once drew people into marriage are exerting less influence. Women have more economic freedom. Society is less uptight about sex outside of marriage. Medical advances make it more possible than ever for single women to mother and raise children. Profoundly, too, there is more caution today around coupling. It's not just high divorce rates but a feeling that, as individuals, we need to be all we can be. The quest for self-actualization can make the compromises of marriage seem unnecessary, even burdensome.

While most single people tell researchers they hope to marry at some point, the threshold for tying the knot has risen. In a 1980 study of sixty-six single women age thirty and older, fewer than one-third (29 percent) of those interviewed said they wished to be married; 11 percent had no desire for marriage, and 60 percent said "it depends." A 1996 study interviewed more than two hundred single, heterosexual adults about their desire for marriage and their reasons for being single. Respondents recorded a median score of 4.04 on a seven-point scale, reflecting "only moderate desire for marriage." The most frequent reason given for being single was that respondents hadn't met the right person. The second most common reason—the respondent doesn't often meet potential partners—endorses what singles say anecdotally and what another study bears out as the fallout of social changes in recent years. The next three reasons deal with the positive aspects of being single, and the next three concern difficulty establishing a relationship, worry that the relationship will fail, or fears about commitment.[11]

The message here is that marriage can be nice but is not an essential event in life. What is striking in interviews with singles today is the tone of calm that surrounds their status. It is a welcome contrast to the frenzy of the 1980s when popular media stories painted single women as desperate beings eager, but unlikely, to marry after a certain age. Today, single men and women are viewed as another constituency and not merely as solo dwellers lacking a mate. Marriage is a choice, and it can happen at any age—or not. As one single forty-three-year-old woman who was adopting a child observed about the timing of her decision, "I can probably always get married. But I can't always have children." And Newsweek included in a special issue called "Tomorrow's Child" a sidebar headlined "I Do, I Do—Maybe." The subject? "Grow up, buy a house, have a kid—and perhaps a wedding. Why marriage may be optional." All this stands in marked contrast to 1942, when results of a youth survey revealed that 90 percent of high school senior boys and 93 percent of girls expected to marry. What's more, 75 percent of boys and 94 percent of girls expected it to happen by the time they reached twenty-five![12]

It's obvious that much has changed. If the numbers have been slowly seesawing in favor of singledom, however, it is only more recently that we have come to embrace this change—and see how it is reshaping the rest of society. The rising number of single people, of course, is not a matter of interest to singles alone. It reflects a changed sensibility about coupling, about the role of the individual, and about the status of marriage in our society. More pointedly, it affects how all of us live. More single people means more focus on the individual, by everyone from TV sitcom writers to human resources departments and niche marketers. It means that we increasingly live in a society that offers the single option. That means that even people who are not single may act singly. More than ever before, it is socially acceptable and easier to dine solo—or sit at the bar, get a movie ticket, or take a vacation.

Consider that workplaces that once offered "work/family" benefits now offer "work/life" benefits, a change made in response to frustrated single employees and married employees without children who were bearing the burden so parents could leave work early—or on time—to pick up children from daycare or to relieve a babysitter. Singles wanted the same flexibility working parents were getting, but they wanted to use their time not for fetching children but going to the gym or socializing with friends. Why should they lose out on flexible work plans just because they don't have children?

The voice of the single person is also being heard in advertising. Ads for products once marketed to families are being repositioned. A radio commercial for deli meats in 1998 had two singles planning sandwich dinners. They meet in line, discuss the features of the cold cuts, and flirt. The message is that this product, once sold as a staple of the family set (remember the Oscar Mayer jingle?), is now food for the solo diner. Other food manufacturers in recent years have offered more single-serve packaging for foods. And a recent television ad for Volvo depicts a single man driving a Cross Country station wagon to a remote spot to go canoeing. Once sold as the quintessential family car, the Volvo station wagon is now the individual's vehicle for exploring both real and emotional terrain. Nowadays, observed one advertising executive at

Hill, Holliday, Connors, Cosmopulos, "marketing is no longer alienating singles" by pitching products to couples and families. But increasing images of single people in advertising does not merely aim to
address the uncoupled. It is a conscious effort to speak with all of us—
regardless of relationship status—as individuals. We are singles all, for
purposes of selling many products and services. Much as television has
moved closer to us in recent decades, so has advertising, speaking today
to us directly. It is a far cry from the first advertising, which tentatively
announced the availability of goods or services. Ads now aim to be like
a pampering conscience whispering messages of deserving indulgence.
Go ahead, you deserve it! You're special! Treat yourself!

The messages are not of personal sacrifice but personal gratification,
and what gratifies is personal, *individual* attention. This has fed the
movement toward the customization of just about everything under the
sun. A world away from Henry Ford's edict that customers could have
any color car they wanted as long as it was black, we today want what
we want. Jeans can now be custom-made. Newspapers offer subscribers
the choice of customizing delivery schedules; no more choosing five
days, seven days, or weekends. Everywhere you turn, whether it's the
espresso bar or the ad for PCs, we're being told we can—and should—
have it made just for us. Perhaps that's why reruns of the classic *Saturday Night Live* restaurant skit with Dan Aykroyd and John Belushi
translating every customer's order into "cheeseburger, cheeseburger,
cheeseburger" have lost nothing to time.

The trend toward serving individuals one at a time instead of en
masse may have sprung from other roots, but the notion of customization caters to the same instinct that makes us careful in selecting a
potential mate. When life is viewed one-at-a-time, everything is more
precious, more needful of consideration. If mates were once chosen
based on economics and from a fairly homogeneous pool, where one
eligible partner was as good as a number of others, we are today exploring every color and pattern we might get in a mate. Do you want someone who likes rock climbing or stamp collecting? Urbanite or
suburbanite? Earring or nose ring? Or neither? And that's just the surface stuff. For some the search is exhausting, frustrating, and demoralizing. Yet people still search.

People may be putting off marriage, but the institution isn't being
scorned altogether. Most still do want to fall in love—just not with the
wrong person. "People are being more and more cautious about whom

they decide to spend the rest of their life with," says Mitch Ribak, president of the Singles Resource Network, an online dating service, and a veteran of the dating service industry. "It's not that they don't think love is possible. It's that they don't think it is permanent."

We live in a world where there are few certainties and fewer things that last. Whether we are talking about jobs, appliances, computers, or relationships, the value of durability that dominated in the early twentieth century has given way to an expectation that all things break or become obsolete. This mindset, when applied to the human heart, demands caution for self-preservation. Coupled with the fact that we have all become conditioned to inventing and reinventing ourselves, it is hard anymore to know whom you can trust or what you can believe. There is nothing so sexy, I realized while glimpsing an attractive man wearing a clerical collar on a soap opera, as a moral man. Or woman. The world (like daytime drama) is full of charlatans and deceivers. The notion of someone dedicated to doing what is right is extremely attractive, even arousing. This is not to say that clerics are the answer—examples from Chaucer to Jim Bakker make us know better—but it is to suggest that there is enormous appeal in honesty and forthrightness. And it is not an accident that such values feel rich now.

The challenge for those who want to couple is how to meet the partner of our dreams. Today, after all, we seek not just someone who will serve well as a mate but someone who will fulfill our ideal. As Bellah and colleagues put it, marriage has become an "individual quest for psychological gratification." What we want—as in so many other matters of our lives—is to have our needs met. In other times and places, people put less pressure on marriage. It was a civil agreement; passion and romance were something else altogether. In considering the subject in 1949, Earl Kennel observed that marriage was a limited pairing: "A wife or a husband is voluntarily chosen—but the choice is ordinarily made for reasons which have little to do with spiritual or mental needs." Yet what we look for today *is* spiritual and material, mental and physical. We want it all. And, we are told, we deserve to have it.[13]

Talk to singles or read what researchers write, though, and you find that it is harder to meet people. It's not just that we want more but that the way we live today makes it more difficult to find a mate. A more complex society, sociologists argue, means there are "fewer traditional, interpersonal routes available to individuals." The old networks that people once relied on to hook them up with the love of their life have simply broken down. Extended family, church acquaintances, and long-time neighbors are no longer matchmakers. The workplace is one of the few social environments that persist for meeting mates. But overall, there are fewer social interactions and occasions for meeting partners—especially once you have left school or if you work on your own. The modern solution, popularized in the late 1980s and 1990s, is personal ads and dating services. These businesses are flourishing, and as more people meet this way it has become a socially acceptable way to partner. But it fundamentally changes the way we approach potential mates. Instead of being hooked up by someone who knows us both or being struck by someone in a chance moment of meeting, we are left to develop wish lists of traits that can be put down on a form. In the end, we have personal ads that read like catalogue copy and dating profiles that look like advertisements. We don't look for love; we shop for it.[14]

"People think they can get exactly what they want," says Ribak, the online dating service president. "They say, 'I want someone five foot one and a hundred and ten pounds,' but is that really important in the scheme of life?" Certainly, many don't pursue such rigid expectations, but even so, the basis on which we decide who interests us and who doesn't has become indistinguishable from the way we think about stuff we want to buy. The ads encourage the illusion that finding a mate is a matter of choosing the right color, size, styles, smoking or non. That's what we have to compare. The online profile of Bobby says he's five foot eight, 165 pounds, brown eyes, brown hair, forty, a never-married nonsmoker who wants children and loves sushi, Super Bowl parties, and romantic walks. Or try out Fran. He's five foot eight, too, 160 pounds, blue eyes, brown hair, thirty-nine, never married, non-smoker, doesn't follow professional sports, enjoys shopping and working with his hands. Hmm. Maybe someone taller? More literary? More exotic? Why shouldn't we get what we want? God knows, we certainly deserve to. Just like shopping online, the profiles offer the option "Click to select this person" or, if not, "Click to start a new search."

No wonder more of us stay single. We may long for the Cinderella–Prince Charming scenario, but as with an extended shopping trip that leaves you drained, jaded, and sick of looking at merchandise, it's tough to keep going when the quest seems endless and disappointing. Maybe there are no jeans that fit comfortably and look great. Maybe there is no one. Ribak says many frustrated seekers simply "settle" at some point because the urge for coupling or marriage and children is great. But many, too, find that there's plenty of company and no stigma in going it alone.

Friends

Our greater expectations are not limited to quests for love. Friendship—that precious but often ill-defined relationship—is being tested in these times, too. There are no neatly rendered academic explorations that clarify the route of friendship on the map of human relations, but clues that spill out suggest we simply are not as available to each other as either we once were or, more critically, we now need to be. As one twenty-seven-year-old man in the insurance business observed during an interview: "I often pine for what is perceived as the 'old way' of doing things: seeing your friends once a week, cocktails every Friday at someone's house." Instead, he says, he often finds himself feeling spent after a long week and doesn't make the effort to see friends. "When you get home on a Friday night, you don't always want to go out to dinner with someone where you have to be 'up,'" he says. "It is so much easier to play cards with myself."

Whether it is lack of time, motivation, or something else altogether, polls suggest this young man is not unique. A Roper Starch poll of two thousand adults found that between 1983 and 1994 the median number of friends people reported seeing in the previous two weeks fell from 6 to 5.3. And time-use researchers John Robinson and Geoffrey Godbey, who have tracked Americans' use of time for three decades, concluded that while much about the way we spend time has remained about the same, there is one notable shift: We now watch more TV and socialize less.[15]

Certainly, the structure of people's interactions with friends has grown more formal. Showing up uninvited, once routine practice among friends and neighbors, today is considered rude. Getting together now requires negotiation and planning. You have to find a mutually agreeable time on the planner and—of course—a purpose. Whether the stated aim is to catch up, have coffee, eat lunch, discuss a problem, shop for something, or go to a movie, just as with a good business meeting, people like get-togethers to have an agenda. There's nothing wrong with this, but it feeds a different, more formal brand of interaction. It also says something about the need to control the reach and demand of friendships. We have, in a sense, become a society of more private people, more careful about the face we present, even to our closest friends.

For the most part, this behavior is not meant as malicious or manipulative. People subject friendships to schedules because they need to. Many of us today are busy and feel pressured for time. As a society, we can no longer handle it when someone unexpectedly gobbles up an hour of the day without warning. Indeed, many of us grow uneasy when someone unexpectedly takes a few minutes. Even if we could afford the time, we are conditioned to stick to a schedule, even a mental one. This makes time, in effect, a currency for measuring the value of relationships. How much is Greta worth? How much is Arnie? Who makes the sacrifice to travel to whom? Time pressures lead us to prioritize and evaluate friendships with an eye toward efficiency. We may not discuss this frankly, but we are all keenly aware of the system. We anticipate that when we see someone unexpectedly, he may not want to stop and talk. If he does stop, we are left to wonder: Who will say "I've got to run" first? He who does holds the power. Time pressures have created a kind of pecking order of friendship akin to what has long existed in the business world. You have all the time in the world for the boss or the customer but little for those beneath you.

Sociologist Carroll Bourg says one of the great impediments to friendship today is the speed of life. Bourg, who has studied loneliness in the elderly and those facing divorce and separation, says people don't take enough time to let meaningful relationships flower—relationships that make people feel connected. "The speed at which we do things doesn't allow much time to meander or saunter. We don't even use those words anymore," he says. "We use quick words, speedy words. People have the experience of forgetting in a moment of distraction and not saying what they wanted to say because the time is so short."[16]

Conversation is one critical vehicle for knowing others and knowing ourselves. It is often in the midst of deep talk that we uncover some small truth or new insight about ourselves. Yet such talk has become endangered. The images described in the Simon and Garfunkel song "The Dangling Conversation," images of a "now-late-afternoon" of slowly consumed coffee, lengthening shadows, and talk that picks up, falls off, and picks up again, now seem dated and hopelessly romantic. We don't converse today so much as embrace the e-mail form of talking: We spit out our point like a press release and wait for a reply. Conversation makes us more vulnerable—something we like to avoid—because it is an act of mutual construction. Minds change, ideas are argued and recast. There are great spurts of insight that catch two people in a rush of shared vision. There is something exciting about a good conversation, something that builds intimacy—not the intimacy of revelation but the intimacy of understanding. It is that understanding that is so critical to well-being. Doesn't each of us want a friend to know us, care about us, and be in our corner?

A great deal has been written about friendship by poets, writers, and scholars. Some is romantic, some practical advice. Much is an effort to define what, exactly, we mean when we call someone a friend. Sociologists have long tried to figure out why people become friends, what elevates someone to status of "best friend," and how same-sex friendships differ between men and women. Not surprisingly, researchers struggle with this inquiry, reaching different conclusions. All agree on one point: Friendship is hard to explain in numbers or theories.

Despite such problems, some studies do hit on relevant ideas. Some research has considered the formation of friendships around activities: tennis friends, golf friends, book-group friends. Others have studied friendships by developing lists of important qualities. And research looking at male and female friendships has found that, despite stereotyped differences, men and women want essentially the same things from their bonds. Many of us know from experience that it's sometimes hard to explain why someone becomes a friend. There are also different levels of friendship, with a select few making it into the inner circle. Some of us have hundreds we call friends. Some of us bestow that label on only a few. Despite so many variables, critical questions remain about how we conduct our friendships today. What do we want?

One answer comes in the pages of popular magazines, which routinely discuss friendship and have for years. In looking at articles on the same subject—What makes a really good friendship?—published between 1951 and 1997, it's possible to make a few observations about the way we view this bond. Several articles over this time span draw nearly identical conclusions about what's important in a good friendship: loyalty, acts of kindness, sharing—the same things researchers find again and again. But what evolves over the time span is the angle and the tone.

A 1951 article in *Woman's Day* focuses on the substance of friend interactions, advising on the importance of being supportive and noncritical. "We know all too well how we stumble and fall and do the wrong thing and wreck our dreams," the article reads. "But let our consciences or our enemies tell us—not our friends." Articles from 1975 in *Woman's Day* and *Seventeen* detail the art of making and keeping friends, with heavy emphasis on how one should behave. In the *Seventeen* article, for example, substantive issues like the importance of honesty between friends is given much focus. One sixteen-year-old girl observes about her friend that "when one of us is busy or preoccupied we don't feel inhibited about saying we're unavailable. I'm a non-stop talker sometimes. Just last Sunday I asked Pat if I could come over and tell her about my date the night before. She said she'd love to get together, but couldn't. There was a big exam coming up the next day. A casual friend might have been uncomfortable about putting me off. But we're straight enough with each other so we don't have to put on airs." It's a pretty sophisticated observation about a friendship from a teen. The observations aren't nearly so thoughtful in a 1985 *Seventeen* article profiling "six picture-perfect pairs" of best friends along with a list of tips on how to make friends—and what behavior will lose them.

By 1996, an article in *Cosmopolitan* is keying into a new problem: that we aren't putting enough effort into our friendships. The article, "Little Things Mean a Lot," is an admonishment to stop slacking off and make the effort to be friendly—even though you may be horribly busy. "Sending a card, photo, funny fax . . . Asking for an update on her job search . . . These and other gestures are so simple, show you care—Why aren't you *doing* them?" the teaser reads. The article is full of anecdotes and advice sympathizing with how hard it is to maintain relationships while pressing the reader to try harder. The tips—keeping tissues handy for a bawling co-worker chewed out by a boss, slipping a candy bar into the interoffice envelope with your overdue expense report ("Heath bars are flat and travel well")—feel more like a superficial script than a thoughtful consideration about what it takes to build meaningful bonds. They are directions on strategies of "friendliness" for personal gain rather than insights on *being* a friend.

For the younger set, the August 1997 issue of *Teen* magazine addresses the issue of friendship in a quiz, but the focus shifts. The headline reads, "How Good Are Your Friends?" The aim of the quiz is to figure out if your friends are "Users, losers or the best buds a girl could have." The catch here is that the questions—and the possible answers—seem shamelessly sassy. There is no room for the honesty that was so important to friendships in the 1975 article. Question 3: "Your parents decide to take a family day trip to the beach. When you ask your pal to come along, she: (A) says sure, then offers to bring snacks. (B) rolls her eyes—there's no way she'd be caught dead with your folks. (C) declines, but asks if you could take her kid sister along—that way she won't be stuck babysitting." Answers to other questions offer a dichotomy of rude behavior (friend flirts shamelessly with a guy you're interested in after she said you didn't have a chance) or excessive self-sacrifice (friend bakes a cake to congratulate you on being named yearbook editor—the post *she* wanted). The possibilities suggest a polarized view of relationships: Either you are using her or she is using you.

There are no questions about how friends make you feel or about how well you connect and what you share. It is not about mutuality but about getting service—but not too much or she'll be classified as needy (in which case you should "cut her loose—or at least see less of her"). Taken together, over time, the articles talk less and less about the meaning and value of bonds and more about how to *collect* friends. We move from more thoughtful considerations to glib tips. The articles are, of course, just articles and a brief anecdotal look, not a scientific sampling. But they do seem to reflect a bigger picture. We desire friends as much as always, but we may be struggling more to grant them space in our lives. The *image* of connection can too easily substitute for the real thing.[17]

What friends offer—beyond the superficial—is human closeness. It is this desire for emotional connection that surfaces again and again in research on friendship. In a 1996 study, researchers from the University of Washington wanted to find out, among other things, what people meant by "closeness" when describing friendships. Strikingly, 71 percent considered self-disclosure as a defining characteristic—about twice the percentage that listed any other characteristic, including providing help and support, having shared interests, comfort and ease of getting along, trust, frequent interaction, or length of friendship.[18]

What we seem to want from close friends is an opportunity to bond emotionally, to share deep personal issues and have someone to listen and empathize with our daily traumas. The idea of baring our souls to friends—making confessions—echoes broader trends in our culture. Much has been said and written about the huge popularity of confessional stories, memoirs, pop songs, talk shows. As a society, we have a burning need to speak our most personal stories. The rise of a therapeutic culture—and the language that goes with it—has given many people a tool for translating pain into narrative. For some, this is an incredibly helpful, even lifesaving development. But the real work of legitimate therapy often gets lost in the popularized version, which offers more ways of talking about ourselves and blaming others for our faults. No wonder therapy-speak is so often parodied. No one wants to be a codependent enabler.

The current fashion for baring secrets is a dramatic contrast to decades ago when the inclination was to keep quiet, especially about problems or anything unseemly. Today, the more unseemly the experience, the better the story. Material gathered by researchers Ida David-off and Marjorie Platt and stored at the Murray Research Center at Radcliffe chronicles the lives of two generations of college-educated women. In the data set are interviews with twenty-five women in 1978 that include questions about their social lives. Although the sample was small, one thing emerged as I pored over data and read transcripts: These women had a lot of social contact—but the contact appeared much less intimate than we'd expect from friends today. Notations from the interviewers make observations that paint a group of very outwardly social women. Comments abound like "R [respondent] has a wonderful 'sense of community'" or "she likes time to herself and finds herself having to fend off social invitations" or "this is a woman who cares about people in every part of her life." Another woman observed that she enjoyed supermarket shopping: "I meet people I know and it's so friendly."

The women belonged to, on average, 2.68 clubs or church groups and reported being friendly with "many" or "several" neighbors, whom they typically visited several times a month (only one respondent said she "never" visited with neighbors). This group also socialized frequently with friends. More than half said they got together with friends *once a week or more*. Only five reported having no "close" friends, while eleven said they had "several" and nine reported having "a few." Interestingly, though, when asked how often they discussed their problems with close friends, thirteen responded "rarely" or "never," while twelve said they "sometimes" did. None said they frequently turned to close friends to talk about their troubles—what today seems one of the essential duties of a close friend.

We expect our friends to be our confessors. It is a role that can be a burden, especially in an age when there appears so much to confess. Yet self-revelation has become central to close friendships. If you have lunch

with a close friend you haven't seen face to face in some time, it is a virtual imperative that neither of you can leave the table until you've both
revealed *something*. Such a drive for intimacy is both touching and
potentially superficial. It is endearing that so many people want to share
information about themselves with friends—certainly an improvement
from a time when people kept troubles to themselves, preferring to pepper Betty with questions about her new fudge recipe. But the eagerness
for self-revelation risks replacing a more valuable way of knowing a close
friend: observation through experience. When you spend time with
someone, you notice things about her. You develop an independent picture that may or may not agree with her own assessment. Without this
time, the information is shallower. The friend's self-reporting becomes
the only basis for our knowing her. Certainly, on some level this seems
very natural and obvious. Self-revelation *is* an important aspect of close
friendships. But when we come to know friends *chiefly* by what they tell
us about themselves and not by what *we discover from being with them*, it
produces a rather thin relationship. Although I am a person who puts
great stock in words, in my own friendships I notice the importance of
observation. As I watch my friend Maureen helping my elder daughter
make a cat's cradle from string, it tells me more about her than anything
she could say herself. She has brought the string and they are working
together, Maureen perhaps not realizing that she is teaching my rather
impatient child about patience.

Pornographic Self-Revelation

There is an important role for self-revelation in friendship.
But this rather special event—revealing private information—has
become utterly common and overused as a shortcut to friendship or
friendship-like encounters. People we hardly know—or don't know at
all—seek the friendship equivalent of the one-night stand. What is the
aim? To win attention or empathy? To feel connection (if only for a
moment)? To be listened to or have someone validate his or her existence? What's most interesting to me is that at this time in our history
so many people want to be heard—and loved. I read it as a desperate
reach for company, for understanding. But it is weak and awkward.
Instant intimacy ultimately feels false.

A "Hers" column in the *New York Times Magazine* for June 12, 1994,
by Martha Gershun is headlined "Presumed Intimate." The essay is

about the intimate secrets revealed by the writer's lunch companion, among them details about the other woman's luck with conception, specifics of her ovulation, her current daycare situation, and the stupidity of her previous boss. Unfortunately, the lunch companion was a woman the writer had met thirty minutes earlier and was meeting over lunch "to discuss how her company could better serve my company's direct-mailing of promotional materials to prospective students." Eek. The woman is trying to act like a friend, using private information as a currency for buying closeness, even just an hour's worth.

A *New York Times* headline writer coined a phrase for the plague of strangers spilling their innermost secrets: "the urge to blurt." It's always an uncomfortable scene when you are trapped on a plane or train or in a line next to someone who feels you're the perfect person to unload on. No one wants to hear the details of a stranger's affair, operation, or plans to enter psychotherapy. And yet giving in to this "urge to blurt" has become something of a commonplace event. Is it because it's safe to tell intimacies to a stranger? Is there more to lose if you tell someone in your life who matters? Or do we simply have fewer people to tell things to? We may be years and studies away from getting an answer—if there is one. But if the why is not so clear, the fallout of such behavior is easier to imagine. As Doug Marlette pleaded in a 1996 column in *Esquire*, "Why can't we all take our pain and our suffering and our gotta-be-me-ness back into the closet?" He describes the discomfort of a job interview with an editor who disclosed that his wife had run off with his best friend and who later showed off "art photos" of naked children fondling their genitals: "His clunky peek-a-boo self-revelations, like the trench-coat flashings of a dirty old man, were his idea of what it means to open up, to connect."[19]

This culture of self-revelation *is* obscene: secrets bared as a come-on, a quick route to the climax of connection. In "The Ecstasy of Communication," Jean Baudrillard describes a culture in which so much is revealed that private space—true privacy—is lost. The media make the most intimate details of our lives public, and "the entire universe comes to unfold arbitrarily on your domestic screen." It is, he says, "like a microscopic pornography of the universe, useless, excessive, just like the sexual close-up in a porno film." We are at once eager for communion but too hurried and nervous to allow it to flower. In the end, we act out the pornography of excessive self-revelation, in which all is open, revealed, and beckoning. There are no taboos, no secrets that cannot be spoken. We can talk dirty in the studio of the Ricki Lake show, air our family secrets on TV, and tell of our psychic angst to whomever will listen. We'll talk about Bill Clinton's penis again and again and again until a penis *is* no different than a cigar or any other ordinary physical object. The turning out of everything we keep within challenges our very ability to have—even to understand the meaning and value of—intimacy. We ache for closeness, for others to penetrate our being, but our desperation too often shows, and the act of consummation is hollow. In these instances, we are not joining, not connecting, but merely rubbing up against one another. In the end, we are left exhausted and alone. There is no shortcut to brotherhood, connections, love, or friendship, no candy bars slipped into reports or truths revealed that can replace knowing through experience. A sixty-eight-year-old woman described to me what she meant by a good friend: someone who knows how you like your coffee without having to ask.[20]

Strained Relations

We want to connect, to have lives rich with family, friends, neighbors, and lovers. There is no doubt about our desires. What is troubling is that for all the attention we pay these subjects, we seem to be slipping further and further from each other. We want, but on our terms. We love the notion of caring, sharing, and knowing others, but we long to steal off and be alone—away from everyone and everything. The family unit is no longer part of a community web but is our private retreat, retrofitted with the means to render interaction with the rest of the world unnecessary.

We have moved from a society in which the group was more important than the individual to one in which the central figure is the self. Even when we are with others, we remain apart, psychologically separate. From the ashes of duty we have risen to claim not merely a healthy dose of freedom but individual supremacy. It is our life's mission to achieve and make ourselves happy. We want success, power, and recognition. We want to be able to buy or command caring, respect, and attention. And today so many of us feel deserving of the service and luxuries once accorded a privileged few. We may live in a more egalitarian society, but we have become puffed full of our own self-worth.

In concrete terms, in the past few decades we have seen an America in which there is less tangible connection between individuals. We see friends less often. We socialize less and watch TV more. We visit less with kin. More of us live alone. Marriage is a goal for fewer and fewer. The studies, the polls, and the anecdotes point to what the Fortune 500 executive observed: We are developing "a lack of need for each other."

We are not blind to this. In the hunger for connection, we grab at shortcuts, quick ways to bond. Some people embrace the electronic as the easy way to do the hard work of visiting, talking, being in someone else's presence and not entirely in control. Others believe they have cracked the code of intimacy in self-revelation (either that or their needs are spilling out willy-nilly). If we tell everything, we believe we are close. Isn't that the very *definition* of connection? In the end, those intimate blurts and the disembodied stabs at managing relationships the quick way leave us going through the motions but taking little sustenance from our bonds. Good love—platonic or erotic—grows with time and effort. People fall into the familiar motions, acting out the role of friend, brother, sister, lover, daughter, son, parent, spouse, neighbor. But it's harder to feel the weight, density, and security that those relationships can have. Too eager for gratification, more of us are left momentarily rosy-cheeked but ultimately alone.

 **us**

The article in the November 1945 issue of *Seventeen* magazine begins ominously. The headline poses the provocative question "Who's a Black Sheep?" We learn in the first paragraph that "Mary J." is fifteen and a half, cute, with "soft brown hair [that] floats around her shoulders," brown eyes, and a "darling button nose." But she wears her clothes too tight. And she wears so much lipstick and mascara that "they add to her weight."

Mary's story is a tale of the transformation of a lonely high school kid into a "bad" girl. A year ago, Mary and her family moved to a new city from a small town, and she doesn't fit in. She is unable to impress classmates, unable to "roll off the kind of glib small talk the city high school crowd used." With no friends and little connection, Mary starts hanging out at the bus terminal "just so she could be in the middle of a crowd and not feel so terribly alone." One night, a sailor speaks to her (he seems lonely, too). The two of them go out for a Coke and to listen to music. Harmless, you say?

Not so, we learn. (This was 1945, after all.) Mary stays out too late and is picked up for vagrancy. She is "hauled into court," bringing embarrassment to her family. Neighbors whisper. Her parents try to keep her at home, but she sneaks out of the house. She meets up with other sailors and men from the factories. Soon, she drops out of school and takes a factory job. One night, she's picked up for prostitution. She is given only probation, but trouble looms. Mary J. "learned to be cagey so the police wouldn't get her again—the next time the court wouldn't be so lenient—but Mary was sliding downhill fast."

Ba-dum.

This anecdotal lead is standard journalistic stuff, a way to get the reader hooked into the story and focused on the subject at hand. If it were written today, we would anticipate the next few paragraphs—the "nut," in journalistic lingo—to drive home the message of the piece. We would expect to be warned: Don't *be* Mary J. We would want tips on combating the loneliness that comes when you move to a new place and don't fit in. In other words, we would expect the writer to warn us about a potential problem and help us to safeguard ourselves against it. Good solid news you can use.

This story doesn't go like that. This story is—or was then—directed to each of us, but it poses a question foreign to magazine readers today: What could *you* have done to help Mary J.? This is not self-help but self-involvement. The reader is scolded about the problems facing teens: crime and pregnancy and out-of-wedlock births. "You know there's no point in pretending the problem doesn't exist," the writer prods. "You *know* it exists; you know that it concerns you, the boy up the street, the girl who works next to you in chem lab, and your brother who's being demobilized any day now."

Again and again, the article hits the messages of responsibility and involvement. "Without your help, there can be no answer. What can you do?" the writer demands, even outlining a "ten-point program" to follow. Readers are urged to "watch out for classmates who look unhappy or underfed. Reach out to the extra slow, the truants and the chronic school-haters." And, they are advised, "it might be a good idea to invite the distressed teen to dinner and a talk with your mother."

The suggestions may seem overly intrusive by today's standards, but there is no confusing the tone or intent of the article. "Don't misunderstand," the writer drives home. "You have a responsibility to your town and to your neighbors." *You have a responsibility.*

The story was written at a time of dramatic change, as World War II was ending and the future seemed potentially bright but uncertain. Other articles written during this time urge people of all ages to do what is described as one's civic duty—looking out for others, even going out of your way to help. The magazine writing at this time assumes a sense of "we-ness," a collective "us" that today strikes the ear as a foreign chord. The notion that it is our *job* to help someone like Mary J. has become alien.

There are many reasons for this. To be sure, the war effort heightened and more clearly delineated social responsibilities. And roles in general were stricter and more stringently defined a half century ago. As Robert

Wuthnow writes in *Loose Connections,* social relations have now become porous. People, pressed for time, view involvement not as a matter of customary expectations but as a matter of personal choice with details to be deliberated and negotiated. As a result, he points out, the picture of activism doesn't look the way it did in the 1950s, 1960s, or 1970s, with people channeling civic energy into well-defined roles with local civic organizations. The nature of involvement has changed. That's one reason, Wuthnow says, that people have a sense that something is amiss. So how can we tell if Americans are more or less involved in civic life today? Are the new ways of networking and connecting as effective as the old? Are virtual communities real enough? Can looser connections still make us feel a part of things? Do we have the close ties we need?[1]

The questions are tough, but critical to ask. The answers today may be harder to discern. What's clear is that regardless of how you view the new social order—that it's falling apart or merely reformatted—there is little doubt that we are more driven by individual needs and desires. We use the words "we" and "us," but the sense has changed. The "we" of today is not a part of a social network with unspoken duties and responsibilities. Our "we" is us—individuals. An observer, a demographer, an ad agency may look at poll numbers and notice how much we share, how similarly we act, how nicely we fit into predictable demographic and socioeconomic slots. And yet *we* don't feel it. Sure, we think people who drive the same car we do are probably more upstanding people than those who drive a make we would never buy. But even as the similar taste sounds a demographic *ding!* the more profound belief in a common fate fades. We choose our own road. It's not our job to pull over and rescue the Mary J.'s of the world, or even, if we can help it, to think about them at all.

There may be a million logical reasons to explain why fewer of us are joining the Kiwanis or the Rotary Club. What is more troubling and essential is how ghettoized our perceptions have become, how quickly and eagerly we retreat into online newsgroups and virtual communities of specialized interests and like-minded others. We seek connection in validation. A humorous but telling article by Elayne Rapping in the December 1996 *Progressive,* "Burrowing Within," suggests that Baby Boomers once so strongly identified with seeking social change are now absorbed in their insular worlds of lawn care, home goods, baby paraphernalia, and personal health and fitness. She cites a *New York Times* headline for an article on increased cosmetic sales to aging female boomers as emblematic: "They Once Wanted to Transform the World; Now They Settle for a Personal Makeover." The image is of a generation turning inward, drawing efforts and energies closer to themselves. Although some research suggests that widespread social activism in the 1960s was a myth—activities were really carried out by a few—the fact remains that the perception of mass involvement fed a sense of shared community. Song lyrics spoke of people as "brothers" and "sisters," and messages of peace and love, even if somewhat superficial, nonetheless elevated those values in public consciousness. Today, our values and our images are very different. The tone of public life is of disinterested detachment. There is less concern for things that affect us collectively, more for things that touch our lives personally.

Fewer and fewer of us read newspapers, an activity that has been linked to civic involvement, or follow major national and international stories. The Pew Research Center for the People and the Press tracks public attentiveness to major news stories. In December 1998, for example, the center found that more people paid close attention to reports of unseasonably warm weather patterns (news that affects us personally) than to the impeachment inquiry against President Bill Clinton (news that affects us collectively). And in an analysis from the 1940s to the present, a Pew Center report observes that, contrary to past eras, people under thirty registered less interest than their elders did in 92 of 110 major news stories. They also scored significantly lower when quizzed about current events. "Those under thirty know less than younger people once did, and they are less interested in what's happening in the larger world around them," the report says.[2]

Declining interest in the collective experience shows up in other places, too, including in our senses of public and personal well-being. These are prosperous times we live in, and most people recognize that. But there is a schism between how people report feeling about their own lives and about the community, society, and nation. Even as we express to pollsters contentment with our personal lot, we express a dwindling optimism about society and a declining sense of trust in government, many institutions, the media, and our fellow citizens. In other words, our vision and our happiness today are solo, confined to the immediacy of our personal experience. We speak of the importance of civic engagement, volunteering, voting, and community participation, but our lives are conceived more and more as solitary pursuits. Even the high drama of the 2000 election only drew 51 percent of eligible voters to the polls, according to tallies by Curtis Gans at the Committee for the Study of the American Electorate in Washington, D.C. The widespread ordinary connection seen in the sense of civic duty that was part of the landscape in 1945 is vanishing.

For about four decades, polls conducted by the Pew Research Center have asked Americans to evaluate their own lives and the state of the nation. In 1996, Americans judged their personal lives much as they have always done in good economic times, expressing optimism for the future and a feeling of satisfaction with their financial stability, health, and family life. But, according to the Pew report of these results, what is most noteworthy is that even as the "public's self-evaluation is very familiar, its appraisal of the *nation* is strikingly different. Americans are much less positive about the state of the country than they have been in fifteen years, and they are even more pessimistic about the prospects for 'national progress.' " Despite a strong economy, Americans rate the state of the nation as being nearly as low as in bad economic times or, as the report notes, in the wake of the demoralizing Watergate scandal in April 1974.

This notion—that individuals are separating their own lot from the lot of the public—also surfaces in figures from the General Social Survey. When respondents were asked about their level of satisfaction with family life, friendships, marriages, and their own general happiness, the trend between 1973 and 1994 showed people just slightly less satisfied than previously. Figures for personal happiness slipped only slightly lower, with increasing numbers reporting themselves "pretty happy" instead of "very happy." Satisfaction with family life and friends declined slightly as well. But the percentage of those reporting a "very great deal" of satisfaction with the city or place they live—the community at large—declined to its lowest level in more than twenty years, with only 15.7 percent expressing the highest level of satisfaction, down from 23 percent. The changes are not dramatic, scale-straining swings, but they are, in question after question, consistent. The picture that emerges is a quiet one, a portrait of a slowly changing state of affairs. It is precisely this consistency and this glacial pace of change that makes it so important to observe. Small shifts, over time, change everything.

If our own happiness is a little less robust these days, our faith in institutions, the glue that holds our society together, is more dramatically on the downswing. Among the questions I find most interesting are those about trust. Trust, after all, cuts to how we view others. While many questions purport to be about fact—questions, for example, on church attendance, which some now believe are tainted by people overstating their religious devotion—questions of trust are about perception, about what is in our hearts. Between 1972 and 1994, the portion of the population who felt others generally could be trusted fell from nearly a half to about one-third. That means that most of us—nearly two-thirds—don't feel we can trust our fellow citizens.

Trust in the media and in institutions of government has also dwindled over the years. The percentage of those answering "hardly any" when asked how much confidence they have in various institutions has increased dramatically in recent decades. Those reporting "hardly any" confidence in the press rose from 15 to 40 percent between 1973 and 1996. Respondents reporting "hardly any" confidence in the executive branch of the federal government rose from 19 to 43 percent over the same time; figures for Congress rose from 15 to 44 percent. These are dramatic numbers. People also expressed an increased lack of confidence in education. The numbers suggest that key institutions—institutions relied upon to create a sense of fair play, to promote unity, and to support public debate—are losing their ability to engage all citizens. Increasingly, they are perceived not as vehicles for collective conversation but as means for a few to have a voice. Those institutions whose confidence levels stayed about the same or rose are those typically removed from people's day-to-day public experience: the military, the Supreme Court, and the scientific community. In the end, what's so striking is not just how dramatically confidence in some sectors has dwindled but how many Americans express "hardly any" confidence in institutions that just a few decades ago were critical to a sense of shared purpose and destiny. Even if any glue remains—and it may, in newer but less discernible forms—the long-standing visible elements of a national life are coming unstuck.

Hail Mary

Two social institutions that have traditionally brought people together, sports and religion, today struggle to command the level of loyalty and dedication from followers and fans that was once taken for granted. We'll talk sports first. To be sure, there have been some wonderful highlights in the sports world recently, including the 1999 World Cup victory and the U.S. women's soccer team. The grassroots excite-

ment that filled stadiums with fans and talk-radio airwaves with boos-
terism caught the sportswriters off guard. The women's team was
refreshing, a feel-good story amid the disillusionment that clouds many
glamour sports. The women's teamwork and competitive verve was a
contrast to what usually commands sports headlines: lockouts, walkouts,
salary disputes, tantrums, and bad off-field and off-court behavior.

At their best, sports can bring strangers together. It is no mere cliché
that they give many men and women who follow them an instant tool
for striking up a conversation. When the Red Sox with pitcher Pedro
Martinez advanced in the 1999 playoffs, all of Boston was behind them.
One day while I was walking through Filene's, a department store, I
stopped and asked a man who was moving display tables—one of the
people we're not supposed to see or notice—about the end of the
game; I'd fallen asleep and missed it. My question brought him to life
and prompted a fifteen-minute back-and-forth. I left the conversation
feeling uplifted, human. In New York, the same thing was happening.
Yankees fans and Mets fans communed over the triumphs of their
teams.

Still, the power of sports as a unifying force is being sorely tested. In
some manner, sports have always been a dirty business, but today the
unseemliness is harder to ignore. On the professional level, battles for
new stadiums, more lucrative deals for players, and fights for broadcast
rights (not to mention the concessions made to accommodate TV)
mean that more of what we read, think, and hear about sports is about
political maneuvering and complaining. Franchises are good or bad
because of how much they can spend, not because of some magic that
happens when a team of athletes and a coach set their sights on playing
well. Good teams like the Dallas Cowboys are "less a sports team than
a brand name," observed writer Eyal Press. The notion of sport as
heroic is growing rare. True, one cannot take away the high-fives we do
over the raw beauty of a stunning completed pass or a no-hitter, but this
is being overshadowed by a mess of bad feeling. Players spit at umpires.
Coaches get thrown out of games. Fans throw trash onto the field
because they are unhappy with the referee's calls.[3]

And bad behavior is not limited to the pros. Most anyone involved
with children's sports, from Little League to Saturday morning soccer,
knows the rudeness, even violence, that erupts between parents on the
sidelines. We seem to forget that this is a game, meant for enjoyment
and that "team experience" we declare so essential to building kids' self-

esteem. This is not to say many teams don't promote positive experiences. They do. But the innocence of amateur athletics is being sorely challenged.

At the college level, as in the pros, some of the threat comes from money. Thad Williamson, a writer and lifelong fan of University of North Carolina basketball, mourns that the team and the college basketball he loves are being consumed by commercialism. "In college arenas the best seats are now routinely reserved not for students and die-hard fans but for big-money boosters and private donors to the universities," he writes. "The arenas themselves are being turned into prime-time advertising venues: Georgia Tech's revamped Alexander Memorial Coliseum, for example, goes so far as to place the McDonald's trademark *M* on the floor." There are also pacts with companies like Nike to provide athletic gear, and television contracts, whose broadcast deals and demands for commercial time-outs are lengthening the games.[4]

The nostalgia we have for athletics is powerful, but the images of great physical feats, of beating great odds, or of being noble in defeat pale in comparison to the way games really look today. The idea of cheering for the home team, of having real loyalty, is even growing scarce. Yes, we cheer when they play well, but when they lose, we grow angry and abandon the team. It is wearying to listen to the complaints of disgruntled fans who call in to sports talk shows. Sports *can* draw us together. But it is an increasingly fragile togetherness, one that can turn with a bad play, a bad trade, or a losing season.

A similar fragility marks our relationship with another important social institution: organized religion. Belonging to and participating in a church or synagogue community was once a basic, taken-for-granted connection. You move to a new home, you locate your new church or synagogue. This still happens, of course, but organized religion is playing a smaller role in people's lives. Although a 1999 poll shows that 39 percent of people say they attend church weekly—a figure that has been remarkably stable for three decades—findings show people less tightly connected to those institutions. More than half of respondents said religions have "unnecessary rules and responsibilities," and 45 percent said they pay more attention to their own views and the views of others than they do to God and religious teachings. Nearly one-third identified themselves as "spiritual, but not religious," including 20 percent of those who declared religion "very important" in their life.[5]

There is a powerful hunger today for spiritual connection. It has prompted some people who spent years away from organized religion to find their way back. It has driven a rise in enrollments in seminaries and theological schools as former bankers, business executives, teachers, engineers, doctors, lawyers—people from all walks of life—seek meaning and connection in a society that offers less and less. It is also what draws people to join organizations like the Promise Keepers, to tune in to *The 700 Club*, and to send money to TV evangelists.

The outward bulge of interest in religion is not necessarily about serving God, however, or even about serving other people. It may instead be rooted in the quest for *personal* fulfillment. Research by University of California professor Wade Clark Roof, author of *A Generation of Seekers: The Spiritual Journeys of the Baby Boom Generation*, found that 20 percent of Baby Boomers returning to the church after having not attended for years feel that since "people have God within them, churches aren't really necessary." The interest is in finding personal inner peace, not in participating in religious community, which requires self-sacrifice and seeks adherence to particular teachings. This very issue, in fact, has made leaders at religious graduate institutions wary when looking at candidates for matriculation. As a result, applicants go through strict screening processes. At Pope John XXIII Seminary in Weston, Massachusetts, for example, the president and rector made it a point to say, when I interviewed him, that applicants may have a dozen interviews and be put through a screening process that lasts for months. "This is not a place to come just to satisfy one's own spiritual quest," he told me.[6]

Many more of us, however, *are* seeking ways to satisfy a spiritual quest. To that end, people want to be able to pick and choose among religious practices and traditions to find something that suits them. Roof describes a woman who grew up in an upper-middle-class Jewish family in the 1960s. Since her teen years, she has explored many spiritual practices, including holistic health, macrobiotics, Zen Buddhism, Native American rituals, and New Age philosophies. As Roof writes, "she dislikes any kind of religion that gets in the way of her more expansive views of unity with people, nature, and animals." She fills the feeling of void in her life with celebrations that draw from a variety of religious and spiritual sources. "She is thinking of organizing a Seder that uses new versions of the Haggadah that incorporate global and feminist themes," writes Roof.

Increasingly, the message is that most of us believe in God (86 percent, according to Gallup), but many of us don't want to go to church or conform to religious teachings. We want more flexibility and convenience. This urge has given a rise to online "churches" and prayer Websites, the most audacious of which claims to connect computer users directly to God.

Some are suspicious of online religion. "It is comfortable, convenient religion, completely individualized: Just go on the Web and pray," said Anne Foerst, a Lutheran theologian who teaches at the Massachusetts Institute of Technology. "Religion should be about commitment and community and self-doubt." Indeed, online religion can feel rather thin, even lonely. In logging on to the Amen Christian Online Church one day, I found myself the only chatter in "the Lounge." While I waited to commune, a rather discordant ad distracted at the top of the screen. "Slap me silly," read the come-on. Maybe I should have. I thought about clicking and asking for some prayers, but something stopped me. The whole thing—as well as visits to a few other online church sites— just felt bogus.[7]

Perhaps I'm being too critical. Personally, I find nothing wrong with the eclectic spirituality or religion that many practice today. But we must recognize that it is fundamentally different from the kind of serious religious commitment that once drew people into dedicated and tightly knit communities. Many people, of course, carry on going to church the way people always have. For some—my older neighbors who are very involved in church life are an example—church is an important social and service connection that both makes demands and offers real community. But for many others of us, church attendance— when we go—is about feeling good. Or it may be about exposing children to a tradition. It may be about personal joy, about being around other people (people whom you may not know), or about hearing something that inspires you. While there is nothing wrong with this, it remains an individual experience, consumed in the presence of others but not *with* others. There is something moving and appealing about the ritual of a religious service, but without connection to others, it is just a good show. Today, we are not missionaries but mercenaries seeking self-awareness and meaning. This is not bad (and it may be good and essential), but it means that religion cannot be the social glue it once was.

And the church is not alone. Many of the institutions we once relied on have grown weak, their strength attenuated by the drive for individualism and by a constellation of new, less communal values. But this has not been wholly negative. The greater recognition of individual values, rights, and differences has also pushed important social strides in recent decades. In many ways we are a more just people, more fervent about embracing values of equity and fairness, more concerned about the environment and animals other than humans. We have rules to ensure that people with handicaps have equal access to public places, jobs, and schools. In our classrooms, we teach tolerance and respect for sexual, racial, religious, and cultural differences.

Yet there is hypocrisy in the progress. Despite a belief in tolerance and understanding as a society, as individuals we trust less and fear more. People readily call on lawyers to address disagreements once worked out on their own. People vote less often, follow the news less, care less about what's happening in Washington. In public, we demand more, drive more aggressively, and forget our manners. Incivility, 89 percent of Americans polled told *U.S. News and World Report* in 1996, is a "serious problem." We talk about community, about connecting with others and being a part of things. But increasingly the "we" we envision is a virtual we, an imagined cohort of comrades, each involved in a private struggle, each loath to be actually engaged or obligated to throw his lot in with everyone else. Too often, the "us" of today is singular.[8]

Insecurity

The question of trust is not merely an abstract issue but is central to how we feel about our society and how connected we feel to others. Since each of us deems himself or herself trustworthy (I assume), being able to trust others implies a relationship, even if it exists only in theory and is never activated. Believing that the other person would do the right thing, help out, or be reliable is comforting. It offers peace of mind and allows us to identify with the other person because, presumably, he or she is also trusting us. On the other hand, not trusting implies the need for caution, protection, even defense.

The belief that people could be trusted, in fact, is one of the Good Old Days ideals people love to talk about. This doesn't mean people today are uniformly untrustworthy; it's just that we can't rely on them to be, well, reliable. When I returned to my car yesterday afternoon, after leaving it parked in a Cambridge garage all day, my heart skipped a beat when I saw that I'd locked it all right, but the metal clip of the seatbelt was caught in the door and it never completely closed. I'd left the car open all day. Sadly, my first assumption was not that I'd made a mistake but that somebody had broken in. Seeing the radio and everything else intact, I then marveled at how completely lucky I was to leave the car open all day and have it sitting there, untouched. Certainly, there are many times when pocketbooks, jewelry, even money are returned. But the gut assumption is that once it's lost, it's gone.

A lack of trust extends to other situations as well. People no longer expect others to be reasonable in the face of a disagreement. Teachers fret about lawsuits from students. I worry each time the New England winter coats my walkway with ice. I worry I'll be sued as my in-laws were, by someone they never knew had slipped on the sidewalk in front of their home. We are trained today to be alert and cautious. We watch our backs and protect our legal standing. Older people love to shake their heads and recall the days when people left their front doors unlocked, the car open and the key in the ignition. They remember when "sue" was a dirty word, and honorable people worked out their differences. Now people hire lawyers to do the talking and surveillance systems to make them feel safe. People install alarms and flashing lights, home security systems and motion detectors, window bars and hidden security cameras. We have million-dollar liability policies. We carry mace, learn self-defense, and expect the credit card company to call when we charge a lot all at once. Really, it's not unreasonable, these days, to watch your back.

When did it all start? It depends on whom you talk to. Many people have their private stories of betrayal. In 1977, my mother learned that it wasn't wise to leave your purse on the front seat of an unlocked car—even if it was in a small town and just for a few minutes. But for many, the bitter awakening came in 1964, in the early hours of a March morning, when a twenty-eight-year-old bar manager named Kitty Genovese was stalked and repeatedly stabbed for more than half an hour near the Kew Gardens train station in Queens. What made her brutal murder the subject of letters, editorials, and much soul-searching was that it was carried out as thirty-eight of her neighbors watched, ignoring her pleas for help. Only after she was dead did one elderly woman phone the police. News accounts and follow-ups focused on the apathy of witnesses. How could they watch and do nothing? "I didn't want to get involved," one man told police. "I was tired," another said. "I went back to bed."

It was the end of innocence. The crime galvanized a fear about the changing nature of our society. The *New York Times* wrote an editorial asking in the headline, "What Kind of People Are We?" Mayor Robert Wagner weeks later spoke out, saying that "we face an urgent need for a renewal, revival and deepening of the brotherly, the neighborly, the community spirit." His plea came after a second woman, an eighteen-year-old typist, was murdered in the Bronx as forty people ignored her screams. A. M. Rosenthal wrote a book about the Kew Gardens murder called *Thirty-eight Witnesses*, and social scientists have studied the "Genovese syndrome" for more than three decades now. But the most powerful fallout of that hideous event remains the stinging public realization that at our moment of greatest need, there may be people present but no one willing to get involved. We cannot necessarily trust others to act. We may be left utterly alone to face a fatal threat. We may also be the recipients of great human kindness and heroic action. But the Genovese killing made it a coin flip. You can't be *sure* someone will help.[9]

It is an inherently lonely realization, and it seems to rationalize the way we now operate: We expect no help, increasingly relying on ourselves for the security and protection once assumed as part of the package deal of participating in society. The fact that so many of us feel we cannot trust our fellow citizens is one factor that plays into the fear of crime. Two decades ago, this fear prompted researchers to observe that "fear of crime in the United States has become a problem as serious as crime itself"—a situation other researchers argue continues in full force today. Researchers at Tulane University and the University of Pittsburgh in 1998 published a study that focused on coping strategies around the fear of crime. They argue that many things people do on their own in the hope of preventing crime—putting bars on windows, installing security systems, not walking alone, carrying a weapon—actually *increase* one's fear of crime, because the precautions are persistent reminders of the risk of being victimized. The researchers looked at various strategies for reducing the fear of crime, and the only effective measure they found was to be in contact with neighbors. "Only neighborhood involvement significantly buffered the individual from the detrimental psychological effects of fear," they report. "This indicates the important role of active neighboring in beneficial social support."[10]

Still, the security industry is booming. It just seems easier to install window alarms and motion sensors than it does to be active and in touch with neighbors. It is little surprise, then, that even as crime rates decline to lows not seen for decades, fear of crime remains robust. In January 1999, the U.S. Department of Justice reported that the nation's murder rate for the previous year fell to its lowest level in three decades—to 20.3 murders per 100,000 population for 1997. (It was 35.5 per 100,000 in 1991.) And yet, in the same year, according to survey results in the *Sourcebook of Criminal Justice Statistics*, 23 percent of the population—nearly one-quarter—worried "very frequently" or "somewhat frequently" about being murdered. Rates for other violent crimes and property crimes also fell. Still, more than one-third of survey respondents feared being beaten up, knifed, or shot, while nearly half worried about their home being burglarized. This is not to diminish the problem of crime in our society but to suggest that some of the crippling effects of the fear may come because we are turning inward and seeking to address collective issues by building walls around ourselves. Ultimately, the walls do little but make us feel isolated and keenly aware of our vulnerability.[11]

Collective action may not end crime or address all the ills in society, but increased trust and contact might improve our psychic state and sense of well-being. A study on urban alienation that blames neighborhood disorder—trash, public drinking, unkempt homes—for feelings of perceived powerlessness among residents also found that one key in diminishing the impact of such surroundings was neighbor ties. "People who visit and talk with their neighbors and help each other out report significantly lower levels of powerlessness than do those without such ties," researchers from Ohio State University report.[12]

The idea that behavior is a potent tool in fighting urban decay and crime was the focus of research by sociologist James Q. Wilson and George L. Kelling, a Rutgers University professor of criminal justice. They found that small antisocial acts can have large consequences. Their "Broken Windows" approach, adopted by many police forces around the country, suggests that battling nuisance crimes like public drinking, graffiti, and urination can do more to improve quality of life and deter neighborhood crime than setting stings for drug kingpins. In their research, Wilson and Kelling found that once police and neighbors developed a consensus about what was—or wasn't—appropriate behavior, even troublemakers adhered to the rules. Kelling cites an instance when he saw a drunk hassling a woman in front of some other drunks. When police showed up, instead of siding with their friend, the other drunks "ridiculed him because they knew he was violating the norms."

The key here was community communication and an articulation of values. Today people hesitate to assert values publicly or to believe that we might be able to collectively agree on anything. We avoid labeling "right" and "wrong" for fear of being branded insensitive to some group's values. But in fact, as civility activists like David Gerzon, author of *A House Divided*, will tell you, people of diverse cultures and religious affiliations share many basic values. It is no coincidence, Gerzon observes, that the Golden Rule is at the heart of nearly every religious tradition in the world. More than likely, there are public values we can articulate—that is, if we can see that one way to reduce the fear of victimization and increase mutual trust is to envision ourselves not just as a collection of individuals, but as a community.[13]

Community

We are, we are told incessantly, part of a "global village." Watch TV ads for Internet services, computer networking companies, even overnight delivery services, and you see bright, smiling faces of people of varied ages and races, from far reaches of the globe. They are chatting, confiding, doing business as if they lived next door. The message is not merely that distance doesn't matter and national borders are meaningless but that we are all part of the same big happy community. We're all friends! Like the word "village," the word "community" evokes a coziness and intimacy that seem comforting in an age when we may be more physically far-flung and more dependent on new technology to do the things we have always done.

This is a useful way of making technology less frightening, even exciting, to the average person, and yet it creates confusion about what we mean by "community." The word has been overused, stretched, and worn thin. Invoking it has become a way of creating positive vibes. We think: If it's *community* he/she is talking about, then it must be a good idea and he/she must be a thoughtful, inclusive person. But in appropriating the language of community—most obviously in dealing with technology—we risk reducing its meaning in our lives.

Because the word has so many shades of definition, it is easy to apply the notion of community, with the common effort it implies, to a range of experiences. "Community" may refer to an involved and committed group of people, or it may be applied to near-strangers who share a single characteristic or job description and gather once a year in a big convention town. The word offers such flexibility, but its use evokes strong images. Think "community" and you think wholesome thoughts of people coming together to support and help one another, often involving some self-sacrifice and inconvenience. Clearly, not just any large unit of people constitutes a community. But the warm draw of the word—especially appealing at a time when we may feel anything but a part of a community—makes it a candidate for overuse.

Is an online community, for example, really a community? In recent years some researchers have concluded that virtual communities can do the same work and provide the same connections as physically located communities. Craig Calhoun of New York University argues, however, that research projects that try to demonstrate the existence of online communities are really only cultivating the "rhetoric of community." They may create a sense of belonging, he says, but in the end they are limited. They may *feel* like real communities, even sound like real communities, as people express online concern and caring. But, he argues, they are limited by some of the very characteristics that make them so appealing to people: the use of pseudonyms; the ultimately anonymous nature of encounters; the ability of participants to log on and off as they please—not necessarily as they are needed—and to focus their attention only on issues or problems that interest them. It may be a network of people, but there is little accountability.[14]

The search for online community is also, at its heart, a search for others of like interests. This is inherently different from a physically based community in which a friend, co-worker, or stranger notices you look tired or happy or are struggling to get through the day. It is different, too, from being pressed into action by witnessing a public act, or from being asked by a stranger for your opinion or your assistance. "What computer-mediated communication adds is a greater capacity to avoid public interaction that would pull one beyond one's immediate personal choices of taste and culture," says Calhoun. We may be more global, but we are more provincial as well.

This is not to say online relationships have no value. Calhoun, in fact, suggests that the Internet is a useful way to enhance existing face-to-face relationships. The screen, like other mass media, offers another way of being involved with people with whom you are already involved. But it does little to create the sense of public or social solidarity that comes when people participate in the daily acts of living with, interacting with, supporting—even merely looking at—one another. The rise of the global village or "virtual community" is a sham of language. The idea that we might experience something as intimate as community on such a massive scale is deceiving. Instead, Calhoun says, we have the sense of being directly linked into what he terms a "superpublic" that is global in scope but offers no local connection. We may communicate internationally, but we have attenuated our relationships with those nearby.

We end up belonging to and identifying with a mass market, a faceless public. We bond in our minds through orchestrated public experiences that we consume privately. We feel familiar, even intimate, with people who arrive every evening on our television screens, who speak with us every morning via radio as we shower or commute, who are faithfully online, who come alive on the big screen and whom we fret over and identify with through the pages of celebrity magazines. We love Oprah (some even expect her to handle our bills). Prepubescent girls are crazy for Leo. We rely on Don Imus to grouse and Dr. Laura to set us straight. These—and many others—are important voices in national life. But even as we identify with particular public figures, we remain alone. We may write, call in, appear in the studio audience, but it remains a one-way relationship that cannot replace local ties. And yet it seems easier to engage as part of this superpublic than as part of a real community drawn into the mess of a public experience.

Being part of the worldwide audience as Barbara Walters interviews Monica Lewinsky—and commenting afterward online—may offer the powerful feeling of communicating with the entire world, but such access does little to build community. People are eager to wear the mantle of community, quick to label nearly any gathering of people as a sign that, indeed, a sense of communal togetherness is alive and well. But as with a family, whose identity and relationships are forged in the daily rituals of living and not during the expensive Caribbean vacation, community-making is a tedious act. It is the accretion of small commonplace experiences—the seeking of advice, the shared childcare, the group project, the thoughtful response or comment, even the dull regularity of seeing the same face week after week—that gives people a belief that they can know and rely on one another and, in turn, that they can be relied upon and known.

The challenge today is to separate the rhetorical from the authentic. Community can be hard to define and easy to mimic. We may all have slightly different visions of what we believe community should be. Calhoun describes community as bringing different people together in common pursuit across lines of difference. Certainly, we don't have to love or agree with everyone in our community, but we do understand a need for each other, and—perhaps most critically—we know that our destinies are bound up with one another. We come together not always because we want to but because we need to.

What's troubling today is that many seek to avoid this coming together, preferring to make an end run around dependence by seeking private solutions to collective problems. One example that comes to mind is school. My children, husband, and I are part of an elementary school community. There are issues of academics, school discipline, safety, and test scores—among many subjects—that are best addressed as a community. How should we handle children who enter kindergarten able to read? How should we handle children who struggle with reading in second grade? Should we have more science? Such issues (and scores more) may seem familiar to many parents. Yet today, it is a struggle to get parents to view themselves as part of a collective enterprise. Some of the most able and involved parents throw themselves into their child's education—but privately. Great reader? Enroll in enrichment classes. Problem reader? Hire a personal tutor. More science? Sign up for Saturday classes at the science museum. To a degree, parents have always done this, but today it is often the first choice, not the last resort, and it is done to the detriment of a group effort. At my children's public school—featured in *Newsweek* on May 17, 1999, for its active, high-achieving population—only a dozen show up for a principal's talk on school placement or standardized testing (considered hot topics). Six or eight people show for a PTO meeting. Less than half of households returned school council surveys designed to find out what changes parents want to see at their child's school. There is a small group of active parents, but for many, many more, it is easier to take care of things yourself and avoid the rigmarole of being part of a community effort.

We don't feel our destinies bound up with one another. There is a certain amount of cutting-edge freedom in going your own way, taking care of your own issues and not leaning on anybody else. Some might even argue that efforts at community-building earlier in this century were overbearing and unnaturally scripted. Certainly, in the midst of World War II and even afterward, the hunger to build a cohesive war effort spurred a rather heavy-handed view of how people ought to behave. Throughout these years such organizations as the Public Affairs Committee, a nonprofit educational organization addressing issues of American domestic and foreign policy as well as everyday information, published pamphlets as wide-ranging as "Your Teeth— How to Save Them" and "South Africa Today." There is a certain overly wholesome flag-waving tone to the writing, yet—like the *Seventeen* magazine article on Mary J.—they offer a valuable perspective.

A 1953 pamphlet called "Let's Work Together in Community Service" describes how critical taxpayer-funded social services are, not only to the troubled Cummings family in St. Paul, Minnesota, but to the rest of us as well. "We, too, are part of a huge social laboratory endeavoring to find out what makes family relationships so unstable at times they can tilt our whole world," it reads. "We *are* affected, whether we like it or not, every time a Sarah Cummings neglects her children out of ignorance and fear . . . every time a Tatum passes on her inherited weaknesses, in or out of marriage . . . every time a Will Cummings gives up and takes his beatings lying down . . . every time a Papa 'hits the road' and the bottle simultaneously because he cannot understand or cope with his problems . . . every time a Raymond withdraws into a secret world from which he may later sally forth to retaliate on the innocent. All these ripples wash many a distant shore."

The idea that private ills wreak public vengeance is all too obvious today. Behind every schoolyard shooting or other heinous act there seems to be a tale of abuse or neglect nearly as horrifying as the crime itself. The point of the pamphlet is not merely to describe the roots of the social problem, however, but to incite the average citizen's sense of obligation to participate in the solution. "We cannot walk by on the other side of the road and let the Humpty-Dumpty families just lie there," the pamphlet exhorts. "They are people, who but for the problems which hamper them from producing an income, might be some of the rest of us."

The message is that we are all cut from the same cloth. It is the job of the community—and the community welfare councils we hear about—to help families like the Cummingses. "Nowhere, unless it is through the local community welfare councils—where health, welfare, and civic organizations, both public and private, hold up a mirror together—does the citizen see himself as a *whole man*, wholly served by a well-knit community plan."

We still serve families and individuals in need today—and perhaps more thoroughly than we did in the 1950s, even with welfare reform. The difference is that we are no longer asked to participate emotionally in the act. There may be a modern-day family like the Cummingses benefiting from programs paid for by our tax dollars, but in our own minds there is a vast space between us and them. *We* are not involved in their issues, the government is. There is no common cloth, no linking threads—one reason, perhaps, why resentment of those getting public assistance has risen over the years: We don't see ourselves as connected to them.

Robert Putnam, public policy professor at Harvard, has made much of the privatization of life experience. He observes that people don't join civic organizations much anymore, that they seek private, not public, forms of entertainment, and—his marquee example—that they increasingly bowl alone, not with others in bowling leagues. It is a provocative argument to explain what he observes as the loss of social capital, that is, the storehouse of civic energy to tackle community and social ills. Some disagree with Putnam's conclusions, but whether he is right or wrong, the question he unearths is a good one: Are we more or less involved with our fellow citizens than we used to be?[15]

As one piece of evidence, Putnam tracks memberships in various civic organizations and notes a decline. Certainly, many of us in our own lives have the sense that once-prominent civic organizations have receded from public consciousness. But the question remains: Have we replaced them with something else? This is more tricky to answer. Robert Wuthnow argues that the nature of people's civic involvement has changed to reflect increased time pressures. Instead of sustaining highly structured organizations with local, regional, and national chapters and a hierarchy that makes major corporations look simple, he says, we have reorganized. There may be a less tangible infrastructure, but the network remains in looser civic connections. Grassroots, volunteer, and nonprofit efforts seek more sporadic, task-oriented involvement from citizens, a departure from the structured time commitments required in the past. City Year, a nonprofit organization that sponsors young people to spend a year in a kind of domestic Peace Corps attacking urban issues, raises some of its money through a weekend Serve-a-Thon. That means people get sponsors and perform a one-shot stint of community service. Spending the weekend painting an elderly woman's home or refurbishing a community playground gives participants a sense of accomplishment and community connection with a minimal time commitment.[16]

There are many examples of such fine efforts, but they make up just one piece of the community puzzle. The sense people have, as Wuthnow observes, that "their communities are coming apart at the seams" exists not just because the Welcome Wagon has stopped going door to door or because the newspaper boy is a relic of the past. It is, rather, what happens when so many of the institutions—formal and informal—that make up community or civic life pull inward. It is not that civic organizations, neighborliness, government, public institutions have disappeared; they haven't. It is that they are more ambivalent, more modest, less reliable elements of public life. Government no longer serves as a trustworthy overseer to keep the playing field level. Partisan political squabbling, behind-the-scenes power plays, and uncivil public behavior have robbed government of its status as the nation's civic soul. We can't know, can't trust, that President Bill Clinton had good reason to bomb a medical building in the Sudan. Was it a chemical weapons plant, or was the bombing a way to distract the nation from the charges against him? Were the House Republicans looking out for the Constitution and the American people in seeking impeachment? Or did they see a ripe political opportunity to attack Clinton? Government, at least in recent years, has ceased to provide a fair and safe forum for public debate. Instead, it offers what we have come to want: entertainment.

Even on the local level, government seems more and more irrelevant to the character of civic life. Residents of many communities don't vote in local elections, don't run for local office, don't follow local events or even see themselves as invested in school budgets, local environmental concerns, community health board policies, traffic issues, or zoning. Small groups mobilize when the strip club is proposed in their neighborhood or a communications company wants to erect another tower to handle burgeoning cell phone usage, but most people remain cloistered in their homes, more interested in investment portfolios, real estate prices, and the speed of their Internet hookup.

Perhaps the most critical piece is the hardest to parse: how we interact with the other people in our community and our lives. What sense of obligation or connection do we feel to others? "Because a strong civil society depends on citizens who interact with one another, one of the most basic questions is whether Americans still have meaningful connections with significant others—people with whom they can share their lives and to whom they can turn when in need," writes Wuthnow. "Such connections may have little to do with politics, voting, or taking part in community organizations. But they are the elemental condition on which all other forms of civic involvement are based."

Do we interact with one another in meaningful ways? It is an impossible question to answer conclusively. Certainly, even though more people do live alone and more families are far-flung, many of us do have people we interact with and rely upon. Work colleagues have become, for many, important social supports. I interviewed a young analyst at Andersen Consulting who lived with another Andersen analyst—one or another was almost always on the road—and said that the major part of his social life revolved around watching sitcoms on Thursday nights with a group of co-workers. Two secretaries likewise said that they had developed an important friendship since being seated next to each another, often confiding personal things they didn't share with others. Once someone moves or leaves for another job, however some contact may continue, but the network dissolves.

It leads you to wonder: How much of the relationship was a real friendship and how much mere convenience? Even so, it suggests that we *need* such connections. We need people to whom we can report the trivia of daily life, not because there is information that must get passed on but because the act of telling—and listening—is an act of human connection. Wuthnow observes: "That people seem not to know their neighbors as well as they did in the past, and that neighborhood soda fountains and taverns and bowling leagues are less abundant, are thus worrying developments not primarily because these were places in which political issues were discussed but because they helped forge bonds among people."

One other piece of community-making is the ability to empathize with others, much as readers in 1953 were encouraged to empathize with the Cummings family. This empathy creates a tone for public discourse and behavior that sets up a mutual exchange: We empathize with others knowing they will empathize with us. It is a critical connection, played out in the language we use, the expression on our face, the tone of voice we call up when dealing with strangers. Too often today, though, there is not a connection but a gap of unexplored space between us and the other guy.

Civility

Early one Saturday morning I sat in a borrowed classroom at a suburban Boston senior center and observed as fourteen men sat around long tables, arms folded across their chests. Their body language said they didn't want to be there. And who would? They had each paid ninety dollars to enroll in a course called Attitudinal Dynamics of Driving, which would consume the next eight hours and would focus on something they would do well to study: rude driving behavior. For these men, who had each committed five driving violations, the course was the key to keeping—or, in some cases, getting back—their driver's licenses.[17]

For the Massachusetts Registry of Motor Vehicles, which began requiring the National Highway Safety Council course in 1995, it was part of what you might call a civility crusade—an effort to teach offenders not the rules of the road but better driving behavior. It was not a subject the class took to readily. In fact, when they were told by the instructor to pair off to discuss their driving violations, the buzz in the room evinced few signs of contrition. "It's small stuff!" huffed one student. "It's bullshit!" steamed another. Complained a third: "I didn't do anything!"

These men—and the rest of us, if we're being honest—have trouble owning up to their own incivility. We tend, as these men did, to see *ourselves* as the victims. Never mind that 60 percent of those questioned in a 1996 Gallup poll admitted shouting, cursing, or making gestures at drivers who upset them. The problem is obvious: As any of the respondents would explain, we only honk at the other guy because he deserves it!

Incivility may seem trivial, little more than the accumulated annoyances of modern life. Increasingly, however, people, from government officials to college presidents and think-tank researchers, are seeing rudeness as more than unseemly public behavior. It is, some argue, threatening the very fabric of society, poisoning relations that build goodwill and a sense of community. Polls suggest that a majority of Americans believe incivility is a serious and worsening problem. Such sentiments point to the fact that we feel alone, that we feel we must be vigilant and focused on our own self-preservation. They paint a world in which others are untrustworthy and uncivil: ready to cut us off on the highway, slip in front of us in line, or ignore more serious requests for help or understanding. We cannot count on others or connect with others when we find them looking through us, ignoring our humanity, focusing exclusively on their own immediate desires.

Start up a conversation on this subject, and the tales of wrong gush forth. The pushy couple at the Bloomingdale's counter; the clerk who gabs on the phone and leaves customers waiting; the bank teller who refuses to make change for a hundred-dollar bill because a man, new to town, doesn't yet have an account there; the parent who stands up to videotape her child and ignores the fact that no one else can see the preschool concert as a result; the California anesthesiologists who deny painkillers to women in labor who are on Medicaid—unless they pay four hundred dollars in cash in advance. Some examples are trivial; some are serious. All reveal a connection gap, a failure to empathize and, in the last example in particular, to acknowledge the other person's humanity.

It is no accident that worry about incivility has come at a time when the rhetoric of community is prevalent. One threatens the other. Civility—and the lack of it—has become a persistent topic of concern among a wide spectrum of people and institutions. Congress in 1997 held a retreat to discuss how members might encourage more mannerly debate. Colleges, high schools, think tanks, police academies, municipalities, retailers—all have made manners, if not a mission, at least a subject of discussion. The Pew Charitable Trusts in 1997 funded creation of the National Commission on Civic Renewal to study civic engagement and the incivility problem.

Although William Galston, the executive director of the commission, was careful from the start to differentiate between social rudeness and what he terms "the full range of concerns about civic issues," neither does he see them as wholly unrelated. Galston says there is no escaping the fact that people's "view of social reality is strongly colored by what they see as the decline of basic decency. If you look at the surveys and focus groups, it comes out loud and clear: Most Americans see a decline of basic civility on the airwaves, in music, on the streets and public spaces, in public institutions such as schools, and on our nation's highways, where there has been an epidemic of bad vehicular manners with dangerous and tragic consequences." When it comes to rudeness and the fraying social fabric, Galston observes, "Americans see these as connected phenomena."

Civility is not just about manners but about the way we regard and relate to others. It cuts to the tone of a society. Pam Solo, a former nun who is president of the Institute for a Civil Society, a foundation created in 1997 with an anonymous thirty-five-million-dollar donation, says what she calls the "vulgarization of society" is both a cause and an effect of incivility, which creates an unending chain of bad feeling. For example, she says, "if you get the message in the workplace that you are disposable, dispensable, undervalued, you internalize that, and you carry that message back out onto the street and into your car and into your personal relationships."

Everyone knows that rudeness can make life unpleasant. A day of being honked at, scowled at, and shouldered aside can frazzle even the best-natured among us. But is it more serious than that? Is incivility simply an annoying thorn in our collective side or a sign of something more distressed in our society? Do all the daily trespasses, the routine acts of rudeness, accumulate? Does our mistreating someone we don't know, and may never see again, have consequences?

Does the fact that a passenger berates a flight attendant for a missed connection (or worse) have anything to do with domestic violence, rape, hate crimes? Or with our indifference to the problem of the homeless? Or with low voter turnouts? It may be too simple to draw a line from the small act to the social trend, but how we treat the most vulnerable members of society or how compelled we feel to participate in the governing process or our local community clearly has some relationship to how we feel about our fellow citizens.

If we once felt directed by strong social norms that created expectations for our behavior, from gender roles to the way we dressed and conducted ourselves in public, that order has been shattered—for good and ill. Incivility has been an important tool for bettering society. Since the nation's inception, fighting injustice has often meant standing up, impolitely, and confronting authority, whether one is Rosa Parks, a member of ACT UP, or a patriot at the original Boston Tea Party. But at what point, we need to ask, does speaking out change from a courageous act to a self-centered and annoyingly uncivil one?

In some part, it may be a matter of perception or one's political leanings. When Sinead O'Connor ripped up a picture of Pope John Paul II on *Saturday Night Live* in 1992, was she registering a powerful abortion-rights statement in front of a huge national audience, or was she just being rude? But even those who see social protest as an important tool worry about its trivialization. Individual rights, once evoked on important occasions, have become the everyday cry not of the gravely wronged but of the merely unhappy. In the name of defending their "rights," people try to get an edge for themselves. No longer are rights buttressed by arguments for equality of opportunity or access to life-prolonging medication. Today, rights are exercised in the name of merchandise returns, travel arrangements, restaurant meals, college credit, and Internet access.

"People used to hesitate to be loud and make a scene," observes one longtime police chief. "Nowadays it seems to be okay. There's a perception that people are standing up for their rights. I just got off a plane last night. There was a guy who had missed a connecting flight because he was five minutes late, and he was using profanity with the stewardess." A college president notes that often when students face a disciplinary hearing today, "they are immediately involved in an assertion of their rights. Very rarely do I get a student who says, 'I was wrong.'" Nobody wants to concede fault. The police chief says stopping drivers who run a red light invariably sets off a debate over whether they actually went through the red light. Twenty years ago, he says, "You'd get an apology. The attitude now is 'Admit to nothing.'"

We may try to justify our lapses: We are busier these days, and the overload contributes to our collective impatience. But some people get angry even when they're not in a hurry. Our language even reflects a less temperate temperament. Jim Lowe, senior editor in charge of new words at Merriam-Webster, points out, for example, that "attitude" earned a new meaning in the tenth collegiate edition. "Attitude used to be something neutral," says Lowe. "Now if you say someone has 'attitude,' you are saying they have a belligerent or hostile attitude." "Dis" is now in the dictionary. So are "in-your-face" and "trash talk." And, Lowe says, "road rage" is vying for entry.

People today routinely backbite, browbeat, and tailgate. They cut others off not only in traffic but in conversation. They ignore NO SMOKING signs and use the ten-item checkout line at the supermarket when they have fourteen. Even if an invitation says RSVP, people don't respond; "you're probably going to have to call," the owner of a Natick, Massachusetts, party-planning firm warns hosts and hostesses. And despite the directive on the VCR tape—"Be a friend, rewind when you reach the end"—a twenty-year-old clerk at Blockbuster Video says people "just don't care about rewinding."

It may seem wrong to mix the trivial and the profound, but both gnaw at our sense of well-being and our willingness to align ourselves with others. Some may say it's hard to judge whether someone is boldly challenging a serious social wrong or just being rude. We can wonder: Have we become victims of our own quest for individual self-empowerment? Or are we stuck in a rut on the road to Utopia? It may be hard to tell, but right now there seems little doubt that many of us feel we have become a ruder, less caring, less civil—and less connected—society.

BRIDGING THE GAP

In this book I have tried to consider the elements of our moment-to-moment, day-to-day lives that have become nearly invisible to us in their familiarity. I have tried to look at them with fresh eyes. Why are our homes so much larger today when our households are smaller? Does it matter that we socialize less with neighbors? That we don't drop in? That we build high fences around our yards and fortify our homes with alarm systems? Is technology drawing us closer or pushing us apart? How is it changing who we are and how we relate? Why has shopping become so central—not just in acquiring stuff but in weighing friends, lovers, or mates?

Just as there is no single force that has brought us to this point, there is no switch to flip that will send a current of connection flowing between us. The challenge is personal and multiple. But it is something that we have the power to control. The future is in our hands, embedded in the myriad choices that present themselves. In the broadest terms, we must take back our lives and more fully inhabit the moments, days, and years that shape relations with ourselves, with our world, and with the people around us. It is the little junk that counts. Unfortunately, even as spiritual gurus and self-help wizards offer up advice and we give a great deal of lip service to "connection," we continue to be pulled along, seeking the very things that isolate us: greater privacy, efficiency, and control.

It's all right, of course, to want these things. I grocery-shop online. I feel great when I get a lot done quickly and at the same time. I long for another bathroom. But we must at the same time be mindful of what we are giving up—and I don't mean just what first comes to mind, like the thrill of no longer pushing faulty carts stuffed with grocery bags through the snow to the car. I mean the real stuff: I lose out on interactions, interactions that seem trivial but that actually make me feel a part of my community and an active participant in my own life. And I have to work to bring those things back into my days. I find myself making supplementary trips to the supermarket and working to do other things myself. I rake my own leaves, do my own gardening, mow my own lawn, paint my own rooms, plaster my own walls, cook my own food, sew my own drapes. I don't intend to sound like Martha Stewart. My results can look pretty shabby sometimes. But they help connect me to myself, my family, and my world. I have never spent a day out gardening or raking leaves—something I often do with the children—that I don't end up exchanges glances, nods, or conversation with someone strolling by. It wouldn't happen if I hired a gardener.

Connection requires sacrifice and action. We can no longer assume that it will "just happen," because it doesn't anymore. People disappear inside their homes and their lives, and we never realize they are missing. To connect, we sometimes must deny ourselves what is not only available but pervasive. We must sometimes choose not to put up the fence, screen phone calls, flip open the cell phone, ignore the person sitting in the next seat on the plane or standing next to us in line. It is all right—no, it is essential—to empathize, to smile, to nod in understanding, even to offer help or to be late because you have stopped to have a real conversation. The rapid changes driven by technological advances and a changing value system have made it easy to excise human interaction—profound and trivial—from our daily lives. We are falling out of practice. We are losing our ability to do such basic things as converse and make ourselves comfortable around others. We must learn not merely to overcome this nervousness with interaction but to find solace and pleasure in the act. We must learn, too, to look more deeply at those around us in an effort to find common ground.

New World, New Challenges

In 1991, in the midst of the Los Angeles riots, Rodney King, a black man whose beating by white police officers was captured on videotape and triggered burning and looting, stood before a bouquet of news microphones and uttered a plea: "Can't we all just get along?" The question seemed not to have been rehearsed or planned, but it could not have been more apt or more perfectly stated if it had. In six words he captured the question on everyone's mind. Was it possible for people of different values, races, experiences, and backgrounds to live together in peace? Years later, that question distills one of the most critical—and explosive—issues facing all of us.

Throughout this book I have harkened back to the past as a means of contrasting current social values, norms, and behaviors with those of long ago. I have tried not to be nostalgic for the Good Old Days or to glorify decades past. It is interesting and informative to trace the transformation from then to now. But when it comes to seeking solutions to the Connection Gap, we must realize that much, though not all, of what worked in the past to create a sense of cohesion and community is no longer applicable today. The world and the issues have changed and grown more complex. We are strange new people living strange new lives.

For the middle class—particularly the white middle class—it was easier decades ago to forge common ground with neighbors and community members, in part because so many people shared the same backgrounds, experiences, and values. Our society today is far more diverse, and that diversity will only grow. We can see this in our own extended families, which increasingly include members of different races, religions, and ethnicities. Likewise, our neighborhoods, our workplaces, our classrooms, and our communities are more diverse. Although Rodney King's plea was for the cessation of violence, it is not enough to not fight. We must find a means for living together, not in silent acceptance but in meaningful concert. The challenge of connection has, in some ways, grown more intense. How do we forge relationships with people who have fundamentally different backgrounds from ours? Who may not want to be like us?

The issue is complex, and its complexity is rooted in our identities. We are searching for who we are, caught between the pull of a bland homogenized culture, in which everyone shops at the Gap and eats at McDonald's, and a desire to boldly express a more potent and original affiliation. It is no accident that, as our society grows more mixed, some African American leaders expound the virtues of segregation over integration and some religious leaders warn of the dangers of interfaith marriage. Nor is the popularity of genealogical searches, return quests to homelands, or searches for birthparents an unrelated development. We have an urgent need to know who we are, where we come from, and why we matter.

While some of us embrace our roots, others have shrugged off ethnic and religious identities as quaint, outmoded, or regressive. Instead these others construct identities of what is left: their jobs, their zip codes, their cars, their clothes, their marital status. Many of us paint ourselves as followers or consumers. We are Goth music fans, food co-op members, Volvo owners, or the Macintosh faithful, to name a few. Even haters like skinheads and white supremacists or those drawn to violence through gang membership yearn for a collective identity— though it may not be desirable. In the end, though, these sorts of affiliations are not very satisfying. They offer no real community or any way to know others or ourselves. They offer instead a parallel experience in which belonging comes from acting on similar values. After years of tracking and cross-referencing the names and activities of white supremacists, for example, federal law enforcement officials concluded, according to an August 1999 report, that there is no cohesive underground movement, only the actions of lone wolves. The philosophical framework is available on the Internet, but individuals without tangible connections plot and carry out terrorist acts. There is no real company in being part of a dark, cultish organization. My point here is not to compare the relatively harmless self-identification with brands or rock bands to those who carry out terror crimes, except in one sense: Often, what looks communal may, on closer inspection, turn out to be simply a grouping of people.[1]

In the end, we are left with a rather fractured picture, a collection of more profound affiliations that might actually foster productive relationships and an excess of group identities that are worth little. In this era of political correctness we are mindful to respect all affiliations, no matter how trite. So we end up highlighting our differences because they are all that seems to make us interesting anymore. At the same time, the effort to "get along" is boiled down to the quaint and irritating command to "celebrate diversity." It is irritating, not because of the message but because it has become an overused catchphrase that, far from encouraging thoughtful interaction, seems to say, "Ah, well, I've taken care of the multicultural thing, let's move on." Its mere utterance has become a broadcast message to play nice while failing to truly consider what it takes to build bridges.

What's striking is that we seem to be waiting for someone to give us directions, to tell us what to do to "get along." We half expect some diversity workshop or a manual of do's and don'ts to clarify the matter.

In the meantime, we try to avoid doing anything that could be wrongly construed. We'll be waiting a long time. Connections are not made en masse or through step-by-step instructions. They happen when you can know yourself well enough to trust that others can know you, not by the trappings of your lifestyle but by what is in your heart. I always tell my children that they cannot act wrongly if they do what they truly believe is right. Unfortunately, today, people don't often challenge themselves to examine their beliefs and their actions. Many of us don't care about being interesting, empathetic, or engaged. Being wealthy, having possessions, being comfortable is enough.

Throughout this book I have looked at the things that keep us from connecting. *So what do we do to bridge the gap?* The answers are highly personal because they require us each to make choices, to become engaged with others, and to act. We each must do it in our own way, but there are some basic goals that can guide us all.

Reviving Conversation

Shortly after my son was born, a friend and neighbor dropped by one morning to visit. This woman, whom I have thought of often while writing this book, breaks many rules of modern-day disconnection etiquette. Her effusive manner, her generosity, and her energy have made the street I live on more neighborly since she moved in a few years ago. This day, she dropped by. It is not every day someone shows up at my door with her own mug of iced tea, wearing a work outfit, and with the mission to check on my well-being. Like my grandmother's neighbor, mine didn't ask if I needed visiting—she presumed I did. She stayed for nearly two hours, and during that time all we did was talk. We talked about this and that, a bit of everything. After the first half hour, I admit, I noticed myself checking the clock on the table. The baby had nodded off. This was my cue to dash up to my office and write. But we kept talking. An hour passed. He woke up. I fed him. I realized my morning writing session, already cut short by the birth of a baby, was being decimated. Finally, though, I just let go. I stopped thinking of the time and began to enjoy what was happening. There we were on a late June morning with the sun filtering into the room, sitting in comfortable chairs from which I could see the tops of the most incredibly tall trees. And we were talking. There was no agenda; the only goal was conversation. It felt indulgent. But it also felt good. We had each decided that the other was worth two hours on a beautiful day in the middle of the workweek. And the act of talking, I found, was oddly refreshing. I hadn't done that in a long time.

Most of us don't. We don't have conversations anymore. We come to another person with a purpose: information to be exchanged. Often we accomplish such data drops more efficiently via e-mail, beeper message, or voice mail. We distill our messages into quick gulps, ignorant that it is not only *what* we say but also *how* we say it that matters. We don't appreciate anymore a perfectly put phrase or a well-described event. It is such a contrast to centuries past, in which the oral tradition was the means for passing on history and showing respect. As Odysseus makes his voyage home after the Trojan War, it is his duty as a dinner guest to talk. He must tell stories; his hosts must listen and respond. It is the evening's entertainment. So powerful was the spoken word that when writing became a dominant form of communication in the Middle Ages, people at first mistrusted the word on the page. How could it do the idea justice? Now, of course, the written record prevails. In our courtrooms, testimony—the spoken account—may be viewed as suspect when it counters printed evidence. The witness may be asked to read the paper record to "refresh" his or her memory. Certainly, our memories are not what they were in Homer's day, when remembering was the dominant means of storing information. Back then, *how* words were spoken, remembered, and respoken was of great importance. Today, our machines do the work. In the process, we have diminished our appreciation of language and dulled our powers of perception. You don't have to see with the same level of clarity when there are street signs and maps instead of trees and stone walls marking your destination.

We have also stopped making room for conversation, in our homes and in our days. Physical spaces once reserved for talking have been phased out of building design. Instead we build rooms for home theaters, computer use, or watching TV. We have also squeezed conversation out of our schedules. There are few circumstances today in which an impromptu two-hour conversation would be welcome. When we do take time to have conversations, we try to multitask. Phone conversations are saved for when we can also be driving a car, cleaning the dinner dishes, folding laundry, or checking our e-mail. We don't value the slow, imperfect entertainment of talking. In fact, it is hardly considered entertaining at all. The standards of what constitutes "entertainment" have grown so demanding that conversation seems dull. Certainly, it offers nothing to look at except another person's facial expressions and body language. In an age of high-speed electronic stimulation, it feels boring to concentrate on a single idea or a single person for very long.

But the loss of conversation is more than a loss of verbal air traffic. It is a loss of companionship and a way of relating that, by its very nature, requires connection. Conversation is a joint venture, like a dance in which each participant has a chance to lead and to follow. It is during that dance that we come to understand not only another person but also ourselves. It is often through conversation, through the act of explaining an incident or an idea to someone else, that we see it clearly for the first time.

There is pleasure, too, in coming to know another person intimately through conversation and in sharpening our own skills of analysis: *What do I think about what she just said?* To be sure, conversation can be taxing and demanding and less controllable than watching TV. But there is something about the issue live, in your living room, instead of on a screen, that excites, enlivens, and engages us. Conversation, the slow participatory act of verbal exchange, offers a way to create something *with* someone else. As we revive the art of conversation, we revive our connections.

Don't Get Sucked Along: Unplug

Long after the Internet had lost its novelty and grown pervasive (something I mark by when my preschooler starting chanting "www-dot-com" whenever the letter *W* came up in talking about the alphabet), I would still read articles by people who were just discovering computers. Typically they were by older people who had put off the inevitable, and the stories were either rather humorous or pathetic. Technological fluency is perceived as a way of staying young. If you are plugged in, logged on, and able to navigate the Web, then you are not dead yet. You may, if you have e-mail (especially if you get a lot of it, though not junk e-mail), be young and hip. In other words, we are clinging to technology as a fountain of youth, better than a facelift or laser skin peel. I like boasting about my mom's abilities at troubleshooting software problems. She used to repair sewing machines; now we call her when the printer doesn't work or we can't open the photo she'd e-mailed. Unfortunately, this predisposes us to greet every new technological advance with an overeager embrace when we should be exercising some judgment. It is okay, we must learn, to say no to some technologies or at some times. Just because we have a cell phone doesn't mean we have to use it when we suddenly find ourselves in a free, unscheduled moment.

Technology *can* literally connect us, but it can also corrupt our ability to connect with others and with our world. Screens of various kinds are recasting the way we live and relate to others. They are altering our perceptions and expectations, and they are doing it without our permission or our overt acknowledgment. Research and our own experiences over several decades show us the powerful influence of television. Although much of the debate around TV viewing focuses on the content of shows, it is not only *what* we watch but also the fact that we watch that changes us. The same is true of the TV's "smart" cousin, the computer. Computers do offer windows to lots of great content, just as well-produced television can. But there is nothing inherently informative, meaningful, or connecting about a PC or the Internet.

Technology has already made us more impatient, more hurried, and less attuned to the nondigital world. It is becoming harder for us to see, hear, smell, touch, and remember the kinds of things that used to give people real pleasure. Who anymore takes time to watch the ant trying to carry the mammoth crumb you dropped from your snack? Who even sees the ant? The dropped crumb? Who notices the eerie late afternoon light cutting through dark clouds? That strange feeling in your stomach when you are outside anticipating a rainstorm? Such experiences and, more critically, our ability to perceive and produce such experiences are being dampened by an overdependence on technology. We must be wise enough to make use of technology's real and stunning benefits without leaning on it for every aspect of daily living. We especially must be wary of this in regard to our children. It may be a proud parent who has an infant, toddler, or older child who loves to sit in front of the screen and may be surprisingly adept for his age, but even educational software is limited and cannot replace the learning that happens off-screen. It is in the great space of unplanned, unscheduled time that children—and adults—practice the skills of imagining, creating, and interacting.

Too often, we just get pulled along. It's time to use our power of choice. Technology extends our reach. It stands in for us when we can't be there. Certainly, it does let us do more, if "doing" means checking off more boxes on the daily planner. But if doing is about living, about having experiences that allow us to learn and interact with our world, then we should think again about precisely what and how much we want to delegate to our electronic machines. It's all right—even critical—sometimes to unplug.

The Restoration of Competence

It used to be that the saying went "If you want something done right, do it yourself." Well, we have pretty much turned that notion on its head. Today, if you want something done right, you hire someone else to do it. Almost daily, we are informed of services that can enhance our lives by removing the drudgery of ordinary tasks. Everywhere there are experts who will not merely do things but do them *professionally*. We call on them to walk our dogs, buy our clothes, organize our closets, send flowers, pick up the dry cleaning, mail packages, whip up a restaurant-quality meal in our kitchens, organize our photo albums, hound us to reach personal goals, decorate our homes for the holidays, or track down a replica of Junior's favorite lost teddy, to mention just a few. Virtually anything you can imagine doing for yourself, there's somebody who can do it for you—and do it better.

The *New York Times* has declared that we are in the midst of a boom. The do-it-yourself movement, a "House and Home" section story reports, has given way to the " 'let others do it' trend." And this trend is not just for the rich but is being priced and marketed for ordinary folk. One executive of an errand-running company quoted in the article boasts that the company wants custodians, administrative assistants, and salespeople to have the same access to services as a CEO. The point is that delegating your life tasks is not a special indulgence but increasingly something that everyone does. This movement assumes that the tasks and skills of daily life—the stuff we once relied on our parents to teach us to do—are not only tedious but best avoided. They are unworthy of valuable time. There is today no glamour in the domestic. No one boasts about his talent at folding a fitted sheet. Even hobbies like planting and caring for a vegetable garden are outsourced to experts who plant, water, and weed—so you can pick. For a *New Yorker* story, Margaret Talbot interviewed a woman who has made a business of tending to other people's lives, a woman Talbot describes as "a person for whom everyday hands-on labor has not become a mystery." The woman, Beth, will show up at your home and help you find missing keys, pack kids' school lunches, pick up their sleeping bags after the sleepover, and throw together an impromptu dinner party for six. She will, it seems, do just about everything except live your life for you (and even that line seems blurred).[2]

Where does this leave us? What, really, are we buying? The ads tell us we are getting more *quality time* as the advertisers do the junk. So we—do what? Work more? Smell the flowers (that have been professionally planted)? While quality time is a nice idea, it really cannot be scheduled. It just happens. This is not to say that we shouldn't delegate some things. A century ago, after all, people—mostly women and female children—spent their entire day producing food and doing chores just to keep a home operational. But neither do we win when we assign too much of our domestic living to others. In the *New Yorker* piece, "Dial-a-Wife," Talbot asks Beth if she would want to hire someone like herself. Beth says she wouldn't. Much of what she does for her clients gives her a good feeling, a feeling they miss out on. She gets satisfaction in planting the flowers along the front walk—more pleasure than one gets just walking by them. "I think I would always want to take care of those basic things in my life," says Beth. "Because if you don't put the work into something, you don't know the worth of it, either."

It is a powerful point—and one often drowned out by the escalating buzz about whom you can get to do what to make your life easier. When we delegate too readily we diminish something that, as a society, we are letting slip away: a sense of competence. When you do something yourself, especially when you do it well, the silent companion to the accomplished job is the knowledge of your own ability. Although it is fashionable to joke about our ineptitude at so much that was once considered basic—fixing cars, sewing, cleaning, home repairs, painting, doing laundry, mowing the lawn (and the list goes on)—the joke is really on us. Being able to do things is a source of confidence that flushes away the insecurity of our place in the world.

The ability to do something—not necessarily professionally, but competently—is also the basis for offering or exchanging that talent with someone else. The old cliché of men gravitating to a neighbor with his power tools out and a project under way may be such a guy-tool stereotype that it borders on the offensive in our politically correct world. But the nut of the image is appealing: that work—not professional work but amateur work—offers openings for engagement. In fact, the experience depends on the willingness of others to offer their wisdom or just their two cents. It is a collaborative effort in a way that the same job done by a professional is not. Will there be mistakes? Maybe (but perhaps no more than when you hire a pro). Collective learning and doing is a valuable—and often overlooked—tool for connection.

Unfortunately, the barn-raising sensibility has given way to a preference for hiring professionals. In the process of giving over chores big and small to experts, we are relinquishing not only the work itself but also our ability to judge the work and faith in our own common sense. We let the professionals dictate the standards, tell us the *right way* to do the job. We become connoisseurs not of doing but of choosing who is best. People today acquire status by selecting that which appears top quality. All the better if you are ahead of the curve, choosing some fabulous-but-little-known product or service company.

Our romance with experts spills over into our relationships with our children. Ever eager to give them more than we had, we enroll them in activities aimed at giving them a head start in specialized training we hope will one day appeal to admissions officers at top colleges. In fact, the scheduled, professionally organized activity has become the way children play. Basketball is not basketball unless it's being taught and organized by an adult. Lessons, tutors, and special camps legitimize what should need no legitimization. One elementary school principal observed that children seem lost at recess, unable to start and run their own games, instead looking for an adult to craft the activity. This is not to suggest there is no room for experts: You need a piano teacher to teach piano. But the level to which the professionalization of children's play has escalated is absurd. I realized this when my elder daughter was five and, after watching her dad and me go running on a regular basis, thought she might like to try it, too. Was it possible, she asked, for her to be enrolled in running lessons?

In the end, the quest for perfection—for our children and for us— is a sign not so much of refinement as of insecurity. The oft-overlooked truth is that one road to connection is through our own competence and, most critically, our willingness to share it with others. The force of progress would have us believe that we are entitled to the best, fastest, newest products and services, that we are too busy to bother with the mundane, too important to do the grunt work ourselves. Not only does such thinking short-circuit our own development, but it removes a potentially enriching avenue of experience and a means of connection.

Do Something, Do Anything

It is the nature of the way we make decisions today to wonder about dividends. Does doing X pay off? Is it worth it? It is tempting to throw out this pattern of thought and argue that human connections—and the efforts they require—should be beyond such calculations. But let's be cynical. What *do* you get out of putting aside some convenience or efficiency? Relinquishing some control and privacy? What can relationships and support networks really accomplish? How can we gain individually and as a society?

One of the most obvious benefits—one that people talk a lot about— is a more civil society, one more connected, more caring, and more tolerant. Certainly, by some standards we are a more compassionate society than we were generations ago. There are more laws and protections for people with disabilities. There is positive attention paid to differences between us. We are more concerned about the environment and animals. Yet we are constantly affronted by the hard edge of everyday public life, meanness, or what seems a lack of empathy for one another's plight. Whether the issue is our driving, street manners, customer service, community action, or noticing someone in need, there is little doubt that changing the tone of public engagement would make everyone's life more pleasant—and perhaps more meaningful. Actually accomplishing this, however, seems an overwhelming, even unattainable goal with little immediate personal benefit. Or does it?

Although we don't much notice it, I'd argue that *dis*connection is costing us, both in dollars and cents and in quality of life. It costs us individually when we hire people to do what others once did—or could do—freely, like watch a child, pay attention to our homes when we're away, visit with an elderly neighbor, or change a lightbulb that's tough to reach. It also costs us as a society in terms of social services and programs—for profit and not for profit—that now provide what friends, neighbors, and family members once just did. Our social isolation has a financial price tag. Physicians will tell you that patients sometimes make appointments not because they need medical attention, but because they are hungry to talk with someone who will listen and care. Pediatricians' offices are jammed with parents who have simple childcare matters needing answers—answers once provided by an involved extended family.

In other areas, too, disconnection extracts a price. A lawyer argued to me that people today hire lawyers to avoid dealing with each other. He said people prefer to resolve differences not through face-to-face discussion of a problem but through legal threats and lawsuits. Not only is this expensive for the individual, but the practice of clobbering one another with lawsuits jams court dockets and slows the wheels of justice.

At the heart of the matter is a breakdown not only in communication but also in the tools for communication. We are relinquishing direct and meaningful avenues for connecting—avenues that become more expensive, more distant, and less satisfying when professionals do the mediating. It is as if the ability to speak and be heard—to express ourselves—is being drowned out by a rising tide of individual gain at any cost. Even restaurants and hotels are accommodating this attitude, finding that "I'm sorry" has lost its meaning as an expression of regret unless accompanied by something of value. A sincere apology is no longer sufficient. People expect to be compensated for a mistake—a compensation that no matter how you slice it ends up costing all of us in higher prices. If a server makes a mistake in a meal, the customer expects a free dessert. One frame shop I frequent automatically hands out 10-percent-off coupons if they make a mistake or fail to have a picture framed on time. While it's always nice to be on the receiving end of these unexpected windfalls, it hardly advances the cause of social compassion and understanding. The message is that the human expression is valueless and that money and prizes talk. This is a real cost, not only in dollars and cents but also in terms of personal relations. We have come to *expect* compensation.

It is, to be sure, much easier to have mediators and coupons stand in for the awkward experience of apologizing and forgiving—of connecting. It is easier to hire a lawyer than to negotiate with your neighbor over the height of his fence. It is acceptable to go see your doctor even when all you want is to have someone to talk with. These are just a few disparate examples taken from a pattern of daily life that has come to offer neat and easy alternatives to the critical and sometimes tough work of human engagement. It is our nature to find the simple way out, but sometimes the hard way can be enriching beyond expectations.

One example of such an experience is the extraordinary tale of Susan, a forty-two-year-old divorced mother of two, who, faced with a fatal cancer, called a dozen of her friends to a meeting at a Manhattan therapist's office. At the meeting, Susan explained her situation and said she would need their help to get through the tasks of living that lay ahead. Before the friends, who had no idea ahead of time why they were called to the meeting, could register a reaction, the therapist posed an interesting question: What did they each think they might get out of being in a group like this?[3]

Get out of being in a group like this? Get out of being inconvenienced and called on to help? The question turned the tables on the assumptions we make about sacrifice. Some in the group clearly felt uncomfortable at first. For one woman, the prospect of being so intimately involved with such grave illness was so frightening she "just wanted to get out of there." In the end, though, all twelve—some of whom had not known each other before—agreed to help, forming teams and ferreting out skills they didn't know they had. They helped plan Susan's elder daughter's wedding. They took her to doctors' appointments and accompanied her to the Bahamas for experimental treatments. They handled insurance paperwork and kept track of medications. They cleaned her house and made sure she could attend social events. The group stayed together for three and a half years, until Susan's death. Over the time, the friends found that they gained far more than they gave. The woman who at first "just wanted to get out of there" said she saw a blossoming of her own sense of competence. She observed that she "got so many things out of it I feel I could really come through for somebody else. I had gone to the doctors with her. I had helped her take a shower," she said. "I had become the kind of person somebody could count on."

It is often easy to overlook the great gains that accompany real in-the-trenches connecting because diving in feels so foreign and overwhelming. Why open the door when it is challenging enough to manage our own lives? And yet, the evidence mounts: We win when we engage.

We all need to do something—to do anything. It does not matter how small the act is, but an act done with the aim of removing barriers is a road to making our individual lives richer and to making our world a more connected place. Social action does not happen in isolation. One person's meaningful act that can have a ripple effect, creating an opening for others to participate. Here in Boston a friend of mine started a program called Citizen Schools, which recruits working people—lawyers, judges, journalists, chefs, writers, dance instructors, massage therapists, carpenters, skateboarders, AIDS researchers, anyone with a talent and a willingness to teach it—to work with middle school children. The children serve as apprentices to the volunteer teachers. They learn how to, say, argue a legal case, publish a newspaper, perform shiatsu massage, and other real-world skills. I'm familiar with this program because I've volunteered in the past. What is striking to me—not just about my own involvement, but what I hear over and over from others who volunteer—is how profound the experience is for the teacher, how much meaning it adds to your daily existence. It is a message I have heard from partners of top law firms. One man in particular claimed that offering lawyers in his firm the chance to work with these children so increases job and life satisfaction that he sees it as a tool for retaining employees.

Certainly, there are similar opportunities in cities and towns across the country, and people who get involved in civic activities or who volunteer offer stories of revelation that make clear the link between connection and personal growth. But this is not a call to volunteerism; it is a call to engagement. Some of us cannot or do not feel able to volunteer, but we can all take some action. We can see ourselves as a part of a larger community; we can shoulder some responsibility for the greater good. It is not all right to be a bystander. We all must be participants. The Connection Gap looms as the consequence of our times, of our particular choices, and of being pulled along. It is how we have responded to a rapidly changing way of life. It is easy to embrace what arrives in our hands, to accept and adapt. We are, after all, skilled at adjusting our living, our thinking, our way of being, in order to survive, but evolution of this sort is not always productive or inevitable. We have the power to set limits. We may dig in our heels. Our challenge is to exercise our authority over our own lives and our relationships. Challenges to connection are present at every turn. But if we can find the opportunities to reach out—and not retreat—we may find that in our quest for meaning and richness we are, in the end, not so alone.

 **NOTES**

Introduction

1. Sven Birkerts, *The Gutenberg Elegies* (New York: Ballantine Books, 1994), 15.
2. Langdon Winner, *The Whale and the Reactor: A Search for Limits in an Age of High Technology* (Chicago: University of Chicago Press, 1986), 9.
3. David Popenoe and Barbara Dafoe Whitehead, "The State of Our Unions: The Social Health of Marriage in America," National Marriage Project, Rutgers University, cited July 19, 1999, http://ur.rutgers.edu/medrel/news/healthandbs/marry.html.
4. "Private Vehicle Occupancy for the United States: 1990 and 1980 Census," U.S. Census Bureau, cited June 18, 1999, http://www.census.gov/population/socdemo/journey/usvehocc.txt. "Trends Show Bathing and Exercise Up, TV Watching Down," Gallup Organization, January 7, 2000, cited January 20, 2000, http://www.gallup.com/poll/releases/pr000107.asp.
5. Maitland Zane, "Psychiatrist Criticizes Pelican Bay Prison," *San Francisco Chronicle*, October 13, 1993, A17. See also Stuart Grassian and Nancy Friedman, "Effects of Sensory Deprivation in Psychiatric Seclusion and Solitary Confinement," *International Journal of Law and Psychiatry* 8 (1986): 46–65; and Sheilagh Hodgins and Gilles Cote, "The Mental Health of Penitentiary Inmates in Isolation," *Canadian Journal of Criminology* 33, no. 2 (April 1991): 175–182.

Shopping

1. Thomas G. Exter, *The Official Guide to American Incomes,* 2d ed. (Ithaca, N.Y.: New Strategist Publications, 1996).
2. *Chicago Tribune*, December 1, 1927, 9, as cited by Roland Marchand in

Advertising the American Dream: Making Way for Modernity, 1920–1940 (Berkeley and Los Angeles: University of California Press, 1985), 158.

3. Leslie Savan, *The Sponsored Life: Ads, TV, and American Culture* (Philadelphia: Temple University Press, 1994), 1–14.

4. Exter, *Official Guide to American Incomes*, 49.

5. Susan Fornier and Michael Guiry, "'An Emerald Green Jaguar, a House on Nantucket, and an African Safari': Wish Lists and Consumption Dreams in Materialist Society," *Advances in Consumer Research* 20 (1993), 352–358.

6. Peter K. Lunt and Sonia M. Livingstone, *Mass Consumption and Personal Identity* (Buckingham, U.K.: Open University Press, 1992), 13, 9.

7. "The Cost of Caregiving to U.S. Business," *1997 National Alliance for Caregiving/AARP National Caregivers Study.*

8. Robert Bly, "Snowbanks North of the House," in *The Man in the Black Coat Turns* (New York: Harper & Row, 1988), 3.

9. Edward W. Cundiff, "The Evolution of Retailing Institutions Across Cultures," in *Historical Perspectives in Marketing*, ed. Terence Nevett and Ronald A. Fullerton (Lexington, Mass.: D. C. Heath, 1988), 148.

10. Exter, *Official Guide to American Incomes*, 236.

11. Colleen McDannell, *The Christian Home in Victorian America, 1840–1900* (Bloomington: Indiana University Press, 1986), 50. Department of Commerce, *Historical Statistics of the United States* (1960), as cited by Elaine Tyler May, "The Myths and Realities of the American Family," in *A History of Private Life: Riddles of Identity in Modern Times*, ed. Antoine Prost and Gerard Vincent (Cambridge, Mass.: Harvard University Press, 1991), 547–548.

12. Thomas Hine, *Populuxe* (New York: Knopf, 1989), 3.

13. William Freeman, "Emotional Appeal Held Key to Sales," *New York Times*, October 21, 1953, 45.

14. Katharine Barrett, "Shopping Malls in Decline," CNNfn (www.cnnfn.com), February 21, 1997.

15. James B. Twitchell, *Adcult USA: The Triumph of Advertising in American Culture* (New York: Columbia University Press, 1996), 159.

16. Susan Fornier, "Consumers and Their Brands: Developing Relationship Theory in Consumer Research," *Journal of Consumer Research* 24 (March 1998): 343–373.

17. Pasi Falk and Colin Campbell, eds., *The Shopping Experience* (London: Sage Publications, 1997), 8. Juliet B. Schor, *The Overspent American* (New York: Basic Books, 1998), 3.

18. "Yearning for Balance: Views of Americans on Consumption, Materialism, and the Environment," prepared by the Harwood Group, commissioned by the Merck Family Fund, July 1995. Clair Brown, *American*

Standards of Living, 1918–1988 (Cambridge, U.K.: Basil Blackwell, 1994), 469.

Screens

1. Ron Stodghill II, "Where'd You Learn That?" *Time*, June 15, 1998, 52–59.
2. Bruce Handy, "It's All About Timing," *Time*, January 12, 1998, 77–81.
3. John P. Robinson and Geoffrey Godbey, *Time for Life: The Surprising Ways Americans Use Their Time* (University Park: Pennsylvania State University Press, 1997), 145.
4. Marshall McLuhan, *Understanding Media: The Extensions of Man* (New York: McGraw-Hill, 1964), iv. Bill McKibben, *The Age of Missing Information* (New York: Random House, 1992), 22–23, 32.
5. Laura Pappano, "Alone Together," *Boston Globe Magazine*, July 26, 1998, 28.
6. Robert Kraut et al., "The Internet Paradox: A Social Technology That Reduces Social Involvement and Psychological Well-Being?" *American Psychologist* 52, no. 9 (September 1998), 1017–1031.
7. Alan Sobel, "Television's Bright New Technology," *Scientific American*, May 1998, 70.
8. David E. Fisher and Marshall Jon Fisher, *Tube: The Invention of Television* (Washington, D.C.: Counterpoint, 1996), 348.
9. Jack Sands and Peter Gammons, *Coming Apart at the Seams: How Baseball Owners, Players, and Television Executives Have Led Our National Pastime to the Brink of Disaster* (New York: Macmillan, 1993), 254–257.
10. Sonia M. Livingstone, *Making Sense of Television: The Psychology of Audience Interpretation* (New York: Pergamon Press, 1995), 3.
11. "Utilization of Selected Media: 1970 to 1995," U.S. Census Bureau no. 888. Neil Postman, *Amusing Ourselves to Death* (New York: Penguin Books, 1985). Patti Doten, "Tuning In and Tuning Out: Families' Members Spend More Time Watching Television . . . Alone," *Boston Globe*, April 6, 1995, L1.
12. Livingstone, *Making Sense of Television*, 4.
13. "Newsbytes," *Virtual Basic Online Magazine*, January 1998, cited February 4, 1998, http://www.vbonline.com/vb-mag.
14. Richard Gibson, "Machine Takes Orders in Test by McDonald's," *Wall Street Journal*, August 11, 1999, B1. Lucas Graves, "But on the Other Hand . . . ," *Marketing Computers*, February 1998, cited July 1, 1998, http://www.marketingcomputers.com/issue/feb98/graves.as.
15. Jon G. Auerbach, "Software Firms Coddle a Growing Market: The Preschool Crowd," *Wall Street Journal*, April 2, 1998, 1. Lisa DeMauro,

"Great Gifts for Kids," *Sesame Street Parents*, December 1998/January 1999, 48, review of JumpStart Baby software by Knowledge Adventure.

16. Auerbach, "Software Firms," 1.

17. Tannis M. MacBeth, ed. and contrib., *Tuning in to Young Viewers: Social Science Perspectives on Television* (Thousand Oaks, Calif.: Sage Publications, 1996).

Mobility

1. Laura Pappano, "Four Score and More: Meet the 85-Plus Generation, the Country's Fastest-Growing Age Group," *Boston Globe Magazine*, November 27, 1994, 18.

2. Stephen Kern, *The Culture of Time and Space, 1880–1918* (Cambridge, Mass.: Harvard University Press, 1983), 111.

3. Arthur Fisher, "What's Next: An SST That's Faster, Quieter, Cleaner, Longer," *Newsday*, April 7, 1998, C11. Jane Holz Kay, *Asphalt Nation: How the Automobile Took Over America and How We Can Take It Back* (New York: Crown Publishers, 1997), 175.

4. For both Sassoon and Kern: Kern, *Culture of Time and Space*, 217.

5. Alan J. Moyer, "The Social History of the Telephone," in *The Social Impact of the Telephone*, ed. Ithiel de Sola Pool (Cambridge, Mass.: MIT Press, 1977), 307.

6. Jean Gottman, "Megalopolis and Antipolis: The Telephone and the Structure of the City," in *The Social Impact of the Telephone*, ed. Ithiel de Sola Pool (Cambridge, Mass.: MIT Press, 1977), 306.

7. The discussion here of the telephone's early years relies on Sidney H. Aronson, "Bell's Electric Toy," in *The Social Impact of the Telephone*, ed. Ithiel de Sola Pool (Cambridge, Mass.: MIT Press, 1977), 18, 22–29, and Marion May Dilts, *The Telephone in a Changing World* (New York: Longmans, Green, 1941), 5–9.

8. Donna Haraway, "A Cyborg Manifesto," in *Simians, Cyborgs, and Women: The Reinvention of Nature* (New York: Routledge, 1991), 161, 163.

9. Jean Baudrillard, "The Ecstasy of Communication," in *The Anti-Aesthetic: Essays on Postmodern Culture*, ed. Hal Foster (Port Townsend, Wash.: Bay Press, 1983), 129.

10. Haraway, "Cyborg Manifesto," 153.

11. Laura Pappano, "Freedom from Chores," *Boston Globe*, July 22, 1997, B1.

12. Laura Pappano, "Too Busy to Play: Are We Overscheduling Our Children?" *Boston Globe Magazine*, February 11, 1996, 16.

13. Laura Pappano, "In Search of the Simple Life: Why Americans Yearn to Pare Down," *Boston Globe Magazine*, August 18, 1996, 20.

14. Kern, *Culture of Time and Space*, 125.

15. William L. Hamilton, "Executives Apply Type-A Eating to Shorter and Shorter Lunches," *Dallas Morning News*, November 20, 1997, 41A.

16. Edward Tenner, *Why Things Bite Back: Technology and the Revenge of Unintended Consequences* (New York: Knopf, 1996), xi.

17. "Annual Geographic Mobility Rates, by Type of Movement, 1947–1996," U.S. Census Bureau, cited March 10, 1998, http://www.census.gov/population/www/socdemo/mig96. "Recent Movers," U.S. Census Bureau, cited April 1, 1999, http://www.census.gov/hhes/www/housing/census/historic/movers.

18. "Ownership Rates," U.S. Census Bureau, Census of Housing, cited March 10, 1998, http://www.census.giv/hhes/housing/census/ownrate.

Home

1. Roderick J. Lawrence, "A More Human History of Homes," in *Home Environments*, ed. Irwin Altman and Carol M. Werner (New York: Plenum Press, 1985), 129.

2. Melanie Rehak, "Questions for Lars Eighner: A Roof of One's Own," *New York Times Magazine*, March 7, 1999, 23.

3. Colleen McDannell, *The Christian Home in Victorian America, 1840–1900* (Bloomington: Indiana University Press, 1986), 20–28.

4. Henry David Thoreau, *"Walden" and "Civil Disobedience"* (New York: New American Library, 1980), 8, 164.

5. Froma Harrop, "Trophy Houses Rarely Reward the Neighborhood," *Sacramento Bee*, September 8, 1997, B8. John C. Kuener, "'Mansionization' Irks Chagrin Residents," *Cleveland Plain Dealer*, June 3, 1997, 1B. Wilma Randle, "Curb Appeal: Park Ridge Citizens' Group Wants Tear-Down Issue Addressed," *Chicago Tribune*, September 14, 1997, 5X, Zone C. Jeff Ortega, "Plans for Home Anger Some Neighbors," *Columbus Dispatch*, November 10, 1997, 1B.

6. "Housing Facts and Figures: Characteristics of New Single-Family Homes, 1971–1997," National Association of Home Builders, cited April 6, 1999, http://www.nahb.com/sf.html. "Characteristics of New Multifamily Buildings, 1975–1998," National Association of Home Builders, cited January 21, 2000, http://www.nahb.com/facts/economics/mf.html. "Households by Size: 1960 to Present." U.S. Census Bureau, cited May 25, 1999, http:///www.census.gov/population/socdemo/hh-fam/htabHH-4txt.

7. Scarf quoted in Laura Pappano, "Too Busy to Play: Are We Over-scheduling Our Children?" *Boston Globe Magazine*, February 11, 1996,

23. Martin Buber, *I and Thou*, trans. Ronald Gregor Smith (Edinburgh: T. & T. Clark, 1952), 8.

8. Jean Baudrillard, *The System of Objects*, trans. James Benedict (New York: Verso, 1996), 19–28. Baudrillard also wrote: "As directly experienced, the project of a technological society implies putting the very idea of genesis into question and omitting all the origins, received meanings and 'essences' of which old pieces of furniture remained concrete symbols; it implies practical computation and conceptualization on the basis of total abstraction, the notion of a world no longer given, but instead produced—mastered, manipulated, inventoried, controlled: a world, in short, that has to be constructed" (28–29).

9. Georjeanna Wilson and Mark Baldassare, "Overall 'Sense of Community' in a Suburban Region: The Effects of Localism, Privacy, and Urbanization," *Environment and Behavior* 28, no. 1 (January 1996): 27–42.

10. Edward J. Blakely and Mary Gail Snyder, *Fortress America: Gated Communities in the United States* (Washington, D.C.: Brookings Institute Press, 1997), 6–7, 3.

11. George Cantor, "Searching for New Living Arrangements: Redefining Neighborhoods," *Detroit News*, April 26, 1998, cited May 4, 1999, http://www.detnews.com/1998/outlook/9804260026.html. Leanne Mieszala, "Safety Gate Proposal Dividing Community," *View*, December 2, 1998, cited May 4, 1999, http://www.viewnews.com/1998/VIEW-Dec-02-Wed-1998/Nwest/10107355.html.

12. Blakely and Snyder, *Fortress America*, 130–135.

13. Randall Crane and Richard Crepeau, "Does Neighborhood Design Influence Travel? A Behavioral Analysis of Travel Diary and GIS Data," *Transportation Research Part D—Transportation and Environment* 3, no. 4 (July 1998): 225–238.

14. Laura Pappano, "Neighborhood by Design," *CommonWealth*, fall 1998, 28–35.

15. Blakely and Snyder, *Fortress America*, 135.

Relations

1. Marvin Opler, "Woman's Social Status and the Forms of Marriage," *American Journal of Sociology* 49 (September 1943): 125-148.

2. Andrew Hacker, "Two Hundred Million Egos," in *The Social Fabric: American Life from the Civil War to the Present*, ed. John Cary and Julius Weinberg (Boston: Little, Brown, 1984), 299–311.

3. Steven Gaines, "Getting What You Want in a Snap," *New York Times Magazine*, November 15, 1998, 79–80.

4. Sheila John Daly, "Dating Data," *Seventeen*, September 1945, 12, 134. Alice Speakman, "Another Time, I Wouldn't," *Woman's Day*, August 1951, 39, 87–88. Shepherd Mead, "Be Well Rounded: More Pertinent Pointers on Succeeding with Women Without Really Trying," *Playboy*, January 1956, 61. Elizabeth Pascoe, "Me First," *Woman's Day*, June 1977, 44, 46, 188–189.

5. Richard Schmitt, *Beyond Separateness: The Social Nature of Human Beings—Their Autonomy, Knowledge, and Power* (San Francisco: Westview Press, 1995), 38, 115, 174.

6. Timothy Stephen, "Communication in the Shifting Context of Intimacy: Marriage, Meaning, and Modernity," *Communications Theory* 4, no. 3 (August 1994): 191–218.

7. Emeline S. Whitcomb, *Home Economics for Boys* (Washington, D.C.: U.S. Department of Labor, Office of Education, April 1930), 15, 17.

8. Notes from "Symposium in the Problems of Youth as a Challenge to the Home, Church, School, and Community," May 1–2, 1934, Schlesinger Library, Radcliffe College, Cambridge, Mass. Arleen C. Otto, *New Designs in Homemaking Programs in Junior High Schools* (New York: Columbia University Teacher's College Bureau of Publications, 1958), 32.

9. Robert N. Bellah, Richard Madsen, William M. Sullivan, Ann Swidler, and Steven M. Tipton, *Habits of the Heart* (Berkeley and Los Angeles: University of California Press, 1996), 112.

10. Ken Bryson, "Household and Family Characteristics: March 1995," *Current Population Reports,* U.S. Census Bureau, October 1996. Projections from middle series tables, "Resident Population Projections of the United States: Middle, Low, and High Series, 1996–2050" and "Projections of the Number of Persons Living Alone by Age and Sex, 1995 to 2010, Series 1, 2, and 3," cited January 19, 1999, http://www.census.gov/population/projections/nation.

11. L. L. Gigy, "Self-Concept of Single Women," *Psychology of Women Quarterly* 5 (1980): 321–340. Patricia Frazier, Nancy Arikian, Sonja Benson, Ann Losoff, and Steven Maurer, "Desire for Marriage and Life Satisfaction Among Unmarried Heterosexual Adults," *Journal of Social and Personal Relationships* 13, no. 2 (1966): 225–239.

12. Laura Pappano, "The Single File," *Boston Globe Magazine*, January 25, 1998, 30. Pat Wingert, "I Do, I Do—Maybe," *Newsweek*, November 2, 1998, 58. Harold H. Punke, "Attitudes and Ideas of High School Youth in Regard to Marriage," *School and Society*, September 12, 1942, 221–224.

13. Bellah et al., *Habits of the Heart*, 85. Earl Kennel, *This Is Friendship* (New York: R. R. Smith, 1949), 60.

14. Debra L. Merskin and Mara Huberlie, "Companionship in the Classifieds: The Adoption of Personal Advertisements by Daily Newspapers," *Journalism and Mass Communications Quarterly* 73, no. 1 (spring 1996): 219–229.

15. John P. Robinson, and Geoffrey Godbey, *Time for Life: The Surprising Ways Americans Use Their Time* (University Park: Pennsylvania State University Press, 1997).

16. Laura Pappano, "The Connection Gap: Why Americans Feel So Alone," *Boston Globe Magazine*, September 24, 1995, 23–24.

17. Rupert Hughes, "The Only True Friend," *Woman's Day*, May 1951, 26, 99. Fredelle Maynard, "Lasting Friendships: What Makes Them Grow?" *Woman's Day*, October 1975, 40, 128–131. Julius Segal, "Choosing a Best Friend," *Seventeen*, December 1975, 102–104. Terri Minsky, "Here's to Best Friends," *Seventeen*, August 1985, 316–323. Charlotte Parker, "Little Things Mean a Lot," *Cosmopolitan*, December 1996, 82, 84. Julie Taylor, "Quiz: How Good Are Your Friends?" *Teen*, August 1997, 98–99.

18. Malcolm R. Parks and Kory Floyd, "Meanings for Closeness and Intimacy in Friendship," *Journal of Social and Personal Relationships* 13, no. 1 (1996): 85–107.

19. Michel Marriott, "The Urge to Blurt Plagues Imperfect Strangers," *New York Times*, December 29, 1996, Styles 33, 36. Doug Marlette, "Out Is In, In Is Out," *Esquire*, December 1996, 54.

20. Jean Baudrillard, "The Ecstasy of Communication," in *The Anti-Aesthetic: Essays on Postmodern Culture*, ed. Hal Foster (Port Townsend, Wash.: Bay Press, 1983), 129.

Us

1. Robert Wuthnow, *Loose Connections: Joining Together in America's Fragmented Communities* (Cambridge, Mass.: Harvard University Press, 1998).

2. "Pew Research Center Database: Public Attentiveness to Major News Stories (1986–1998)," cited February 8, 1999, http://www. people-press.org/database.htm; "The Age of Indifference," cited February 8, 1999, http://www.people-press.org/agerpt.htm; and "Politics, Morality, Entitlements Sap Confidence: The Optimism Gap Grows," cited July 13, 1998, http//www.people-press.org/unionrpt.htm.

3. Eyal Press, "The Heart of the Matter," *Nation*, cited December 21, 1999, http//www.thenation.com/1998/issue/980810/0810pres.htm.

4. Thad Williamson, "Bad as They Wanna Be," *Nation*, cited December 21, 1999, http//www.thenation.com/1998/issue /980810/0810will.htm.

5. "Americans Remain Very Religious, but Not Necessarily in Conventional Ways," Gallup Organization, December 24, 1999, cited January 20, 2000, http://www.gallup.com/poll/releases/pr991224.asp.

6. Wade Clark Roof, "The Baby Boom's Search for God," *American Demographics*, December 1992, 56. Laura Pappano, "Inspired Choices," *Boston Globe Magazine*, December 22, 1996, 23.

7. Judith Gaines, "New Ways to Pray are Just a Mouse-Click Away," *Boston Sunday Globe*, January 9, 2000, B1.

8. John Marks, "The American Uncivil Wars," *U.S. News and World Report*, April 22, 1996, 66-72.

9. Martin Gansberg, "37 Who Saw Murder Didn't Call the Police," *New York Times*, March 27, 1964, 1, 38. Charles Mohr, "Apathy Is Puzzling in Queens Killing," *New York Times*, March 28, 1964, 21, 40. "What Kind of People Are We?" *New York Times,* March 28, 1964, 18. Irving Spiegel, "Neighborly Spirit Asked by Wagner," *New York Times*, May 8, 1964, 42.

10. Lesley Williams Reid, J. Timmons Roberts, and Heather Monro Hilliard, "Fear of Crime and Collective Action: An Analysis of Coping Strategies," *Sociological Inquiry* 68, no. 3 (August 1998): 312-328.

11. "Nation's Largest Cities Lead the Way as Homicides Fall to Lowest Rate in Three Decades," U.S. Department of Justice, Bureau of Justice Statistics, cited February 23, 1999, http://www.ojp.usdoj.gov/bjs/pub/press. *Sourcebook of Criminal Justice Statistics, 1997,* Tables 2.31, 2.35, 2.40, Bureau of Justice Statistics, cited February 23, 1999, http://albany.edu/sourcebook.

12. Karyln J. Geis and Catherine E. Ross, "A New Look at Urban Alienation: The Effect of Neighborhood Disorder on Perceived Powerlessness," *Social Psychology Quarterly* 61, no. 3 (September 1998): 232-246.

13. Laura Pappano, "The Crusade for Civility," *Boston Globe Magazine*, May 4, 1997, 43.

14. Craig Calhoun, "Community Without Propinquity Revisited: Communications Technology and the Transformation of the Urban Public Sphere," *Sociological Inquiry* 68, no. 3 (August 1998): 373-397.

15. Robert Putnam, "Bowling Alone: America's Declining Social Capital," *Journal of Democracy* 6, no. 1 (January 1995): 65.

16. Wuthnow, *Loose Connections*, 204.

17. Interviews in this section are from my "Crusade for Civility."

Bridging the Gap

1. Jo Thomas, "New Face of Terror Crimes: 'Lone Wolf' Weaned on Hate," *New York Times*, August 16, 1999, 1.

2. Jenny Lyn Bader, "Relying on the Competence of Strangers," *New York Times*, April 1, 1999, D1.

3. Michael Ryan, "How One Woman's 12 Friends Became a Family," *Parade*, March 30, 1997, 8-10.

INDEX

About the Author

Laura Pappano, a Yale graduate, is a freelance journalist, social observer, and visiting scholar at Northeastern University. Pappano researched and wrote *The Connection Gap* while serving as a visiting scholar at the Murray Research Center at the Radcliffe Institutes for Advanced Study at Harvard. Pappano writes a weekly column on education for the *Boston Globe* and has written more than a dozen cover stories for the *Boston Globe Magazine*. She is a contributing writer for *CommonWealth*, a political quarterly. Her work has also appeared in *Good Housekeeping*, the *Cleveland Plain Dealer Magazine*, the *Detroit Free Press Magazine*, and the *Washington Post*. She has volunteered to teach journalism to nine- to thirteen-year-olds through Citizen Schools, is involved at her children's school, and has coached soccer for the YMCA. She does order her groceries online, but she sews (and sometimes pins, staples, or tapes!) her own draperies, does her own gardening, spackles, sands, and paints the rooms in her house herself—and is trying to make more time for conversation. She lives in Newton, Massachusetts, with her husband, Tom, and their three children.